LOUISIANA LAW OF CONVENTIONAL OBLIGATIONS
A PRÉCIS

LexisNexis Law School Publishing Advisory Board

William D. Araiza
Professor of Law
Brooklyn Law School

Lenni B. Benson
Professor of Law & Associate Dean for Professional Development
New York Law School

Raj Bhala
Rice Distinguished Professor
University of Kansas, School of Law

Ruth Colker
Distinguished University Professor & Heck-Faust Memorial Chair in Constitutional Law
The Ohio State University, Moritz College of Law

Richard D. Freer
Robert Howell Hall Professor of Law
Emory University School of Law

David Gamage
Assistant Professor of Law
University of California, Berkeley School of Law

Craig Joyce
Andrews Kurth Professor of Law & Co-Director, Institute for Intellectual Property and Information Law
University of Houston Law Center

Ellen S. Podgor
Professor of Law
Stetson University College of Law

David I. C. Thomson
LP Professor & Director, Lawyering Process Program
University of Denver, Sturm College of Law

LOUISIANA LAW OF CONVENTIONAL OBLIGATIONS

A PRÉCIS

ALAIN A. LEVASSEUR
Hermann Moyse, Sr. Professor of Law
Director, European Studies
Jean Monnet Chair
Louisiana State Unversity, Paul M. Hebert Law Center

2010

ISBN: 978–14224–7703–8

This publication is designed to provide accurate and authoritative information in regard to the subject matter covered. It is sold with the understanding that the publisher is not engaged in rendering legal, accounting, or other professional services. If legal advice or other expert assistance is required, the services of a competent professional should be sought.

LexisNexis and the Knowledge Burst logo are registered trademarks and Michie is a trademark of Reed Elsevier Properties Inc., used under license. Matthew Bender and the Matthew Bender Flame Design are registered trademarks of Matthew Bender Properties Inc.

Copyright © 2010 Matthew Bender & Company, Inc., a member of the LexisNexis Group.
All Rights Reserved.

No copyright is claimed in the text of statutes, regulations, and excerpts from court opinions quoted within this work. Permission to copy material exceeding fair use, 17 U.S.C. § 107, may be licensed for a fee of 25¢ per page per copy from the Copyright Clearance Center, 222 Rosewood Drive, Danvers, Mass. 01923, telephone (978) 750-8400.

> **NOTE TO USERS**
> To ensure that you are using the latest materials available in this area, please be sure to periodically check the LexisNexis Law School web site for downloadable updates and supplements at www.lexisnexis.com/lawschool.

Editorial Offices
121 Chanlon Rd., New Providence, NJ 07974 (908) 464-6800
201 Mission St., San Francisco, CA 94105-1831 (415) 908-3200
www.lexisnexis.com

MATTHEW●BENDER

Louisiana Code Series

CIVIL CODE SERIES

LOUISIANA POCKET CIVIL CODE
2010

LOUISIANA CIVIL CODE PRÉCIS SERIES

LOUISIANA LAW OF OBLIGATIONS IN GENERAL
3RD ED. 2009

LOUISIANA LAW OF CONVENTIONAL OBLIGATIONS
2010

LOUISIANA LAW OF SALE AND LEASE
2007

LOUISIANA LAW OF TORTS
2010

LOUISIANA LAW OF PROPERTY
2010

LOUISIANA FAMILY LAW
2010

LOUISIANA LAW OF SUCCESSIONS
2010

ABOUT THE AUTHOR

Professor Alain Levasseur is a graduate of the Universities of Paris (France) and Tulane. He was an associate with the Paris firm of Mudge, Rose, Guthrie & Alexander for a while but left the firm to become a technical assistant at the World Bank in Washington, D.C. Professor Levasseur taught at Tulane Law School from 1970–1977 when he joined the LSU Law Faculty. He is a member of the International Academy of Comparative Law, the Société de Législation Comparée, and the Louisiana State Law Institute; he serves on the editorial or advisory boards of the American Journal of Comparative Law, the Revue Internationale de Droit Comparé, the Revue Trimestrielle de Droit Civil, the Revue Générale de Droit, the Foro de Derecho Mercantil, and e-Competitions. He is a member of the Scientific Committee of the Fondation pour le Droit Continental; he is president of the Louisiana Chapter of the Association Henri Capitant and of the International Association of Legal Methodology. He has published extensively in the fields of Comparative Law, Civil Law (Civil Law System/Tradition, Obligations, Contracts, Sale/Lease, etc.), EU/EC Law, and U.S. Law (in French with Dalloz). He has been a regular visiting Professor at the Universities of Aix-Paul Cézanne and Lyon III. He has been honored with two Doctorats Honoris Causa, one from the University of Aix-Marseille Paul Cézanne (1999) and another from the University of Paris-Panthéon Assas (2010).

Table of Contents

INTRODUCTION 1

Chapter 1	**Classification of Contracts (General Principles) LSA-C.C. Arts. 1906 to 1917** **3**	

Article 1   Unilateral Contracts and Bilateral or Synallagmatic Contracts 4
Article 2   Onerous and Gratuitous Contracts 5
Article 3   Commutative and Aleatory Contracts 7
Article 4   Principal and Accessory Contracts 11
Article 5   Nominate and Innominate Contracts 12
Article 6   Implied Kinds of Contracts 12
  § 1.6.1.   Consensual, Solemn, and Real Contracts 12
  § 1.6.2.   Mutually Negotiated Contracts and Contracts of Adhesion 14
FORMATION OF CONTRACTS Chapters 2 to 7 17

Chapter 2	**Capacity LSA-C.C. Arts. 1918 to 1926** **19**	

Article 1   Incapacity of Enjoyment 20
Article 2   Incapacity of Exercise 21
  § 2.2.1   Scope and Effect of Nullity for Incapacity 22

Chapter 3	**Consent LSA-C.C. Arts. 1927 to 1947** **25**	

Article 1   Existence and Expression of Consent 25
  § 3.1.1.   Offer 26
  § 3.1.2.   Acceptance 29
Article 2   Binding Nature of Offer — Meeting of Minds — Revocation 32
Article 3   Offer of a Reward and the Public 33

Chapter 4	**Integrity of Consent LSA-C.C. Arts. 1948 to 1965** **35**	

Article 1   Error 35
  § 4.1.1.   Concept of Error 36
  § 4.1.2.   Seriousness of the Error 36
  § 4.1.3.   Kinds of Serious Errors: Error of Fact-Error of Law-Error as to the Person 38
  § 4.1.4.   Effect of Error 44
Article 2   Fraud 45
  § 4.2.1.   Concept of Fraud 46
  § 4.2.2.   Constitutive Elements of Fraud 46
  § 4.2.3.   Effects of Fraud 49
Article 3   Duress [Violence] 50
  § 4.3.1.   Constitutive Elements of Duress 50
  § 4.3.2.   Characteristics of Duress: Author-perpetrator, Reasonableness, Unlawfulness 51
  § 4.3.3.   Legal Consequences 53
Article 4   Lesion 53

Table of Contents

Chapter 5	**Cause LSA-C.C. Arts. 1966 to 1970**	**55**
Article 1	Brief Historical Survey of "Cause"	55
§ 5.1.1.	Contemporary Theory of Cause and its Legal Regime	57
§ 5.1.2.	Legal Regime of Cause	59
Chapter 6	**Object and Matter of Contracts LSA-C.C. Arts. 1971 to 1977**	**65**
Article 1	Legal Characteristics or Features of an Object	66
§ 6.1.1.	Lawfulness of the Object	66
§ 6.1.2.	Determination of the Object: Kind, Quantity, Quality	67
§ 6.1.3.	Possibility or Impossibility of the Object	70
Article 2	Promesse de Porte-Fort	71
§ 6.2.1.	Promesse de Porte-Fort: Description and Nature	71
§ 6.2.2.	Effects of a Promesse de Porte-Fort	73
Chapter 7	**Third-Party Beneficiary — Stipulation pour Autrui LSA-C.C. Arts. 1978 to 1982**	**75**
Article 1	Notion of a Stipulation for the Benefit of Another	75
Article 2	Conditions for a Valid Stipulation	76
§ 7.2.1.	Conditions Pertaining to the Contract Between Stipulator and Promisor	76
§ 7.2.2.	Conditions Pertaining to the Stipulation Itself	77
Article 3	Effects of a Stipulation for the Benefit of Another	77
§ 7.3.1.	Effects Between Stipulator and Promisor	77
§ 7.3.2.	Effects between the Stipulator and the Third Party Beneficiary	78
§ 7.3.3.	Effects between the Promisor and the Third Party Beneficiary	79
Chapter 8	**Effects of Conventional Obligations or Contracts LSA-C.C. Arts. 1983 to 2012**	**81**
Article 1	General Effects of All Contracts: Effect of Law — Good Faith	81
§ 8.1.1.	Effect of Law	81
§ 8.1.2.	Good Faith	86
Article 2	Specific Performance and Putting in Default	86
§ 8.2.1.	Specific Performance	86
§ 8.2.2.	Default; Putting in Default; Effects and Manners	88
Article 3	Damages	91
§ 8.3.1.	Stipulated Damages	92
§ 8.3.2.	Court Assessed Damages	94
Chapter 9	**Dissolution and Nullity LSA-C.C. 2013-2024**	**99**
Article 1	Dissolution	99
§ 9.1.1.	Grounds for Dissolution	100
§ 9.1.2.	Mechanism of Dissolution	102
§ 9.1.3.	Effects of Dissolution	104
Article 2	Nullity	106
§ 9.2.1.	Kinds of Nullity and Extent of Nullity: Absolute and Relative	107

Table of Contents

§ 9.2.2. Effects of Nullity 110

Chapter 10   **Interpretation of Contracts LSA-C.C. Arts. 2045-2057 . 115**

Article 1   Rules of Interpretation 115
Article 2   Bending the Rules: Interpretation Is Not Revision 117
§ 10.2.1. Bending the Rules 117
§ 10.2.2. Interpretation Is Not Revision 118

Chapter 11   **Revocatory and Oblique Actions LSA-C.C. Arts. 2036 to 2044 .... 119**

Article 1   The Revocatory Action 119
§ 11.1.1. Conditions for the Existence of a Revocatory Action 119
§ 11.1.2. Principal Effect of a Revocatory Action: Nullity of the Act 121
§ 11.1.3. Revocatory Action and Onerous Contracts 121
§ 11.1.4. Revocatory Action and Gratuitous Contracts 123
§ 11.1.5. Exceptions 124
§ 11.1.6. Additional Requirements and Effects of a Revocatory Action 124
Article 2   The Oblique Action 125
Article 3   Simulation [Arts. 2025 through 2028] [To be included in the next edition of this Précis. See Appendix III, Chapter XI]

Appendix I   **Louisiana Civil Code 2010 .... 129**

Appendix II   **Louisiana Code of Civil Procedure 2010 .... 147**

Appendix III   **Cases—Illustrations 151**

Index I-1

INTRODUCTION

LSA-C.C. Art. 1757 states: "**Obligations arise from contracts and other declarations of will. They also arise directly from the law, regardless of a declaration of will, in instances such as wrongful acts, the management of the affairs of another, unjust enrichment and other acts or facts.**" As a "legal" consequence, an obligation that arises from a contract or another declaration of the will, "**is a legal relationship whereby a person, called the obligor, is bound to render a performance in favor of another, called the obligee. Performance may consist of giving, doing, or not doing something.**" Particular attention should be given to the last words of **LSA-C.C. Art. 1757** where they refer to "**other acts or facts.**" As stated in a previous Précis,[1] "a juridical act, *stricto sensu*, in the technical sense of the words, is any manifestation of the will of a person meant" to create a legal relationship (Art. 1756) which carries legal effects as outlined in **LSA-C.C. Art. 1758**:

"**A. An obligation may give the obligee the right to: (1) Enforce the performance that the obligor is bound to render;**

(2) Enforce performance by causing it to be rendered by another at the obligor's expense;

(3) Recover damages for the obligor's failure to perform, or his defective or delayed performance.

B. An obligation may give the obligor the right to:

(1) Obtain the proper discharge when he has performed in full;

(2) Contest the obligee's actions when the obligation has been extinguished or modified by a legal cause."

That particular source of obligations referred to in LSA-C.C. Art. 1757 as "contract(s)" is defined in **LSA-C.C. Art. 1906** in these words: "**A contract is an agreement by two or more parties whereby obligations are created, modified, or extinguished.**" A contract is, therefore, a juridical act because by their "agreement," or exchange of wills, the parties to it *create, modify or extinguish obligations.*

One will notice that the words that make up Title IV of Book III refer, first, to "Conventional Obligations." Although "titles" are not part of the substantive law of the civil Code,[2] and, therefore, should not be given any legal authority, the fact that this Title IV uses the preposition "**or**" and, thereby, equates "Conventional Obligations" with "Contracts" prompts to making two brief comments. The word "convention" comes from the Latin "*conventio*" which

---

[1] Précis, Louisiana Law of Obligations in General, § 1.1.2.

[2] Revised Statutes 1:13.

meant "to get together, to agree," such as in an assembly or meeting, but not necessarily with the intent to create legally binding obligations.[3] So, a contract being the creation of at least two minds, therefore being an "agreement," with the intent to create legal effects, was also a particular type of a convention.

In a different context, we read in **LSA-C.C. Art. 544** that **"The usufruct created by juridical act is called *conventional*. . . ."** Comment (b) under this Art. explains that "conventional usufructs are of two kinds: either contractual, created by inter vivos juridical act, or testamentary, created by mortis causa juridical act." The Comment should have been more specific in using the proper legal terminology to describe a "contractual usufruct" as being the creation of a "bilateral juridical act" (because two wills are exchanged in such a contract), and a "testamentary usufruct" as being the creation of a "unilateral juridical act" because a testament is the expression of one will only, that of the testator. Thus a "testament" is neither an agreement nor a contract, and furthermore, it is not a convention.

Be that as it may, today, in civil law jurisdictions and in Louisiana, the terms "conventional obligation" and "contract" are considered as interchangeable or legally equivalent as illustrated by the wording of **Title IV: Conventional Obligations or Contracts.**

We will analyze the Louisiana law of "Contract" or "Conventional Obligations" under the following titles: **Chapter 1: Classification of Contracts;**[4]**Chapter 2: Formation of Contracts; Chapter 3: Consent; Chapter 4: Vices of Consent; Chapter 5: Cause; Chapter 6: Object and Matter; Chapter 7: Stipulation for the Benefit of Another; Chapter 8: Effects of Contracts; Chapter 9: Dissolution, Simulation, Nullity; Chapter 10: Interpretation of Contracts; and Chapter 11: Revocatory and Oblique Actions.**

---

[3] One can think of the ABA Convention; the Geneva Conventions; the Law of the Sea Convention of 1982.

[4] Referred to, in part, in the Louisiana civil Code as "Chapter 1. General Principles," Arts. 1906–1917.

Chapter 1

CLASSIFICATION OF CONTRACTS (GENERAL PRINCIPLES) LSA-C.C. ARTS. 1906 TO 1917

A reason for classifying legal concepts is to be able to bring a given factual situation under a concept or another so that the factual situation will flow automatically from the proper classification under the appropriate concept. For example, when one can accurately describe a thing as a "corporeal animate" or "inanimate thing" under LSA-C.C. Art. 471, rather than as an "immovable" under LSA-C.C. Articles 462 or 463, one will automatically associate this corporeal thing with the rules on the acquisition of ownership under LSA-C.C. Art. 2439 as opposed to 2440; or the rules on acquisitive prescription under LSA-C.C. Art. 3489 rather than Art. 3473. To a legal concept is associated a legal regime, a set of legal rules which govern a carefully described factual situation matching the proper legal concept.

Another reason behind a classification of legal concepts and their definitions is to protect against the danger of polysemy or a possible plurality of meanings being given to the same word. One need only think about the word "act": is that word to be taken in the sense of "juridical act," or "written act" or "physical act" or "act of nature"? The word "cause" can be taken in the sense of a requirement for a valid contract (LSA-C.C. Art. 1966), in the sense of the cause of an accident (LSA-C.C. Art. 2315), or the cause of an action (LCCP Art. 425).

For these reasons, as well as for purposes of education and legal analysis, the Louisiana civil Code has classified "contracts" under a series of "definitions" to which are attached specific legal regimes which are distributed all over the civil Code and which can be fully grasped only as a consequence of an understanding of the structure of the whole civil Code. Let us illustrate the above statements with an analysis of the different kinds of contracts defined in Code Articles 1907 to 1917.

A preliminary remark must be made here to call the reader's attention to the typical civil law "architecture" of these Articles in this particular **Chapter** on **General Principles**: they go "two-by-two"; each set of two Articles forms a "tandem," except for one major recent and discordant instance which, as we hope to convincingly explain below, does not make much sense.

ARTICLE 1
UNILATERAL CONTRACTS AND
BILATERAL OR SYNALLAGMATIC CONTRACTS
LSA-C.C. ARTS. 1907–1908

LSA-C.C. Art. 1907 defines a unilateral contract in these terms: "**A contract is unilateral when the party who accepts the obligation of the other does not assume a reciprocal obligation.**" By contrast, LSA-C.C. Art. 1908 states that "**A contract is bilateral, or synallagmatic, when the parties obligate themselves reciprocally, so that the obligation of each party is correlative to the obligation of the other.**"

A contract, an agreement between two parties at least, is unilateral when only one of the two parties owes an obligation to the other; only one party is a debtor whereas the other party is the creditor of that debtor. We can analogize such a unilateral contract to a "one-way street," the obligation moving in one direction only. Some examples of such unilateral contracts are the contracts of loan,[1] deposit,[2] an option contract,[3] the right of first refusal[4] as well as gratuitous contracts[5] such as a donation.[6]

It is most important to distinguish a "unilateral contract" from a "unilateral juridical act." In the latter case only one person is bound by her/his single will; such would be the case of an "offer" which binds the offeror only until it expires or is revoked. If it should be accepted, we will then have a 'bilateral juridical act' or contract. That contract will be "unilateral" if it creates obligations on one party only, or it will be "bilateral/synallagmatic" if both parties owe obligations to each other. A bilateral or synallagmatic contract is, therefore, a "two-way street" because the obligations flow in both directions. Each one of the two parties is, at the same time, an obligor and an obligee. Typical bilateral/synallagmatic contracts are the contracts of sale, lease.[7] In a sale, the seller is the obligor of the obligation to deliver the thing sold to the buyer but he is also the obligee of the buyer's obligation to pay the price.

Why is such a distinction relevant? Elements of the specific legal regime that make up each one of these two types of contracts should help in illustrating the importance of the distinction. For example, should a party to a bilateral/synallagmatic contract fail to perform, the other party may raise the *exceptio non adimpleti contractus* as a defense if asked to perform: one party cannot be required to perform if the other cannot or is unwilling to perform. As an illustration, **LSA-C.C. Art. 2487** states that "**the seller may refuse to deliver the thing sold until the buyer tenders payment of the price, unless the seller has**

---

[1] Code Arts. 2891-2913. A loan does not exist until the thing "loaned" has actually been delivered to the borrower. Thereafter, the latter is the only one bound by an obligation: to return the thing to the lender.

[2] Code Arts. 2926-2945.

[3] Code Arts. 1933; 2620-2622.

[4] Code Arts. 2625-2626.

[5] See infra Chapter 1, Article 2.

[6] Code Arts. 1468-1469

[7] On Sale and Lease, see Précis, Louisiana Law of Sale and Lease.

granted the buyer a term for such payment."[8] Another right vested in a party-obligee to a bilateral/synalllagmatic contract is the right to demand the judicial dissolution of the contract **"when the obligor fails to perform"** or **"to regard the contract as dissolved. In either case, the obligee may recover damages."** (LSA-C.C. Art. 2013). So, in a bilateral/synallagmatic contract, the obligations are not only juxtaposed but they are also "interdependent" in the sense that, for each one of the parties, the 'credit' she/he is entitled to and the "debt" she/he owes cannot be dissociated; they cannot be treated separately.

It could happen that a contract, unilateral in its essence or by nature, may look like a bilateral contract because it appears to create some obligations on both sides. Such is actually the outcome of the parties' intent or will. A good illustration of this "ambivalent" situation can be found in the definition of an onerous donation. **LSA-C.C. Art. 1524** states that **"The onerous donation is not a real donation, if the value of the object given does not manifestly exceed that of the charges imposed on the donee." "In consequence, the rules peculiar to donations inter vivos do not apply to onerous and remunerative donations, except when the value of the object given exceeds by one-half that of the charges or of the services." LSA-C.C. Art. 1525.** So, by their intent, the parties to a unilateral contract can modify its "nature" for their own purposes and turn it into a bilateral contract. Such a modification in the nature of the unilateral contract will occur when the value of the object given by the "wanted-to-be-donor" is inferior by one-half to the value of "the charges or of the services" provided by the "wished-to-be-donee."

ARTICLE 2
ONEROUS AND GRATUITOUS CONTRACTS
LSA-C.C. ARTS. 1909–1910

"A contract is onerous when each of the parties obtains an advantage in exchange for his obligation." LSA-C.C. Art. 1909. In such a contract, for example a contract of sale, each one of the two parties owes some performance to the other and is entitled to receiving a performance from that other party. Each performance is incurred with the perspective, the anticipation of obtaining a counter-performance. In a contract of sale, the seller who agrees to make the object of his own obligation the transfer of the ownership of "his" thing to the buyer, expects to receive the "price" which is owed in return by the buyer, price which is the object of that buyer's obligation. The same type of onerous relationship is created by a contract of lease.[9]

It follows, as experience shows, that most contracts we enter into are onerous and that, therefore, most onerous contracts are also bilateral/synallagmatic contracts since such contracts create obligations to perform on both sides of the contractual relationship.

"A contract is gratuitous when one party obligates himself towards another for the benefit of the latter, without obtaining any advantage in return." LSA-C.C. Art. 1910. It is the gratuitous motivation or intent of that

---

[8] See Précis, Louisiana Law of Sale and Lease, § 4.1.1.

[9] See Précis, Louisiana Law of Sale and Lease, Chapter 1.

party who obliges herself towards another "without obtaining any advantage in return" that actually determines the nature of that contract. The typical and most common example of such a kind of contract is the **"donation purely gratuitous . . . which is made without condition and merely from liberality."**[10] Another example of such contracts can be found in **LSA-C.C. Art. 2891** which states: **"The loan for use is a gratuitous contract by which a person, the lender, delivers a nonconsumable thing to another, the borrower, for him to use and return."**[11]

There exist some important legal and practical reasons for this distinction between onerous and gratuitous contracts. Three reasons will help illustrate. For example, most gratuitous contracts are "formal or solemn" contracts in the sense that their validity is conditional upon the fulfillment of some requirement of "form." Illustrations are provided by LSA-C.C. Articles 1536 and 1538.[12]

As far as a manual gift is concerned, because it creates on the donor an obligation to vest a real right in the donee, it is possible to look at the "real" or actual delivery of the thing from the donor to the donee as some form of publicity or formality that is binding on the parties and will be binding on third parties once carried out. The purpose of formalities being required of gratuitous contracts is to protect as much as possible the party motivated by a gratuitous intent. Fulfilling a "formality" makes someone think more seriously about giving away some assets without receiving a counter-performance.

Another reason for the distinction focuses on the "person" of the donee or the recipient of one's generous intent. Gratuitous contracts can be annulled more easily than onerous contracts in case of "error as to the person."[13] A combined reading of LSA-C.C. Articles 1949 and 1950 suggests that when the "cause," or consideration of the person who receives the benefit, is one without which the donor would not have made a gratuitous transfer, then the consent of the latter has been vitiated and the contract would be null of a relative nullity for lack of informed consent. Such contracts are said to have been entered *intuitu personae*, because of the very "person" who is to receive a benefit — the "donee" in a donation.

A third illustration of this important difference between gratuitous and onerous contracts can be found in **LSA-C.C. Art. 2039** under the title of the **"Revocatory Action":**[14] **"An obligee may attack a gratuitous contract made by the obligor whether or not the other party knew that the contract would cause or increase the obligor's insolvency."**

---

[10] LSA-C.C. Art. 1523 in part.

[11] As stated above, a loan is also a unilateral contract; see supra Article 1.

[12] LSA-C.C. Art. 1536: "An act shall be passed before a notary public and two witnesses of every donation inter vivos of immovable property or incorporeal things, such as rents, credits, rights or actions, under the penalty of nullity." Art. 1538: "A donation inter vivos, even of movable effects, will not be valid, unless an act be passed of the same, as is before prescribed. Such an act ought to contain a detailed estimate of the effects given."

[13] See infra, Error, Chapter 4, Article 1.

[14] See infra, Chapter 11.

In general, a party who provides a "benefit" to another is not held to the same standard of performance as a party to an onerous contract who, therefore, receives a counter-performance. A donor of a "horse" is not held to the same obligation of "warranty" to which a seller is held precisely because the donor of the horse did not impose any burden on the donee in such a way that the latter could be justified in trying to get his "money's worth" by an action in warranty or equivalent (such as damages). Donation and warranty by the donor do not fit together!

ARTICLE 3
COMMUTATIVE AND ALEATORY CONTRACTS
LSA-C.C. ARTS. 1911–1912

This classification as it exists in the Louisiana civil Code is, we believe, problematic. From the point of view of the "architecture" or "formal structure" of the Code Articles which make up this Chapter, the appearance (in a formal sense) of the "tandem," or "two-by-two" approach, is saved.

In civil law jurisdictions, like France and Québec, commutative contracts and aleatory contracts are, from a presentation or formal point of view, contrasted one with the other as they "appear" to be in the Louisiana civil Code. However when one looks at the "substance" of the Articles and the concepts they describe, the "appearance" is mere window dressing and sets the Louisiana civil Code apart and in a very odd situation as we hope to point out in the following comments.

LSA-C.C. Art. 1911 defines a commutative contract as follows: "**A contract is commutative when the performance of the obligation of each party is correlative to the performance of the other.**" As regards the aleatory contract, **Art. 1912** states that "**A contract is aleatory when, because of its nature or according to the parties' intent, the performance of either party's obligation, or the extent of the performance, depends on an uncertain event.**"

Let us compare the above two articles with code articles taken from the Louisiana civil Code of 1870 (until revised by Acts 1984, No.331 § 1), the French civil Code and the Québec civil Code.

Louisiana civil Code of 1870: Art. 1768: "*Commutative contracts are those in which what is done, given or promised by one party, is considered as equivalent to, or a consideration for what is done, given, or promised by the other.*" *Article 1776*, in its first paragraph, stated: "*A contract is aleatory or hazardous, when the performance of that which is one of its objects, depends on an uncertain event.*" *Article 1104 of the French civil Code states that "The contract is commutative when each party binds herself to give or do something which is considered as the equivalent of what she is given or of what is done for her advantage. When the equivalent consists in the chance for each one of the parties, of winning or losing something as a result of an uncertain event, the contract is aleatory.*" Lastly, the *civil Code of Québec* states in *Article 1382* that "*A contract is commutative when, at the time it is formed, the extent of the obligations of the parties and of the advantages obtained by them in return is certain and determinate. When the extent of the obligations or of the advantages is uncertain, the contract is aleatory.*"

In other words, according to the above three definitions, in a commutative contract each party knows in advance the extent of the advantage she is to receive from the performance of her obligation by the other party. Whenever the existence or the extent of this advantage is unknown in advance, is uncertain, the contract is aleatory.[15] The above definitions preserve not only the well balanced architecture of the Code articles, but also, and most importantly, the contrast in the substance of the two concepts of commutative contract and aleatory contract.

There lies the problem with the substance of the new Louisiana civil Code Article 1911. Must the "correlation" be between the actual "performances" of the obligations or between "the same thing," "the extent," "the consideration" of the reciprocal obligations? It is our position that Article 1911 first does not add to the definition of bilateral/synallagmatic contract and, second, fails to emphasize the difference between a truly 'commutative' contract at civil law and an aleatory contract as it is defined in LSA-C.C. Art. 1912.

What does "correlative" mean and how can its meaning fit in the definition of both LSA-C.C. Articles 1908 and 1911?

According to Webster's II New College Dictionary, correlative means: "corresponding: related. Indicating a reciprocal or complementary relationship." Black's Law Dictionary (abridged 7th ed.) defines correlative in these terms: "Related or corresponding; analogous. Having or involving a reciprocal or mutually interdependent relationship." So, correlative simply means "reciprocal, interdependent."

As seen above, it is the very essence of a bilateral or synallagmatic contract to create obligations going both ways in the relationship in such a manner that each party's obligation has for its "object" to give, to do or not to something.[16] It is inherent in any bilateral/synallagmatic contract that each party owes to the other the performance of the object of her own obligation. A seller must transfer the ownership of a thing to the buyer because such is the object of his obligation to "give," i.e. transfer the right of ownership of the thing. Likewise, the buyer in return is under the obligation to "give" the price which is the object of his obligation. Of what purpose would it be for parties to enter into a bilateral/synallagmatic contract if it were not to expect the faithful and reciprocal performance of the object of each other's obligation? Would any seller be willing to enter into a contract of sale (a bilateral/synallagmatic contract, par excellence) if he did not intend to be "paid," if he did not expect the reciprocal performance of his obligation by the buyer to pay the price? In a bilateral/synallagmatic contract, not only the obligations themselves are "reciprocal, correlative" as LSA-C.C. Art. 1908 states, but so are the performances by the very fact that they are inherent to the very nature of any bilateral/synallagmatic contract. Such a contract by itself can only create the reciprocity, the correlation, of the performances which are necessarily engendered by the reciprocity, or correlation of the obligations without which no performance could exist. We believe,

---

[15] In an aleatory contract, the extent or existence of an obligation owed by one party is contingent upon the occurrence of a suspensive condition as in gambling. On a suspensive condition, see Précis, Louisiana Law of Obligations in General, § 2.2.-B.1.B.

[16] LSA-C.C. Article 1756; see Précis, Louisiana Law of Obligations in General, Chapter 1.

therefore, that LSA-C.C. Art. 1911 adds absolutely nothing to Art. 1908.[17]

There is, possibly, an alternative interpretation of this Art. 1911. This interpretation is suggested by the reference made to the "*exceptio non adimpleti contractus*" in Comment (c) to this Article. The Comment relates this "traditional defense of non performance" to "correlative performances." We read this to mean that this defense can only be raised when the performances are "reciprocal" in the sense that they have to be performed at the same time, tit for tat in a sense. If the performances are not to be carried out at the same time, it is either because we have a suspensive condition[18] attached to the existence of an obligation (and, therefore, we cannot speak in terms of performance because no obligation exists yet and its "progeny" the performance cannot exist either) or we have a suspensive term attached to one performance and in that case the relationship, or timing of the performances, is affected either by the nature of the obligation or the intent of the parties. The contract remains bilateral/synallagmatic and it remains commutative in the original and commonly accepted civil law meaning of this adjective, but it ceases to be commutative in the Louisiana civil Code meaning if that meaning is that of time-related or time-interdependent performances of obligations. If such is the interpretation to be given to LSA-C.C. Art. 1911, we believe that it is a poor substitute for the Code articles on "term"[19] and "condition"[20] and that it does not add to the civil Code (except for confusion and redundancy).

As regards "aleatory contracts" a brief analysis of LSA-C.C. Art. 1912 may help in understanding the contrast made in most civil Codes, outside of Louisiana, between onerous commutative contracts and onerous aleatory contracts which are merely sub-divisions of onerous contracts. **LSA-C.C. Art. 2982** describes in clear legal terms what an aleatory contract is: "**The aleatory contract is a mutual agreement, of which the effects, with respect both to the advantages and losses, whether to all the parties or to one or more of them, depend on an uncertain event.**" The specific legal terms to focus on are that an *aleatory contract* is a *mutual agreement* which *creates effects*, i.e. advantages and losses, *vis-à-vis one or more parties*, and the occurrence of *which effects depend on an uncertain event*. The uncertain event, winning the jackpot, catching a lot of fish, depends on a "suspensive condition" happening, which translates into winning the jackpot, or actually catching a lot of fish.[21]

The Louisiana civil Code gives two examples of "aleatory contracts": the sale of a hope and the rent of lands.

As we wrote in another Précis,[22] "the sale of a hope is neither the sale of a non-existing thing nor the sale of a future thing. . . ." **LSA-C.C. Art. 2451**

---

[17] Is it not strange, and meaningful, that, as of today, no Louisiana Court has ever cited and relied on this Art. 1911 ever since it was revised in 1984?

[18] On Suspensive Condition, see Précis, Louisiana Law of Obligations in General, § 2.2.-B.1.

[19] On Term, see Précis, Louisiana Law of Obligations in General, § 2.2-A.1.

[20] On Condition, see Précis, Louisiana Law of Obligations in General, § 2.2-B.1.

[21] Id.

[22] Précis, Louisiana Law of Sale and Lease, § 2.3.4.

describes this sale in these terms: "**A hope may be the object of a contract of sale. Thus, a fisherman may sell a haul of his net before he throws it. In that case the buyer is entitled to whatever is caught in the net, according to the parties' expectations, and even if nothing is caught the sale is valid. . . .**" Since the "hope" is the thing bought — the object of the contract of sale — it is like an incorporeal thing that exists at the moment the sale is entered into with that sale carrying immediately one of its essential effects, the transfer of ownership of that hope to the fishermen.

The "rent of lands," as the second example of an aleatory contract, is a little more difficult to grasp. **LSA-C.C. Art. 2779** describes this contract in the following terms: "**The contract of rent of lands is a contract by which one of the parties conveys and cedes to the other a track [tract] of land, or any other immovable property, and stipulates that the latter shall hold it as owner, but reserving to the former an annual rent of a certain sum of money, or of a certain quantity of fruits, which the other party binds himself to pay him.**" Most important to bring about the aleatory element of this kind of sale is **LSA-C.C. Art. 2780**; it states that "**It is of the essence of this conveyance that it be made in perpetuity. If it be made for a limited time, it is a lease.**" The greater or lesser aleatory nature of this contract depends on the relationship between the market value of the tract of land conveyed to the "new owners," the annual amount of the rent paid by these "new owners" to the parties who conveyed the land to them, and the length of time that will elapse between the conveyance of the land made "in perpetuity" and the death of the parties who receive the annual rent. The longer these parties live, the longer the "new owners" will have to pay the "annual rent". If the recipients of the annual rent die shortly after the "conveyance" of the land has been made, the "new owners" will have paid a very low or low price, and thus made a substantial profit by "gambling" on the life expectancy of those parties from whom they "bought" the land. Conversely, if "those parties" who conveyed the land should live a long or very long time, it could happen that the total amount of the annual rents paid over that long or very long time will far exceed the market value of the land at the time the conveyance took place, may be years back! In this instance, the aleatory aspect of the contract, the death of the parties who conveyed the land, will come to haunt the "new owners" who will certainly come to the conclusion that they made a "bad deal," their gambling on the life expectancy of the parties who conveyed the land to them turned against them and that, therefore, they surely did not get their money's worth.

These two examples help show that not all onerous contracts are commutative, in the traditional civil law sense, because the objects of the obligations created by an onerous contract may not come to be equal or close to equal in value. It follows that an aleatory contract could not be rescinded on account of lesion,[23] that error as to the object could be almost impossible to argue.[24]

---

[23] On Lesion, see Précis, Louisiana Law of Sale and Lease, Chapter 2, Article 5.

[24] See infra, Error, Chapter 4, Article 1.

ARTICLE 4
PRINCIPAL AND ACCESSORY CONTRACTS
LSA-C.C. ART. 1913

This Article is made up of two paragraphs, each one describing one kind of contract. The "two-by-two" architectural structure or "tandem" of these Code Articles is reinstituted.

LSA-C.C. Art. 1913 states that "**A contract is accessory when it is made to provide security for the performance of an obligation. Suretyship, mortgage, pledge, and other types of security agreements are examples of such a contract.**

When the secured obligation arises from a contract, either between the same or other parties, that contract is the principal contract."

There is no need to dwell on this distinction which is not of much importance and is self-explanatory.[25]

A principal contract is one which can stand on its own; it needs no legal (contractual or otherwise) support than its own to exist; it does not need to *arise* from any other contract. A contract of sale can stand on its own; so can a donation or marriage contract.

On the other hand, when a contract needs the support of another contract (or legislation), when "**it is made to provide security for the performance of** [a principal] **obligation**" then it is an "accessory" to the principal contract. Article 1913 illustrates this concept of accessory contract with "**suretyship, mortgage, pledge . . .**"

The justification for this distinction consists in that the existence and validity of an accessory contract is contingent upon the existence and validity of the principal contract of which it is the accessory: if a contract of sale is invalid, if it cannot exist, the suretyship contract that was meant to "guarantee" or secure the right of the seller to a payment of the price will also be automatically invalid and non-existent. Its "support," the principal contract of sale, failed to come into existence.[26]

By contrast, the invalidity of an accessory contract does not carry with it the invalidity of the principal contract. The principal contract can survive without the "support" of the accessory contract. A sale can be perfectly valid even though the accessory contract of mortgage may be flawed.

It is therefore most important to ascertain that a principal contract is valid and, therefore, exists, before turning to an examination of the validity and, thus, the existence of its accessory contract. If the principal contract is invalid, the accessory contract itself will automatically be invalid.

---

[25] It appears neither in the civil Code of Québec nor in the French civil Code.

[26] The applicable Latin maxim reads "*accessorium sequitur principale*," or "the accessory follows the fate of the principal". (D.34,2, 19, 13). See as illustrations, LSA-C.C. Arts. 482 and 485.

ARTICLE 5
NOMINATE AND INNOMINATE CONTRACTS
LSA-C.C. ARTS. 1914-1915-1916

The substance of each one of these three Articles is so self-explanatory that a restatement of these Articles here should be sufficient.

Art. 1914: "Nominate contracts are those given a special designation such as sale, lease, loan, or insurance. Innominate contracts are those with no special designation."

Art. 1915: "All contracts, nominate and innominate, are subject to the rules of this title."

Art. 1916: "Nominate contracts are subject to the special rules of the respective titles when those rules modify, complement, or depart from the rules of this title."

ARTICLE 6
IMPLIED KINDS OF CONTRACTS

The kinds or categories of contracts listed in this "Chapter 1. Classification of Contracts" do not offer an exhaustive list of all conceivable kinds of contracts. Some kinds or categories of contracts can be implied from a combination of articles all through the civil Code. We will mention here only two implied kinds of contracts on account of the distinctive legal features of each kind and the practical consequences flowing from these distinctive features.

§ 1.6.1. CONSENSUAL, SOLEMN, AND REAL CONTRACTS.

A reading of Articles 1918 to 1982 which list the four requirements for a contract to exist, i.e. "capacity," "consent," "cause," and "object," leads to the conclusion that parties can be bound without the requirement of a writing to formalize their contract.

The rule is, indeed, that parties can be bound by a contract which is merely *consensual*, which results from the oral exchange of their wills. The most common *consensual* contract we enter into just about every day, and sometimes more than once, is the contract of sale of a movable thing. Such is very clearly stated in **LSA-C.C. Art. 2439 § 2:** "**Sale is a contract whereby a person transfers ownership of a thing to another for a price in money.**

The thing, the price, and the consent of the parties are requirements for the perfection of a sale." The binding force of "consent" is such that "**Ownership is transferred between the parties as soon as there is agreement on the thing and the price is fixed, even though the thing sold is not yet delivered nor the price paid.**"(LSA-C.C. Art. 2456.)[27]

---

[27] See Précis, Louisiana Law of Sale and Lease, Chapter 2; see also LSA-C.C. Art. 518. A contract of Lease is also a consensual contact; see same Précis, Chapter 1, Article 2 (". . . it does not appear that any particular form at all is necessary for a lease to be valid")."

To the contrary, and as an exception to the rule that contracts are consensual, there are instances of contracts, in the civil Code, which require a "form," a writing, for some contracts to be valid and binding. They are called *solemn* or *formal* contracts. We read, for example, in **LSA-C.C. Art. 2440** that **"A sale or promise of sale of an immovable must be made by authentic act or by act under private signature, except as provided in Article 1839."**[28]

Likewise a form is required for a compromise. **"A compromise shall be made in writing or recited in open court, in which case the recitation shall be susceptible of being transcribed from the record of the proceedings."(LSA-C.C. Art. 3072)**.

One important legal and practical difference between consensual and formal or solemn contracts concerns the burden of proof as has been explained in *Louisiana Law of Obligations in General, A Précis.*[29] Another legal and practical difference in determining whether a contract ought to be consensual or, on the contrary, should be in writing, is the need to ascertain the reason for the formality. Whose interest is the formality supposed to protect, what purpose is to be achieved in imposing a formality for some contracts and not for others? In a compromise, the law aims at protecting the interests of both parties; in a contract of sale of an immovable, the law aims at protecting the interests of the parties (the seller mainly) in making sure that they realize how important the sale of an "immovable" is, the impact it will have on their patrimony. But the law is also concerned about protecting the interests of third parties by requiring that the contract in "writing" be recorded.[30]

The category of contracts which are identified as "real contracts" is based on the Latin word "res" which means "thing." Such are contracts which come into existence not only when the four basic requirements[31] for any contract are met but, most importantly, when the thing, which is the object of the obligor's obligation, is "delivered" to the obligee. Consent alone is not sufficient to create the contract unless there has occurred an actual transfer of the possession of the thing from one party to the other. The delivery or transfer of the thing takes on the same role as the formality in formal contracts. Illustrations abound in the civil Code. **LSA-C.C. Art. 2891** states that "[t]**he loan for use is a gratuitous contract by which a person, the lender, delivers a nonconsumable thing to another, the borrower, for him to use and return."** In other words, there is no contract of loan for use in existence, may be only a promise of such a loan, until and when the thing to be used has been delivered to the borrower. Likewise, **"[t]he manual gift, that is, the giving of corporeal movable effects, accompanied by a real delivery, is not subject to any formality." LSA-C.C. Art. 1539.** Again, unless the thing given has been actually delivered into the "hands" of the donee, there is no "manual gift," only perhaps, a promise of such a gift.

---

[28] See Précis, Louisiana Law of Sale and Lease, § 2.5.3; see also LSA-C.C. Art. 517.

[29] See Proof of Obligations in Précis, Louisiana Law of Obligations in General, Chapter 6.

[30] See Précis, Louisiana Law of Sale and Lease: Rights of the Parties in Case of Eviction, § 4.1.2.B.

[31] See infra the requirements of Capacity, Chapter 2; Consent, Chapter 3; Cause, Chapter 5; and Object, Chapter 6.

§ 1.6.2. MUTUALLY NEGOTIATED CONTRACTS AND CONTRACTS OF ADHESION.

As a general rule, contracts are negotiated between two parties who mutually agree on their reciprocal obligations and rights. A buyer of a house will, usually, negotiate with the seller over the price and other elements [such as the time of occupation of the home] of the contract of sale or promise of sale. Any buyer of a car has gone through the experience (or "game") of bargaining with the salesman! Such contracts resulting from a mutual agreement between the two parties are presumed to fully reflect the principles of "autonomy of the will" and "freedom of contract" which are the foundations of the law of contracts at civil law. In such contracts, if there arises any claim of vice of consent[32] it will be an issue of be argued and debated between the two parties to the contract.

However, today, contracts are less and less negotiated on equal basis and more and more either non-negotiable at all or negotiable in part only. Such contracts are often referred to as "contracts of adhesion" or "adhesion contracts." Furthermore, if in some instances of adhesion contracts one may enjoy some freedom not to enter into such contracts, in many other instances that very freedom is denied to the "weaker" party, the consumer for example. Illustrations abound: insurance contracts, electricity supply contracts, transportation contracts, etc. One may not contract a life insurance policy but if one does one's freedom to "bargain" or "negotiate" with the insurance company is rather limited. Under the law, one "must" have a car insurance policy but negotiating such a contract for as one would like this contract to read is vel non impossible. At the same time, one is denied the freedom not to enter into such a contract and one's freedom to negotiate such a contract is very limited. Basically one must "adhere" to one of the few offers made by the insurance company. One does need electricity for all sorts of vital purposes and, yet, one may have neither the choice of the supplier of electricity nor any choice between alternative provisions in the contract. It is, basically, "take it or leave it."

The civil Code makes no difference between these two kinds of contracts, whether "negotiated" or "adhesion contracts." All contracts, states **LSA-C.C. Art. 1915, "are subject to the rules of this Title."** Among those rules are the rules on the requirements for the formation of a contract, consent and vices of consent in particular.[33]

With respect to contracts which the courts will qualify and describe as "adhesion contracts," it is the responsibility of the courts to attempt to re-establish some balance between the unequal bargaining powers of the parties, to protect the "weak" against the "strong." The courts can intervene by focusing on the requirement of "consent" under a variety of forms, such as the possible absence or limitation of the "freedom to contract," the **"misrepresentation or suppression of the truth made with the intention either to obtain an unjust advantage for one party or to cause a loss or inconvenience to the other,"**[34]

---

[32] See infra Vices of consent,, Chapter 4.

[33] See infra, Chapters 3 and 4.

[34] LSA-C.C. Art. 1953.

or still **"a reasonable fear of unjust and considerable injury to a party's person, property, or reputation."**[35] One could also bring to bear the concept of "cause" and particularly error as to a substantial quality of the thing or the qualities of the other party.[36]

The Louisiana jurisprudence has adopted a variety of very sensible and "codal" approaches to this issue. The courts have read out of a "boiler plate contract," or adhesion contract, a provision to which the "weaker" of the two parties could not possibly have "freely" consented. The courts will also interpret the "adhesion clause" of a contract against the drafter of that contract, in most instances the much stronger party. Thereby the courts re-establish some equilibrium between the unequal bargaining powers of the parties by substituting their sense of fairness in their attempt to protect the party who is, economically speaking, the weaker party to the contract.

---

[35] LSA-C.C. Art. 1959.

[36] See infra, Error, Chapter 4, Article 1.

Chapters 2 to 7

FORMATION OF CONTRACTS

Chapters 2 to 7, Title IV, Book III, of the civil Code, deal with the four requirements for any contract to be formed as was previously stated in LSA-C.C. Art. 1915. We will analyze these four requirements in the order in which they appear in the civil Code: Chapter 1: Capacity; Chapter 2: Consent and Vices of Consent; Chapter 3: Cause; Chapter 4: Object and Matter of Contracts; Chapter 5: Third Party Beneficiary.

Chapter 2

CAPACITY
LSA-C.C. ARTS. 1918 TO 1926

The concept of "capacity," in its legal sense, must be distinguished, first, from the concept of "personality" and, second, from the notions of "authority or power."

"Personality," in the sense of the civil Code, is the ability to hold rights and owe obligations. Personality is therefore proper to "persons," be they natural persons or juridical persons[1], i.e. legal entities, because upon birth (and even conception) or incorporation, persons are automatically holders of a "patrimony." "Patrimony" can be described as the sum total of the rights and obligations of a monetary value vested in the person. LSA-C.C. Arts 25 and 26 clearly identify this concept of 'personality" as concerns natural persons.[2]

Art. 25 states: "**Natural personality commences from the moment of live birth and terminates at death**". Art. 26 vests "personality" in the unborn under a condition: "**An unborn child shall be considered as a natural person for whatever relates to its interests from the moment of conception. If the child is born dead, it shall be considered never to have existed as a person, except for purposes of actions resulting from its wrongful death.**" Natural personality vests in any natural person the legal ability to hold rights and owe obligations as is stated in **LSA-C.C. Art. 27:** "**All natural persons enjoy general legal capacity to have rights and duties.**" The words "legal capacity" as they are read in this Art. are a little confusing as they seem to equate "capacity" with "personality." Actually, if these same words are read, as they should be, in conjunction with the verb "enjoy" they actually refer to a form of "capacity" which is the capacity to enjoy all those rights which are derived from one's personality except in those few instances where this capacity to "enjoy" rights can be denied or restricted. This particular situation is discussed below where a distinction is made between "incapacity to enjoy" and "incapacity to exercise" a right.

As regards the notions of "authority or power," they are related to the concept of "Representation" as this concept is described in LSA-C.C. Arts 2985 and 2986.

---

[1] LSA-C.C. Art. 24: "There are two kinds of persons: natural persons and juridical persons.

A natural person is a human being. A juridical person is an entity to which the law attributes personality, such as a corporation or a partnership. The personality of a juridical person is distinct from that of its members."

[2] See also LSA-C.C. Art. 1474: "To be capable of receiving by donation inter vivos, an unborn child must be in utero at the time the donation is made. To be capable of receiving by donation mortis causa, an unborn child must be in utero at the time of the death of the testator. In either case, the donation has effect only if the child is born alive."

Art. 2985: "A person may represent another person in legal relations as provided by law or by juridical act. This is called representation."

Art. 2986: "The authority of the representative may be conferred by law, by contract, such as mandate or partnership, or by the unilateral juridical act of procuration."

It is now possible to look at the two facets of 'capacity" or, rather, "incapacity". Indeed the general rule laid down in the Civil Code is that **"All natural persons enjoy general legal capacity to have rights and duties."** (LSA-C.C. Art. 27). In other words, the principle is that of "capacity" and "incapacity" is the exception. Thus, when considering a factual situation involving persons, a contractual relationship in particular, one should assume "capacity" on the part of the parties unless there is a ground for incapacity which will have to be proven and argued as regards one party or the other.

ARTICLE 1
INCAPACITY OF ENJOYMENT

As stated above, this Article 27 can be read as targeting an "incapacity of enjoyment" as opposed to an "incapacity of exercise" dealt with in Articles 28 and 29 as we shall see below.

There exists an incapacity of enjoyment when a person is deprived of the ability to "enjoy" a particular right. For example, under LSA-C.C. **Art. 941** "**A successor shall be declared unworthy if he is convicted of a crime involving the intentional killing, or attempted killing, of the decedent or is judicially determined to have participated in the intentional, unjustified killing, or attempted killing, of the decedent. An action to declare a successor unworthy shall be brought in the succession proceedings of the decedent.**

An executive pardon or pardon by operation of law does not affect the unworthiness of a successor." The so-called successor who falls under these circumstances is denied, by law, the right to claim an inheritance from the "decedent" vis-à-vis whom he has been **"declared unworthy."** Conversely, under **LSA-C.C. Art. 1471:** "Capacity to donate inter vivos must exist at the time the donor makes the donation. Capacity to donate mortis causa must exist at the time the testator executes the testament." And LSA-C.C. Art. 1472 states: "Capacity to receive a donation inter vivos must exist at the time the donee accepts the donation. Capacity to receive a donation mortis causa must exist at the time of the death of the testator." It follows that under the circumstances described in these two articles some persons cannot qualify as "donees" because they are deprived of the right to enjoy receiving a donation and, therefore, "**A donation in favor of a person who is incapable of receiving is null.**" (LSA-C.C. Art. 1475). The donation is null and, even more important, nobody can receive that donation "on behalf of" or as a "representative" of that donee because the latter is denied the very right to receive in these circumstances. These "incapacities" of enjoyment necessarily carry with them the lesser incapacity of "exercise" (reasoning *a fortiori ratione* from the greater to the lesser). The lesser right of "exercise" is included in the greater right of "enjoyment."

Another illustration of an incapacity of enjoyment can be found in **LSA-C.C. Art. 2447** which states: "**Officers of a court, such as judges, attorneys, clerks, and law enforcement agents, cannot purchase litigious rights under contestation in the jurisdiction of that court. The purchase of a litigious right by such an officer is null and makes the purchaser liable for all costs, interest, and damages.**" An attorney who finds himself in such a situation is denied the right to purchase a litigious right under contestation in the jurisdiction of the court in which he practices and no "representative" can do it in his place. However, outside the jurisdiction of that court, and assuming "good faith" on the part of the attorney, he could enter into a contract of sale bearing on a litigious right. The attorney's incapacity of enjoyment is restricted to a particular set of circumstances.[3]

In conclusion, incapacities of enjoyment are always, and can only be, special, restricted, limited in scope, because they amount to depriving a "person" of a necessary component of her "personality" which is the ability to be a holder of all rights under the law as from conception or birth. The "personality" of a natural person ends with death as **LSA-C.C. Art.25** states, in part: "**Natural personality commences from the moment of live birth and terminates at death.**"

Juridical acts entered into in violation of incapacities of enjoyment are null, either of relative nullity or of absolute nullity depending on the kind of interest which is protected by the nullity of the act.[4]

ARTICLE 2
INCAPACITY OF EXERCISE

Incapacities of exercise are much more common than incapacities of enjoyment, so much so that the concept of "incapacity" is used, in general, to refer to incapacities of exercise. The reason is easy to understand: it is much more dramatic and violative of a person's rights to deprive that person of the "enjoyment" of her rights than it is to deny her the ability to "exercise" a right she actually "enjoys" as a component part of her patrimony. For example, under **LSA-C.C.Art. 28** "**A natural person who has reached majority has capacity to make all sorts of juridical acts, unless otherwise provided by legislation.**" And **Article 29** to add: "**Majority is attained upon reaching the age of eighteen years.**" Under **LSA-C.C. Art. 395**: "**A full interdict lacks capacity to make a juridical act. A limited interdict lacks capacity to make a juridical act pertaining to the property or aspects of personal care that the judgement of limited interdiction places under the authority of his curator, except as provided in Article 1482 or in the judgment of limited interdiction.**" In the field of "Conventional Obligations," **LSA-C.C. Art. 1922** states: "**A fully emancipated minor has full contractual capacity.**" On the other hand "**A contract by an unemancipated minor may be rescinded on grounds of incapacity except . . .**" (LSA-C.C. Art. 1923, in part).

---

[3] One can also find an incapacity of enjoyment on the part of a tutor in contracting with the minor: LSA-C.C. Art. 339. We will not address here the types of incapacities of exercise which affect persons of age, persons above the age of majority: see, for example, LSA-C.C. Arts 389 et seq.

[4] See infra, Relative Nullity and Absolute Nullity, Chapter 9, Article 2.

As is implied in the Code Articles above, incapacities of exercise are enacted for the purpose of protecting a person on account of her age or her state of mind. Incapacities of exercise can, to a large extent, be assimilated to "vices of consent", particularly the lack of informed consent because of error, duress or fraud.[5]

§ 2.2.1. SCOPE AND EFFECT OF NULLITY FOR INCAPACITY.

The scope of application of an incapacity of exercise varies with the age of the incapable person.

As regards "minors," **LSA-C.C. Art. 1919** lays down the general rule that a contract entered into by **"a person without legal capacity is relatively null and may be rescinded."**[6] Such a minor is under a general incapacity of exercising the rights of which he has the enjoyment as a person. These rights will be exercised by a representative such as the parents or a tutor. However the civil Code provides for exceptions to the incapacity of exercise of a minor in a few limited instances. **LSA-C.C. Art. 1923** states that **"A contract by an unemancipated minor may be rescinded on the grounds of incapacity except when made for the purpose of providing the minor with something necessary for his support or education, or for a purpose related to his business."** These can be considered as "ordinary living" juridical acts. One can therefore assume that a minor falling under any one of the situations referred to in Art. 1923 has manifested enough knowledge, or maturity to understand and weigh the consequences of his acts as would have been the case of an ordinary person of age. We are here touching on the requirement of consent for the formation of a contract.

Under **LSA-C.C. Art. 1924**, to the extent that the minor represents to a party of age that he is himself of age and that the equities of the situation would not impoverish the "false" minor and when the contract was not entered into in bad faith by the party of age, **"the contract may not be rescinded."**[7]

As regards the effect of the relative nullity of the contract, it means that the contract must be considered as having never been entered into; it is an application of the retroactive effect of nullity. **LSA-C.C. Art. 1919** states that **"A contract made by a person without legal capacity is relatively null and may be rescinded only at the request of that person or his legal representative."** And **LSA-C.C. Art. 1921** adds that **"Upon rescission of a contract on the ground of incapacity, each party or his legal representative shall restore to the other what he has received thereunder. When restoration is impossible or impracticable, the court may award compensation to the party to whom restoration cannot be made."**

---

[5] See infra, Vices of Consent, Chapter 4.

[6] For the whole text of Art. 1919 see Appendix 1; see also LSA-C.C. Art. 1923.

[7] Art. 1924 states: "The mere representation of majority by an unemancipated minor does not preclude an action for rescission of the contract. When the other party reasonably relies on the minor's representation of the majority, the contract may not be rescinded."

Since such contracts entered into by persons without legal capacity are struck by a "relative nullity" which is meant to protect the interest of the person without legal capacity (hence the relative effect of the nullity),[8] such a nullity can be dispensed with, cured, by a juridical act of confirmation or an act of ratification.[9] **LSA-C.C. Art. 1920** states: "**Immediately after discovering the incapacity, a party, who at the time of contracting was ignorant of the incapacity of the other party, may require from that party, if the incapacity has ceased, or from the legal representative if it has not, that the contract be confirmed or rescinded.**"

---

[8] LSA-C.C. Art. 1919 stresses the protection granted by law to the person without legal capacity where it states that the contract "may be rescinded only at the request of that person of his legal representative."

[9] On acts of "confirmation", see LSA-C.C. Art. 1842 and Précis, Louisiana Law of Obligations in General" § 6.1.1.C.1.; on acts of "ratification", see LSA-C.C. Art. 1843 and Précis, Louisiana Law of Obligations in General § 6.1.1.C.2.

Chapter 3

CONSENT
LSA-C.C. ARTS. 1927 TO 1947

LSA-C.C. Art. 1927 is most important in three respects. It states, first, that "consent" is an *essential* (in the sense that consent is of the *essence* of a contract) requirement for any contract since **"A contract is formed by the consent of the parties. . . ."** This requirement applies to **"All contracts, nominate or innominate. . . ."**[1] A second reason why Art. 1927 is important is because it tells us that consent is **"established through offer and acceptance."** In other words, consent is made of two components parts and makes a contract a "bilateral juridical act" because two "wills" are exchanged. The opposite would be a "unilateral juridical act" which is the expression of one "will" only but sufficient, nevertheless, to create a juridical act.[2] A third important statement made in LSA-C.C. Art. 1927-2 is that, as a matter of principle, contracts are consensual **"Unless the law prescribes a certain formality for the intended contract, offer and acceptance may be made orally, in writing, or by action or inaction that under the circumstances is clearly indicative of consent."** The governing principle at civil law is that of **"consensualism,"** the freedom to enter into contracts (within limits set for all by law, public order,..) and the freedom to negotiate the terms of a contract.[3] In this respect, the parties may want their contract to meet a particular form agreed upon; the parties make the form of their contract an essential, and yet consensual, requirement of their contract. Such is provided in **LSA-C.C. Art. 1947: "When, in the absence of a legal requirement, the parties have contemplated a certain form, it is presumed that they do not intend to be bound until the contract is executed in that form."**

Without "consent," where consent is lacking, the contract is "vitiated."

We will consider, first, the existence and the expression of consent and, second, the integrity of that consent.

ARTICLE 1
EXISTENCE AND EXPRESSION OF CONSENT

In the traditional or classical type of contract (as opposed, for example, to e-contracts) described in the Civil Code, the contract "exists" when the "offer" and the "acceptance" are "expressed" in such a way that there is a "meeting of

---

[1] LSA-C.C. Art. 1915, see supra Chapter 1, Article 5.

[2] See Précis, Louisiana Law of Obligations in General, § 1.1.2.

[3] It is beyond the boundaries of this Précis to discuss the limitations to one's freedom to contract, to one's freedom to choose a co-contracting party, to one's freedom to negotiate all or some provisions in a contract; see supra "Consensual contracts" and "Contracts of Adhesion," §§ 1.6.1. and 1.6.2.

the minds" of the parties.[4]

§ 3.1.1. OFFER.

We will consider, first, the features or characteristics that an "offer" must meet to be in existence and we will address, then, the issue of the binding nature of an "offer."

1. *Preliminary Negotiations; Unilateral Promise.*

(a) Preliminary Negotiations

Chapter 3 of Title IV of the civil Code on "Consent" does not provide a list of the legal features that an offer must meet to qualify as an "offer." It might be difficult, therefore, to distinguish between an "offer to enter into a contract" and "an offer to contract."

In an offer to enter into a contract in the future, one could say that the parties to the negotiations are "testing, feeling out" each other for a certain period of time until either these preliminary negotiations fail or lead to an "offer to contract." There can exist a kind of "pre-contract"[5] consisting in the negotiations meant to prepare what could eventually become a "contract." These preliminary negotiations must be entered into and conducted in good faith by the parties. **LSA-C.C. Art. 1759** is imperative: **"Good faith shall govern the conduct of the obligor and the obligee in whatever pertains to the obligation."**[6] In addition, one can find in LSA-C.C. Art. 2315 a ground for holding one party liable to the other for the damage that the former may have caused "the other."[7]

(b) Unilateral Promise

There may exist also a "unilateral promise to contract." Such is a contract between two parties wherein the offeror is bound unilaterally to keep the offer open until the offeree exercises his right to "accept" or not the offer to contract. A typical example of such a unilateral promise to contract is the "option contract" as illustrated in **LSA-C.C. Art. 1933: "An option is a contract**

---

[4] Assuming the other three requirements are met: capacity, cause, and object.

[5] On Pre-Contracts, see Précis, Louisiana Law of Sale and Lease, Chapter 1.

[6] See Précis, Louisiana Law of Obligations in General, § 1.4.2.

[7] LSA-C.C. Art. 2315: "A. Every act whatever of man that causes damage to another obliges him by whose fault it happened to repair it.

B. Damages may include loss of consortium, service, and society, and shall be recoverable by the same respective categories of persons who would have had a cause of action for wrongful death of an injured person. Damages do not include costs for future medical treatment, services, surveillance, or procedures of any kind unless such treatment, services, surveillance, or procedures are directly related to a manifest physical or mental injury or disease. Damages shall include any sales taxes paid by the owner on the repair or replacement of the property damaged."

whereby the parties agree that the offeror is bound by his offer for a specified period of time and that the offeree may accept within that time." As regards the specific option to buy, **LSA-C.C. Art. 2620** states: "An option to buy, or an option to sell, is a contract whereby a party gives to another the right to accept an offer to sell, or to buy, a thing within a stipulated time.

"An option must set forth the thing and the price, and meet the formal requirements of the sale it contemplates."[8]

2. *Features of an "Offer": Precise and Firm/Definite.*

An offer, in its legal and technical sense, is a firm and definite proposal to enter into a contract, of a kind[9] agreed upon, under pre-arranged precise conditions. Such a definite proposal or offer, when accepted, will bring about the existence of the very contract the parties intended to enter into.

The offer must be precise in the sense that it must contain the "essential" component parts of the nominate or innominate contract to be entered into upon the offeree's acceptance. The civil Code does provide a few examples of the contents of a precise offer to enter into a nominate contract. We can find one in **LSA-C.C. Art. 2439** which defines a sale as "**a contract whereby a person transfers ownership of a thing to another for a price in money.**

The thing, the price, and the consent of the parties are requirements for the perfection of a sale."[10] An offer to enter into a sale requires, for that sale to exist, that the parties exchange their consent (offer and acceptance), that there be an agreement on the thing that will be transferred from the seller to the buyer and an agreement on the price that will be paid by the buyer to the seller. Likewise, **LSA-C.C. Art. 2668** defines a contract of lease as ". . . **a synallagmatic contract by which one party, the lessor, binds himself to give to the other party, the lessee, the use and enjoyment of a thing for a term in exchange for a rent that the lessee binds himself to pay.**

The consent of the parties as to the thing and the rent is essential but not necessarily sufficient for a contract of lease." As the second paragraph of Art. 2668 states, there are two essential elements to a contract of lease: consent of the parties bearing on the thing and consent bearing on the amount of the rent. However, by common agreement, the parties can add a requirement, a writing for example, to the two essential requirements of a thing and the rent.

If an offer does not refer precisely to the "essential" component parts of the contract the parties wish to enter into, it will not qualify as an offer.

As to the element of "firmness" or "seriousness" of the offer, it means that the offeror must be willing to enter into the contract he proposes to an offeree. It is usually understood that such is the case when the offer is made without any "reservation." However, even though some of the reservations, express or tacit, are made by the offeror, the proposal could still be considered a "firm" offer.

---

[8] See Précis, Louisiana Law of Sale and Lease, § 1.1.3.

[9] See supra, "Classification of Contracts", Chapter 1.

[10] See Précis, Louisiana Law of Sale and Lease, Chapter 2.

For example, an offer to sell made by a merchant "as long as the merchandise is in stock": this reservation, like a suspensive condition, does not prevent the merchant from being bound to sell until he is out of merchandise. On the other hand, if the reservation is somewhat general and enables the offeror to exercise some discretion in controlling the contents of his so-called offer or to choose an offeree among many, there may not exist, then, a firm offer. For example, an "offeror" may want to enter into a contract on the basis of a particular offeree's human or professional characteristics: such could be the case in a contract for services of a portrait painter, for instance. Such a kind of contract, as is often the case of gratuitous contracts,[11] would be referred to as *"intuitu personae."* Such an offer is obviously not "firm" since the offeror has "reserved" to himself the power to choose his co-contractor. Whenever *"intuitu personae"* contracts are "offered," the offeror <u>reserves</u> to himself much discretion which affects the "firmness" of the offer.

3. *Form of the Offer and Addressee of the Offer.*

Under the second paragraph of **LSA-C.C. Art. 1927, "A contract is formed by the consent of the parties established through offer and acceptance.**

Unless the law prescribes a certain formality for the intended contract, offer and acceptance may be made orally, in writing, or by action or inaction that under the circumstances is clearly indicative of consent. Unless otherwise specified in the offer, there need not be conformity between the manner in which the offer is made and the manner in which the acceptance is made."

Whatever the form of the offer, it remains that it must include the "essential" component parts of the contract which is offered. If an item in a store window does not include its price, it is most likely not offered "firmly and precisely" to a customer. If the same item is "offered" with a price attached, there could still be an "implied reservation," such as that the displayed item would "fit" the buyer. When a taxi is waiting for customers at a train station, the taxi's offer is expressed under the form of "waiting" to enter into a contract of transport. Is it a "firm" offer? Again there may exist some "undisclosed reservations" such as this particular taxi being restricted to some parts of a town, not being licensed to transport more than three passengers, etc.

There may exist some ambiguity, therefore, as to whether there is a firm offer under the facts of a case, particularly when the offer is made **"by action or inaction,"** unless **"under the circumstances"** they are clearly indicative of consent.

As regards the addressee of an offer, there are at least three possibilities: either the offer is made to a particular person, or to several persons or to the public at large. **LSA-C.C. Art. 1944** states that **"An offer of a reward made to the public is binding upon the offeror even if the one who performs the requested act does not know of the offer."** A person who makes an "offer," in the legal sense of the word, to several persons or to the public could be bound by

---

[11] See LSA-C.C. Art. 1910 and gratuitous contracts, supra Chapter 1, Article 2.

his offer as appears clearly from **LSA-C.C. Art. 1946**: "Unless otherwise stipulated in the offer made to the public, or otherwise implied from the nature of the act, when several persons have performed the requested act, the reward belongs to the first one giving notice of his completion of performance to the offeror."

4. *Duration of the Offer or Its Binding Nature.*

The issue is that of the right, or not, of the offeror to withdraw his offer before it has been accepted; is an offer freely revocable or is the revocability of an offer subject to conditions?

The civil Code is rather clear and explicit in this regard. A distinction is made according to whether or not the offeror has specified a period of time for an offeree to accept the offer.

If the offeror has specified a period of time for the acceptance then, according to **LSA-C.C. Art. 1928**, such an **"An offer that specifies a period of time for acceptance is irrevocable during that time."** The same Article adds that **"When the offeror manifests an intent to give the offeree a delay within which to accept, without specifying a time, the offer is irrevocable for a reasonable time."** It follows logically that **"An irrevocable offer expires if not accepted within the time prescribed in the preceding Article."**(LSA-C.C. Art. 1929).

In the event an offer is not irrevocable (under LSA-C.C. Art. 1928) then, under **LSA-C.C. Art. 1930** it "may be revoked before it is accepted." Furthermore, **"A revocable offer expires if not accepted within a reasonable time."** (LSA-C.C. Art. 1931). It might be difficult, under some circumstances, to agree on what a reasonable time is. It is therefore advisable to set a time in an offer so as to make it irrevocable if one is determined to enter into a contract. Furthermore, in such a case, the contract will be formed only when the offeror receives the acceptance, thus giving some control to the offeror over the moment of formation of the contract.[12]

Regardless of the nature of the offer, whether it is irrevocable or revocable, it will expire **"by the death or incapacity of the offeror or the offeree before it has been accepted." (LSA-C.C. Art. 1932)**. In other words, such an offer lapses for lack of a party who could receive the acceptance and proceed with the obligations then created by a contract.

§ 3.1.2. ACCEPTANCE.

If the offer is one side of consent, acceptance by the offeree is the other side. If an offer must meet certain conditions, an acceptance must also meet some conditions if it is to carry any legal effect, in particular contribute to the meeting of the minds so as to form the contract.

---

[12] See infra, Moment of Formation of the Contract, Meeting of the Minds, Chapter 3, Article 2.

1. *Conditions of Substance.*

LSA-C.C. Art. 1943 states that **"An acceptance not in accordance with the terms of the offer is deemed to be a counteroffer."** Reading this Article *a contrario*, it is easy to conclude that an acceptance, pure and simple, is one which meets the terms of the offer in such a way that the **"consent of the parties has been established." (LSA-C.C. Art. 1927)**

Such an acceptance is not complete and ceases to be pure and simple, or firm, whenever the offeree expresses some reservations of substance or suggests some conditions to his acceptance. There will be, then, a "counteroffer" by the offeree as stated in LSA-C.C. Art. 1943. In other words, the offeree will become, in a certain sense, an offeror in return and the original offeror will become the offeree of the counteroffer. Obviously this "counteroffering" could go on for a while through a series of successive offers taking on the forms of successive counter offers . . . until one party "gives up."[13] It is important to recall here that an offer, to be so qualified, must bear on the "essential" component parts of the contract, such as the thing and the price in a contract of sale. Likewise, the acceptance, to be so qualified, must bear on the same "essential" component parts. If the offeror-seller did not make an agreement on the methods of payment of the price an essential element of the contract of sale, a subsequent exchange of views between seller and buyer as regards the method of payment will not amount to "counteroffers" between the parties. Indeed, a method of payment of an agreed price is an accessory component part of a contract of sale which does not prevent the sale from being entered into and the ownership of a movable thing from being transferred by mere consent.[14] Likewise, if in a contract of sale the parties, the buyer in particular, have not agreed on the quality of the thing that the seller is to deliver to the buyer and have not made that agreement on the quality of the thing of the essence of their contract, then the seller **"obligor need not give one of the best quality but he may not tender one of the worst." (LSA-C.C. Art. 1860)**[15] Most illustrative of this issue of distinguishing between a pure and simple acceptance and a counteroffer is LSA-C.C. Art. 2601: **"An expression of acceptance of an offer to sell a movable thing suffices to form a contract of sale if there is agreement on the thing and the price, even though the acceptance contains terms additional to, or different from, the terms of the offer, unless acceptance is made conditional on the offeror's acceptance of the additional or different terms. Where the acceptance is not so conditioned, the additional or different terms are regarded as proposals for modification and must be accepted by the offeror in order to become a part of the contract.**

Between merchants, however, additional terms become part of the contract unless they alter the offer materially, or the offer expressly limits the acceptance to the terms of the offer, or the offeree is notified of the

---

[13] An action may then be available under LSA-C.C. Art. 1757 or Art. 2315.

[14] See Précis, Louisiana Law of Sale and Lease, Chapter 3, Article 1, Transfer of Ownership. See also LSA-C.C. Art. 1816 and Précis, Louisiana Law of Obligations in General, Article 4, Divisible and Indivisible Obligations, § 4.4.1.

[15] See Précis, Louisiana Law of Obligations in General, § 7.1.1.B. Object of the Performance.

offeror's objection to the additional terms within a reasonable time, in all of which cases the additional terms do not become a part of the contract. Additional terms alter the offer materially when their nature is such that it must be presumed that the offeror would not have contracted on those terms."[16]

2. *Conditions of Form.*

As regards the form of the acceptance, the civil Code contemplates different situations. As a general principle, "Unless the law prescribes a certain formality for the intended contract, offer and acceptance may be made orally, in writing, or by action or inaction that under the circumstances is clearly indicative of consent." (LSA-C.C. Art. 1927). Likewise "A medium or a manner of acceptance is reasonable if it is the one used in making the offer or one customary in similar transactions at the time and place the offer is received, unless circumstances known to the offeree indicate otherwise." (LSA-C.C. Art. 1936). In other words, like an offer, an acceptance can be *express* or *tacit*. A tacit acceptance, besides being sometimes difficult to prove, may open the door to questions of determination of the facts in a particular case when the acceptance may consist in "beginning a performance" or in "completing a performance."

Consider the following **Code Articles. Art. 1939: "When an offeror invites an offeree to accept by performance and, according to usage or the nature or the terms of the contract, it is contemplated that the performance will be completed if commenced, a contract is formed when the offeree begins the requested performance."**

Art. 1940: "When, according to usage or the nature of the contract, or its own terms, an offer made to a particular offeree can be accepted only by rendering a completed performance, the offeror cannot revoke the offer, once the offeree has begun to perform, for the reasonable time necessary to complete the performance. The offeree, however, is not bound to complete the performance he has begun.

The offeror's duty of performance is conditional on completion or tender of the requested performance."

These two Code Articles are further explained by **Art. 1941: "When commencement of the performance either constitutes acceptance or makes the offer irrevocable, the offeree must give prompt notice of that commencement unless the offeror knows or should know that the offeree has begun to perform. An offeree who fails to give the notice is liable for damages."** These Articles leave in the "offeree" the "discretion" to decide when he has commenced performance, the extent of that commencement . . . and the timing of the so-called "prompt notice of that commencement" to the offeror. Furthermore, since the notice to the offeror of the commencement of his performance by the offeree is apparently not required whenever **"the offeror**

---

[16] See Précis, Louisiana Law of Sale and Lease, Chapter 2, Article 2, § 2.2.1.

knows or should know that the offeree has begun to perform," it is very unlikely that "**An offeree who fails to give the notice**" would be "**liable for damages.**"

As we interpret these Articles, they are bound to raise important issues. These issues that will arise in a conflict between a party "offeror" and a party "offeree" will be, first of all, to properly qualify these parties as either "offeror" or "offeree" for all legal purposes because that qualification will decide, in second place, which party "has commenced performance" and "should issue a prompt notice," which party "knew or should have known" and thus no notice would be necessary, "which party may owe damages" to the other. A combination of "commenced performance"on the part of the offeree and "should have known" on the part of the offeror, should be beneficial to that party whom the courts would qualify, consistently, as the "offeree."[17]

Acceptance by silence, as a matter of principle, does not meet the requirements of a binding acceptance: silence is not acceptance. However, "**When, because of special circumstances, the offeree's silence leads the offeror reasonably to believe that a contract has been formed, the offer is deemed accepted.**" **(LSA-C.C. Art. 1942).** An illustration of silence, or conduct, as an acceptance, is provided by **LSA-C.C. Art. 2602: "A contract of sale of movables may be established by conduct of both parties that recognizes the existence of that contract even though the communications exchanged by them do not suffice to form a contract. In such a case the contract consists of those terms on which the communications of the parties agree, together with any applicable provisions of the suppletive law.**" Another form of silence as an acceptance is well illustrated by **Art. 2721: "A lease with a fixed term is reconducted if, after the expiration of the term, and without notice to vacate or terminate or other opposition by the lessor or the lessee, the lessee remains in possession:**

(1) For thirty days in the case of an agricultural lease;

(2) For one week in the case of other leases with a fixed term that is longer than a week; or

(3) For one day in the case of a lease with a fixed term that is equal to or shorter than a week."

ARTICLE 2
BINDING NATURE OF OFFER
MEETING OF MINDS-REVOCATION

Whenever a contract is to be entered into between parties who are not negotiating face to face but who are separated by some distance, the moment of formation of their contract becomes a crucial issue. We have seen that when an offer is "irrevocable" the offeror must leave his offer open for the period of time stated. To put it another way, when an offer is irrevocable, it cannot be revoked by the offeror once the offeree has become aware of the offer. The offeror is bound unilaterally to keep his offer open. However, this same irrevocable offer

---

[17] The cases that help illustrate these Articles are not always that decisive; see Appendix III.

represents a great benefit for the offeror since the **"acceptance of an irrevocable offer is effective when received by the offeror."** (**LSA-C.C. Art. 1934**) In other words, the offeror will be the first one to know when the contract is formed since the formation of the contract will occur upon "receipt" of the acceptance within the time given to the offeree to accept. Once should interpret the word "receipt" to mean "physical or material receipt" of the acceptance (receipt of the letter of acceptance, email, telephone message, etc.) rather than to mean "receipt-knowledge" in the sense that the offeror should have knowledge of the acceptance by opening his email or the letter. It cannot be left to the offeror to delay unduly, intentionally in particular, the timing of formation of the contract following his receiving of the acceptance within the time given to the offeree to accept. Such is the meaning of **LSA-C.C. Art. 1938**: **"A written revocation, rejection, or acceptance is received when it comes into the possession of the addressee or of a person authorized by him to receive it, or when it is deposited in a place the addressee has indicated as the place for this or similar communications to be deposited for him."**

On the other hand, when an offer is revocable, the offeree is given control over the moment of formation of the contract. As **LSA-C.C. Art. 1935** states: **"Unless otherwise specified by the offer or the law, an acceptance of a revocable offer, made in a manner and by a medium suggested by the offer or in a reasonable manner and by a reasonable medium, is effective when transmitted by the offeree."** As a result of this "transmission theory," or "mail box theory," or, still, "dispatch theory," the contract is formed when the offeree releases his control over his acceptance, when the latter is placed in the mail box, when it is transmitted at the flick of a button. It is not until then that the offeree has "accepted" the offer. Therefore, an offeree of a revocable offer should act promptly lest the offeror should change his mind within a reasonable time before the acceptance has been transmitted. Indeed, in the words of **LSA-C.C. Art. 1937**: **"A revocation of a revocable offer is effective when received by the offeree prior to acceptance."**

ARTICLE 3
OFFER OF A REWARD AND THE PUBLIC

The Louisiana civil Code addresses this particular kind of "offer" in two Articles. **Article 1944** exemplifies very clearly the principle that a party can be bound unilaterally by expressing her will:[18] **"An offer of a reward made to the public is binding upon the offeror even if the one who performs the requested act does not know of the offer."** Any offeror may be allowed to withdraw his offer depending on the conditions which are attached to the offer, such as whether the offer is revocable or irrevocable. Since an offer of a reward made to the public is not made to a particular offeree or a particular group of offerees, it is difficult, vel non impossible, to apply the rules governing revocable or irrevocable offers. It is the reason why, on the one hand, **LSA-C.C. Art. 1944** states that the offeror of a reward is bound **"even if the one who performs the requested act does not know of the offer"** and why, on the other hand, **LSA-**

---

[18] On these conditions or requirements, see infra: Vices of Consent, Chapter 4; Cause, Chapter 5; Object, Chapter 6.

C.C. Art. 1945 states that **"An offer of reward made to the public may be revoked before completion of the requested act, provided the revocation is made by the same or an equally effective means as the offer."** It is legitimate and fair to bind the offeror so that he will not be "enriched" as the expense of the person who acted, even unknowingly, upon the offer of a reward. One can find in this situation an analogy with *Negotiorum Gestio* or the Management of the Affairs of Another.[19]

---

[19] LSA-C.C. Art. 2292: "There is a management of affairs when a person, the manager, acts without authority to protect the interests of another, the owner, in the reasonable belief that the owner would approve of the action if made aware of the circumstances."

Art. 2297: "The owner whose affair has been managed is bound to fulfill the obligations that the manager has undertaken as a prudent administrator and to reimburse the manager for all necessary and useful expenses."

Chapter 4

INTEGRITY OF CONSENT, VICES OF CONSENT
LSA-C.C. ARTS. 1948 TO 1965

To the extent that "consensualism" is the founding principle of the law of contract, it explains why rules had to be laid down to ensure that "consent," as an "essential" element for the formation of a contract, is, first of all, "free," in the sense that it does reflect the true manifestation of a party's own independent will and, second, that consent be "informed," in the sense that a party's consent is enlightened by the advantages and drawbacks of entering into a particular contract. Following the influence of canonical law on protecting the integrity of consent, it is the underlying purpose of the Code Articles[1] on "Vices of Consent" to ensure the integrity of a party's consent when entering into a contract. However, one should add to the Code Articles on "Vices of Consent" some Code Articles on "Capacity," particularly capacity or incapacity of exercise, as having also for their purpose the protection of the incapable person considered as incapable of formulating a free and well informed intent to enter into a contract.[2]

We will consider, here, three well recognized vices of consent: "error," "fraud" and "duress" (violence). **LSA-C.C. 1948** states: **Consent may be vitiated by error, fraud, or duress.**[3] Because **"Lesion"** is included, albeit in one single Code Article,[4] under the same title "Vices of consent," it will be necessary to briefly address this concept.

ARTICLE 1
ERROR

After a description of this concept of error, we will focus on the several conditions which must be met for an error to be a ground for nullity of a contract. We will consider thereafter a series of situations in which, despite the existence of error on the part of one party, the contract ought to be maintained for reasons

---

[1] LSA-C.C. Arts. 1948-1965. At Roman law, vices of consent in contracts were not of much concern because contracts, being essentially "formal," once the form had been met the contract was considered binding. Violence (duress) and fraud fell under the law of delicts. Subsequently, the praetor, through the jus honorarium, created exceptions (*doli* and *metus*) of a contractual nature in cases of non performance of a contract.

[2] See supra Capacity, Chapter 2, Incapacity of Exercise, Article 2.

[3] From the point of view of structure and methodology, to have placed this Art. 1948, which lists the three existing vices of consent, under "Section I. Error" is totally misguided. Indeed, the Article has for its purpose to announce which are the vices of consent, including Error. Article 1948 should have been listed as a "stand alone" Article outside the legal regime of any one of the three vices: Error, Fraud and Duress. Such was the presentation of the Code Articles on "Defects of Consent" in the Civil Code of 1870 where Art. 1819, standing alone under its own title, listed the "Defects of Consent" before each Defect was covered under a separate title.

[4] LSA-C.C. Art. 1965.

of fairness, "**equity, justice, reason, and prevailing usages.**"[5]

§ 4.1.1. CONCEPT OF ERROR.

The civil Code does not include a definition of error and it was wise not to define such a concept in the Code.[6] The concept of error is a combination of subjective and objective elements which the courts have to weigh under the existing circumstances of each case. An error in one case may not be an error in another case because the combination of these elements can lead to different evaluations of the nature and the degree of the error.

LSA-C.C. Article 1949 contains a hint at providing some understanding of this concept of error: "**Error vitiates consent only when it concerns a cause without which the obligation would not have been incurred and that cause was known or should have been known to the other party.**" It is possible, also, when combining Articles 1954 and 1955 on Fraud,[7] to extract some understanding of the meaning of error in the absence of fraud.

We shall borrow from Articles 1821 and 1822 of the Civil Code of 1870 two descriptions of the concept of error. **Art. 1821** provided: "**That is called error of fact, which proceeds either from ignorance of that which really exists, or from a mistaken belief in the existence of that which has none.**" Art. 1822 stated: "**He is under an error of law, who is truly informed of the existence of facts, but who draws from them erroneous conclusions of law.**" All in all, an error consists in considering something as true when it is actually false or, conversely, in considering as false something which is actually true. Thus, any idea of justice as a foundation of the principle of consensualism would lead to declare null any contract tainted with an error because error would prevent the giving of an informed consent; consent would be vitiated. On the other hand, to grant the nullity of a contract whenever an error would have affected a party's consent would seriously impair the security and reliability of any and all transactions. Therefore, a balance had to be reached between the following two considerations: protect all parties to a contract and ensure the security of transactions. This balance is to be found in the interplay of the conditions which determine the legal regime of "Error" as a vice (defect) of consent.

§ 4.1.2. SERIOUSNESS OF THE ERROR.

An error must be serious, as must the intent to enter into a contract. As stated in **LSA C.C. Art. 1949**, "**Error vitiates consent only when it concerns a cause without which the obligation would not have been incurred and that cause**

---

[5] LSA-C.C. Art. 4: "When no rule for a particular situation can be derived from legislation or custom, the court is bound to proceed according to equity. To decide equitably, resort is made to justice, reason, and prevailing usages." See infra, Limitations, to the effect of nullity of a contract on the ground of error, Chapter 9.

[6] Indeed, definitions can only restrict and confine the ability of the courts to decide whether or not a certain factual situation falls squarely under the concept as defined by law. Definitions prevent expanding a rule of law by an *a pari ratione* reasoning.

[7] On Fraud and these Articles, see infra Chapter 4, Article 2.

was known or should have been known to the other party." The insertion of the word "cause" in this Article would require, under other circumstances, an extensive analysis as it could be standing for the legal concept of "cause" as this concept is presented in the civil Code as a requirement for a binding contract.[8] Since we will analyze this concept at length in its proper place as one of the four requirements for a valid contract,[9] suffice it to say here that the word "cause" in Art. 1949 should not be given the restrictive meaning of the requirement of "cause"defined as **"the[10] reason why a party obligates himself."** (LSA-C.C. Art. 1967 in part). Evidence of the broad analysis to be given to the word cause in Art. 1949 is provided by **LSA-C.C. Art. 1950: "Error may concern a cause when it bears on the nature of the contract, or the thing that is the contractual object or a substantial quality of that thing, or the person or the qualities of the other party, or the law, or any other circumstance that the parties regarded, or should in good faith have regarded, as a cause of the obligation."** Since a "natural person who has reached the age of majority has capacity to make all sorts of juridical acts,"[11] as well as exercise his/her right to vote, to drive . . . one must therefore assume that only serious errors that an average reasonable and capable person could make on account of some "difficulty, inconvenience," or lack of "special skill"[12] could be grounds for nullity of a contract that person would enter into. Furthermore, the need that any capable person meets, daily, to enter into contracts dictates that the security and binding nature of these contracts should not be questioned for any "cause" whatsoever. A contract is the "private law" of the parties to it and that "law" should not be "repealed" at the whim of any party or for any light and unreasonable "cause." As the limitations to the nullity of contracts on the ground of error will show, even some serious errors may not lead to the nullity of a contract if a greater or more valuable interest than the private interest of the party under error requires that the contract as a whole, or in part, be preserved.[13]

The seriousness of an error can only bear on an essential requirement for a contract to exist. Otherwise the error would bear on an accessory element of the contract and such an error could not bring about the nullity of the contract (unless the parties have made such an accessory element a suspensive condition of their contractual obligations[14]) as long as its essential requirements have been met. In this respect, for an error to be a ground for nullity of a contract it can bear **"on the nature of the contract, or the thing that is the contractual object or a substantial quality of that thing, or the person or the qualities of the other party, or the law, or any other circumstance that the parties regarded, or should in good faith have regarded, as a cause of the obligation." (LSA-C.C. Art. 1950).**

---

[8] LSA-C.C. Arts. 1966-1970.
[9] See infra, Cause, Chapter 5.
[10] Emphasis ours.
[11] LSA-C.C. Art. 28.
[12] LSA-C.C. Art. 1954 in part.
[13] See infra, § 4.2.1.C.
[14] On suspensive conditions, see Précis, Louisiana Law of Obligations in General, Chapter 2, Part B.

§ 4.1.3. KINDS OF SERIOUS ERRORS: ERRORS OF FACT, ERRORS OF LAW, ERRORS AS TO THE PERSON.

A. Error of Fact.

There can be an error made by the parties as to the *nature* or *kind* of contract they wish to enter into. The parties can make an error as to the type of arrangement, affairs or "negotium" they thought they were entering into. This type of error can then be called *"error in negotio."*[15] For example: a party may think she is negotiating a contract of loan[16] when the other party thinks that she will be a party to a contract of deposit[17]; or a party thought she would become a party to a contract of lease[18] when the other party was considering the contract to be a sale.[19] In these instances of error, the obstacle to the formation of a contract is such that the error could be called *"error-obstacle"* because the parties were not at all on the same wave length as regards the nature and legal characteristics of the contract (nominate or innominate) they intended to enter into.

The error can bear on the identity of the *thing* as the principal object of their contract. For example, in a contract of sale, the buyer may truly believe that he is buying a certain tract of land, the Laurentine Plantation, when the seller has in mind selling another and different tract of land, the Bayou Bleu Plantation. Or the buyer of a car may believe that he is buying car "A" when the seller believes he is selling car "B" very much different from car "A." In those instances there is error as to the identity of the principal object and, as a result, there can be no contract because the agreement lacks one of the four essential requirement for a contract to exist: an "object," be it a movable, an immovable, or services. Such an error can be called *"error in corpore"* or error as to the very identity of the thing which should have been the object of the contract.

Instead of bearing on the identity of the thing itself, an error can bear on **"a substantial quality of that thing"**[20] or the **reasonable fitness** of the thing for its **ordinary use.**[21] The traditional illustration of an error as to the substantial

---

[15] The word "negotium" or affairs is used here in the same sense as it is used in "Negotiorum Gestio" or Management of Affairs in LSA-C.C. Art. 2292: "There is a management of affairs when a person, the manager, acts without authority to protect the interests of another, the owner, in the reasonable belief that the owner would approve of the action if made aware of the circumstances."

[16] Loan, LSA-C.C. Arts. 2891–2913.

[17] Deposit and Sequestration, LSA-C.C. Arts. 2926–2951.

[18] Lease, LSA-C.C. Arts. 2668–2777.

[19] Sale, LSA-C.C. Arts. 2438–2659.

[20] LSA-C.C. Art. 1950.

[21] LSA-C.C. Art. 2524 states: "The thing sold must be reasonably fit for its ordinary use.

When the seller has reason to know the particular use the buyer intends for the thing, or the buyer's particular purpose for buying the thing, and that the buyer is relying on the seller's skill or judgment in selecting it, the thing sold must be fit for the buyer's intended use or for his particular purpose.

If the thing is not so fit, the buyer's rights are governed by the general rules of conventional

quality of a thing is taken from Pothier: a sale is null when the buyer acquires silver plated candlesticks actually made of bronze whereas he intended to buy candlesticks made of silver.[22] There would also be a subjective error where a party wanted to buy an authentic 17th c. piece of furniture but ended up buying a "made in 2010" copy.

An error can bear also on **"the cause"**[23] of the contract or "reason why a party obligates himself"[24] since "cause" is an essential requirement for the formation of any contract. If "cause" is defined as the "objective cause,"[25] the error would bear then on the **lack of existence** of the counter-performance expected and necessary in synallagmatic contracts. In such a case there would be nullity of the contract for lack of "cause" as an essential requirement for the existence of a contract. We are dealing to a large extent with an error as to the nature of a contract, as discussed above, because the cause of a contract determines the nature of that contract.

However, both parties to a contract may want to achieve a certain goal although they may be mistaken, unclear or fail to agree as to the cause of "the" contract that would lead them to achieve that goal. This uncertainty or ambiguity on the part of parties to a contract can be remedied by the courts which are empowered to keep the contract in existence under a legal qualification or characterization different from the qualification the parties had or failed to have in mind. As **LSA-C.C. 1970** states: **"When the expression of a cause in a contractual obligation is untrue, the obligation is still effective if a valid cause can be shown."** An "intended sale" by one party could be considered by the courts as actually a "donation"; the courts would then change the legal qualification of the contract from a bilateral or synallagmatic contract (the sale) to a unilateral gratuitous contract of donation. We are, here, touching on the second meaning of "cause" in its subjective sense, as being the "subjective" reason why a party enters into a contract.[26]

A **"subjective"** determination of the concept of **cause** raises the important question of its legal nature. Should cause be a subjective or objective concept?.[27] Should the subjective determination of the error be made "individually," taking into consideration only the "person" who made the error, so that the

---

obligations." On Article 2524, see Précis, Louisiana Law of Sale and Lease § 4.1.4. Warranty of Fitness and Warranty against Defects, § 4.1.4.

[22] Oeuvres de Pothier, Traité des Obligations, Dabo Jeune, Libraire, Paris, 1825 p.92. Article 1843 of the 1870 Louisiana Civil Code read: "There is error as to the substance, when the object is of a totally different nature from that which is intended. Thus, if the object of the stipulation be supposed by one or both the parties to be an ingot of silver, and it really is a mass of some other metal that resembles silver, there is an error bearing on the substance of the object." Article 1844 read: "The error bears on the substantial quality of the object, when such quality is that which gives it its greatest value. A contract relative to a vase, supposed to be gold, is void, if it be only plated with that metal."

[23] On Cause, see Chapter 5.

[24] LSA-C.C. Art. 1967 in part. See infra, Cause, Chapter 5.

[25] See Objective Cause, infra, § 5.1.1.

[26] See Subjective Cause, infra, § 5.1.1.

[27] See Cause, infra, Chapter 5.

determination of the subjectivity of the error would be made "*in concreto*"? or should that determination of the subjective nature of the error be made against the background of "the average reasonable or abstract person" in which case the determination would be made "*in abstracto*"? If one looks at **LSA-C.C. Art. 2524** we find, in the first short paragraph, a reference to the *in abstracto* standard, "**the thing must be reasonably fit for its ordinary use,**" and a reference to the *in concreto* standard in the second and longer paragraph:

"**When the seller has reason to know the particular use the buyer intends for the thing, or the buyer's particular purpose for buying the thing, and that the buyer is relying on the seller's skill or judgment in selecting it, the thing sold must be fit for the buyer's intended use or for his particular purpose.**

If the thing is not so fit, the buyer's rights are governed by the general rules of conventional obligations."[28]

We find also in **LSA-C.C. Art. 1949** an implicit reference to the two standards[29]: the *in abstracto* standard in the statement "**a cause without which the obligation would not have been incurred**" and an *in concreto* standard in the statement "**that cause was known or should have been known to the other party.**"

Since a subjective cause that motivates one party to enter into a contract must be communicated to the other party so that it will shared by both parties and become the cause of their contract,[30] it will up to the courts to decide which standard to apply in each particular case. The courts will be, then, in a position to maintain in existence as many contracts as they will deem reasonable to maintain or to declare null as many or as few contracts they will deem reasonable to declare null. The burden of proof as to the error concerning the cause of the contract will be lesser or greater depending on the circumstances of each case. If a buyer expects to buy an antique "clock" from a bazaar or a garage sale, it is very likely that his burden of proof bearing on the "subjective cause," or "antique nature of the clock," that prompted him to buy will be far

---

[28] One can find in the law of warranty and redhibitory defects an analogy with an error in the nature of an objective standard: LSA-C.C. 2520 states, in part:

The seller warrants the buyer against redhibitory defects, or vices, in the thing sold.

A defect is redhibitory when it renders the thing useless, or its use so inconvenient that it must be presumed that a buyer would not have bought the thing had he known of the defect. The existence of such a defect gives a buyer the right to obtain rescission of the sale.

A defect is redhibitory also when, without rendering the thing totally useless, it diminishes its usefulness or its value so that it must be presumed that a buyer would still have bought it but for a lesser price.

The existence of such a defect limits the right of a buyer to a reduction of the price." An average reasonable buyer would want to buy a thing without a defect when he pays the price of a thing without apparent defects. On the other hand, one can find an analogy with an error in the nature of a subjective standard in LSA-C.C. Art. 2524 (see text immediately above). See Précis, Louisiana Law of Sale and Lease, § 4.1.4.

[29] LSA-C.C. Art. 2524 is a good illustration of the necessarily general statement made in LSA-C.C. Art. 1949 which is meant to apply to all contracts.

[30] See Cause, Chapter 5; sharing of cause, unilateral or bilateral cause, § 5.1.2.B.

greater than the burden of proof bearing on a buyer purchasing "an antique clock" from a professional seller of antiques. In the latter case there would actually exist a strong "presumption" that the buyer intended to buy an antique clock, and not a modern day clock, from that professional seller because of that seller's dealing in antiques. In this particular situation, it may not be even required that the buyer should "share" with and "communicate" to the seller his "subjective" cause, buying an antique clock, because the circumstances are such that the professional seller ought to be presumed to know the subjective cause that motivates buyers to deal with him. In addition, the amount of the price that the buyer is asked to pay should be a clear indication as to the kind of clock the buyer would be buying. An average reasonable buyer motivated by an objective cause, [price to be paid in comparison with the kind of thing bought], would not be acting reasonably if he expected to purchase an antique clock at a bargain price from a professional dealer of antiques. Conversely, if this same average reasonable buyer did not intend to buy an antique clock from the professional seller of antiques, that buyer should be expected to communicate his "subjective cause" to the seller, i.e. the purchase of a contemporary and modern clock, so as to "share" with that seller a cause or motive different from the "objective cause" that the seller of antiques is entitled to expect from the average reasonable buyer.

B. Error of Law.

LSA-C.C. Art. 5 states that **"No one may avail himself of ignorance of the law."** Once a statute has been promulgated, no party to a contract can argue that she made an error as to the existence of that statute. Yet, one may enter into a contract under some misunderstanding of the statute, such as the nature or extent of one's rights. As **Art. 1822** of the **civil Code of 1870** stated: **"He is under an error of law, who is truly informed of the existence of facts, but who draws from them erroneous conclusions of law."** If "A" agrees to repair a damage under the belief that she caused that damage when, actually, someone else "B" was guilty of causing that damage, "A" could argue that she made an error of law because the facts lead her to believe, falsely, that she was bound by law to repair the damage. The technical rules on the distribution of successions could be argued by an heir who renounced a succession to be the reason for his mistaken decision to renounce that succession.

However the civil Code provides for instances where an error of law, even though legitimate, cannot be raised as a ground for the nullity of some contracts or juridical acts. For example, under **LSA-C.C. Art. 1761:** **". . . whatever has been freely performed in compliance with a natural obligation may not be reclaimed."**[31] Another example of a contract that cannot be rescinded for error of law is the contract of *compromise or transaction*. **LSA-C.C. Art. 3080** states: **"A compromise precludes the parties from bringing a subsequent action based upon the matter that was compromised."**[32]

---

[31] On Natural Obligations, see Précis, Louisiana Law of Obligations in General, § 1.3.1.

[32] See also "Judicial confession," LSA-C.C. Art. 1853, in part: ". . . Judicial confession is

C. Error as to the Person.

"**Error may concern . . . the person or the qualities of the other party**" (LSA-C.C. Art. 1950). These are the only words in the Civil Code to address this issue of error as to the person, the other party to the contract. Such an error as to the person must, necessarily, concern a *cause* of the contract as stated at the beginning of **Art. 1950**. Contracts which might be annulled on this ground of error are most likely to be *gratuitous contracts*[33] or, more generally, contracts entered into *intuitu personae* wherein the consideration of the person of the co-contracting party is foremost in the mind of the other party. For example in a contract of marriage, each party expresses his/her consent to "**take each other as husband and wife.**" (LSA-C.C. Art. 87).[34] It would appear logical to conclude that an error made by one of the parties as regards the identity of "**the person or the personal qualities of the other party**" (LSA-C.C. Art. 1950) should be an error as to the cause of the contract of marriage and carry with it the nullity of the contract of marriage. It is difficult, we believe, to think of a contract in which the reciprocal consideration of each party's person and personal qualities would be greater than in a contract of marriage in which "**Married persons owe each other fidelity, support and assistance**" (LSA-C.C. Art. 98). Yet, and somewhat surprisingly, **Article 93** states that "**Consent [to a marriage] is not free when given under duress or when given by a person incapable of discernment.**" **Article 95** adds that "**A marriage is relatively null when the consent of one of the parties to marry is not freely given. . . .**" It follows that the grounds for the relative nullity of a marriage are restrictively listed in the civil Code and that those grounds do not include "error."[35] Yet, the *civil Code of 1870* included an *Art. 91* which stated that *"No marriage is valid to which the parties have not freely consented. Consent is not free: . . . 3. Where there is a mistake respecting the person, whom one of the parties intended to marry."* And *Art. 1834* added that *"Error as to the person, with whom the contract is made, will invalidate it, if the consideration of the person is the principal or only cause of the contract, as it always is in the contract of marriage."*

---

indivisible and it may be revoked only on the ground of error of fact." *A contrario*, an error of law cannot be a ground of revocation.

[33] See supra, Classification of Contracts, Chapter 1, Onerous and gratuitous contracts, Article 2.

[34] Note that among the three requirements for the contract of marriage, "free consent . . . expressed at the ceremony" is one of those three. [Emphasis ours].

[35] More surprising is that even "fraud" committed by one party at the expense of the other is not listed as a ground for nullity of the marriage. Even more surprising to us are the contents of the second paragraph of Art. 1954, which is part of the law of Conventional Obligations, Contracts. Art. 1954 states that "Fraud does not vitiate consent when the party against whom the fraud was directed could have ascertained the truth without difficulty, inconvenience, or special skill.

This exception does not apply when a relation of confidence has reasonably induced a party to rely on the other's assertions or representations."

If one reasons *a contrario sensu* and *a fortiori ratione* on these two paragraphs, one can only conclude that, because a contract of marriage is based on the "confidence" the two spouses have in each other, the exception mentioned in the first paragraph of Art. 1954 should not apply, i.e. a spouse should not have to undertake to discover whether fraud had been committed by the other party. So, here we are: the most intuitu personae contract, the contract of marriage, can be annulled neither on the ground of error as to the person, nor even on the ground of fraud.

§ 4.1.3. KINDS OF SERIOUS ERRORS 43

The puzzling situation arrived at in the Louisiana civil Code where error and fraud in a contract of marriage are excluded as possible vices of consent is difficult to understand in light of the codal definition of marriage as **"a legal relationship between a man and a woman created by a civil contract."**[36] The explanation for this deletion of error as a vice of consent is provided in comment (e) to La. Acts 1987, No. 886.[37] Strangely enough, this same comment (e) has never been included in the commercial editions of the Louisiana civil Code. It is our opinion, based on methods of interpretation which take into consideration both the wording of Code articles and the "ratio" or reason which provides the foundation of these Articles, that Art. 93[38] should not be interpreted "literally and narrowly" so as to exclude "error" as a vice of consent in the formation of a contract of marriage.[39]

A contract of mandate is defined as follows: **"A mandate is a contract by which a person, the principal, confers authority on another person, the mandatary, to transact one or more affairs for the principal."** (LSA-C.C. Art. 2989). **"The mandatary is bound to fulfill with prudence and diligence the mandate he has accepted. He is responsible to the principal for the loss that the principal sustains as a result of the mandatary's failure to perform."**(LSA-C.C. Art. 3001). And **"In the absence of contrary agreement, the mandatary is bound to fulfill the mandate himself . . ."**(LSA-C.C. Art. 3006-1). Since **Art. 3024** tells us that **"in addition to causes of termination of contracts under the Titles governing 'Obligations in General' and 'Conventional Obligations or Contracts'. . . ."** it follows that we can apply to the contract of mandate Arts. 1948 and 1950 on vices of consent and error on the cause of a contract. The contract of mandate being *intuitu personae*,[40] the

---

[36] LSA-C.C. Art. 86.

[37] "This Article (93) omits reference to 'mistake respecting the person' as a cause of invalidity. The jurisprudence strictly interpreted that language as referring only to mistakes of physical identity, and not to mistakes concerning some quality or qualities of personality that one party believed the other to possess. . . . As so limited, the omitted language was never applied to invalidate a marriage in Louisiana."

[38] The Article merely states that "consent is not free when given under duress or when given by a person incapable of discernment." The Article Does not say: "the only vices of consent . . ." or "by exception to the rules on vices of consent in conventional obligations . . ." An analogy, *a pari ratione*, can easily be made between a "person incapable of discernment," described in comment (d) to Art. 93 as "a person under the influence of alcohol or drugs . . . or a person too young to understand . . ." and a person whose emotions and feelings for another may, temporarily like drugs or alcohol, deprive that person of the ability to ascertain the "truth" about the other party to a marriage. Furthermore, the somewhat restrictive title of this Art. 93 — "Vices of consent" — is not part of the law of the Article itself [R.S. 1:13]

[39] Our arguments are, first of all, that Art. 93 does not lay down an exclusive list of vices of consent in a contract of marriage; second, that since the contract of marriage has been made a "civil" contract it should be governed by the rules and principles of the Law of Conventional Obligations, including the rules on Vices of Consent in the formation of "all contracts, nominate or innominate" (LSA-C.C. Art. 1915); third, that an analogy with the contract of mandate leads, *a fortiori ratione*, to include error as to the person in the vices of consent in a marriage contract; fourthly, that the duties imposed on "husband and wife" are a legal expression of the foundation of marriage as being an *intuitu personae* contract.

[40] Mandate, past participle of mando; mando [manus + do (dare)] Oxford Latin Dictionary, Oxford at Clarendon Press, 1976. [manus= hand; dare = give] hence giving a handshake as the

mandatary being chosen by the principal on account of the mandatary's "qualities," error as to the person or the qualities of the mandatary should be considered as a ground for nullity of the mandate.

§ 4.1.4. EFFECT OF ERROR.

Not every error leads to the nullity of a contract. Not every kind of error listed in Art. 1950 will necessarily carry with it the nullity of the contract which is the consequence of an error. Some conditions are attached to the error made by one party in her relation with the other party and some limitations can affect the extent of the effects of the nullity of the contract.

A. Conditions.

1. *Principal Cause.*

One first condition is that the error made by one party must have been determinant of the will of that party. However, it is unlikely that a party to a contract will be motivated by only one reason to enter into that contract. It is more likely that several reasons will merge into the expression of the intent to enter into a contract. How, then, is a court to draw a distinction between those reasons and single out one as having tainted the consent and induced the party to make an error as to the "cause" of the contract? For example: suppose "A" wishes to buy a house to make it his domicile. However, unbeknownst to him, the house is about to be torn down because it is an obstruction to a highway to be built in the near future. Is there error as to a cause making the contract of sale null? Suppose that "A" is a candidate for a job in the far distant town of "Ville" and that the prospect of "A" getting that job looks very good. So "A" buys a house in "Ville" while waiting for his appointment to be finalized. Unfortunately, "A" is not appointed. Is there "error" on his part as to becoming owner of the house? In the first instance, the house itself was the immediate reason for the purchase and it is possible to say that "A" made an error as to the very "thing that is the contractual object," the house and the house becoming his domicile. In the second instance, the house itself had nothing to do with "A" being appointed or not being appointed; "A's" intent to buy the house was secondary to his appointment which was the principal reason for his moving to "Ville." So, if "A" made an error as concerns the house, that error was not the determinant reason or cause for buying the house. In this latter case, the contract for the purchase of the house could remain binding on "A".

2. *Sharing. Communication.*

Such could be the outcome unless "A" had made his purchasing the house in "Ville" conditional upon his being appointed, that is to say, unless "A" had communicated to the seller that one of the reasons why he was buying the house was because he expected to be appointed, even though at the time of the sale his

---

"form" of the contract of mandate meant that one party, the principal, was face to face with another party, the mandatary, who was "given" the trust of the principal.

appointment was not final. By communicating those reasons, his anticipated appointment in particular, to the buyer, "A" made the buyer aware of the "causes or reasons" which made him want to buy the house. In a sense, both parties can be said to have made the same error as to the appointment as a cause for the contract of sale of the house. That cause, to some extent, became common to both parties because of the sharing by "A"; from "subjective" to "A" the cause became "objective," in a sense, by entering the realm of the negotiations between the parties. A "subjective" error, as long as it remains "unilateral" and privy to the first party, cannot become a ground for nullity of a contract. If it is communicated to the second party as being determinant or if the circumstances are such that the second party to the contract knew or should have known the cause or reason that prompted the first party in error to enter the contract, then the error can become a ground for nullity of the contract.

3. Limitations

The error can become a ground for nullity of the contract except when that error could be considered so excessive or negligent that it should not be excused: The equities of the situation may indeed favor the other party to the contract and justify that the contract remain binding.

In addition **"A party may not avail himself of his error when the other party is willing to perform the contract as intended by the party in error."(LSA-C.C. Art. 1951).** Since the party in error would suffer no prejudice from the performance of the contract, the other party should be allowed to perform her obligations as per the "modified" intent of the party in error.

The civil Code makes it very clear that to seek the nullity of a contract because of one's error is a right based on the accepted rule of the integrity of one's consent. That right, however, cannot be exercised so as to cause a prejudice to the other party in good faith. That party's good faith will serve as a shield for the protection of her own rights. **LSA-C.C. Art. 1952 states clearly that "A party who obtains rescission on grounds of his own error is liable for the loss thereby sustained by the other party unless the latter knew or should have known of the error.**

"The court may refuse rescission when the effective protection of the other party's interest requires that the contract be upheld. In that case, a reasonable compensation for the loss he has sustained may be granted to the party to whom rescission is refused."

ARTICLE 2
FRAUD

"Fraud," as the second vice of consent listed in the Louisiana civil Code, is governed by Arts. 1953 to 1958. These few Articles describe the concept of fraud, outline the constitutive elements of fraud and warn of its effects.

§ 4.2.1. CONCEPT OF FRAUD.

LSA-C.C. Art. 1953 describes fraud in these terms: **"Fraud is a misrepresentation or a suppression of the truth made with the intention either to obtain an unjust advantage for one party or to cause a loss or inconvenience to the other. Fraud may also result from silence or inaction."** We are told, in a comment, that "Fraud, like its French equivalent, '*dol*' . . ." can be an intentional fault of a quasi-delictual nature sufficient to constitute the kind of fraud that vitiates a party's consent.[41] In Roman law "dolus" (fraud) was a part of the Lex Aquilia, or legislation on delicts that created an action for injurious damage.[42] From this Roman law origin in delict (tort), fraud has kept one of its component parts, the intent to cause a prejudice to another.

Fraud is not, therefore, in itself a vice of consent. It is, rather, either an action such as a misrepresentation or a false assertion meant to hide the "truth" and therefore to "induce an error,"[43] or an inaction such as a failure to act or the withholding of the "truth" so as to "induce an error." The "error" is provoked by the fraud as opposed to being a "spontaneous" error as is the "error" under LSA-C.C. Art. 1949 discussed above. What is then the purpose of combining "fraud" with "error" when the latter is already, by itself, a vice of consent?

There are two reasons to consider: with respect to proof, it is easier to "prove" fraud as an outward fact under the form of maneuvers, schemes, actions or inactions, than it is to prove "error" as a purely internal psychological occurrence. The second reason is provided by **LSA-C.C. Art. 1955**, which states that **"error induced by fraud need not concern the cause of the obligation to vitiate consent, but it must concern a circumstance that has substantially influenced that consent."** In other words, other errors than an error bearing on the principal cause of the contract can lead to the nullity of the contract when they have been provoked by "fraud."

§ 4.2.2. CONSTITUTIVE ELEMENTS OF FRAUD.

They are of two kinds: material and psychological/moral.

A. Material Element.

As the description of fraud in Art. 1953 suggests, the material element of fraud may consist in maneuvers, a scheme, a behavior, lies, withholding information or silence,[44] such that a reasonable person would be led to make an

---

[41] Comment (c) to Art. 1953.

[42] See, for example, The Institutes of Justinian Lib. IV. Tit. III De Lege Aquilia § III, De casu, dolo, et culpa.

[43] LSA-C.C. Art. 1955 reads "Error induced by fraud need not concern the cause of the obligation to vitiate consent, but it must concern a circumstance that has substantially influenced that consent."

[44] LSA-C.C. Art. 1953 uses the words "suppression of the truth" and "silence"; it can be argued that "suppression of the truth" is a positive act, an action, whereas "silence" can be interpreted to mean that a party does not disclose a piece of information or withholds some information that the other party cannot discover "without difficulty, inconvenience, or special skill." On the basis of Art. 1953 and Art. 1954, as well as 1759, it is possible to make the argument that the Louisiana civil Code

error. Such maneuvers [and] schemes . . . would qualify as *"dolus malus"* under Roman law terminology; they are, literally, the "bad fraud" because of the psychological and detrimental impact they have on the consent of a reasonable person. On the other hand, there may exist factual circumstances which are such that maneuvers [and] schemes . . . ought not lead a reasonable person to make an error. Such circumstances would fall under the wording of **LSA-C.C. Art. 1954-1,** which provides that **"the party against whom the fraud was directed could have ascertained the truth without difficulty, inconvenience, or special skill."** A reasonable person should not be a "gullible" person. A salesman's pitch, "puffing," should not under normal circumstances lead a reasonable person to make an error, as such "puffing" is expected from a salesman anxious to sell his wares. A reasonable person is expected to exercise some "average" caution and display some "average" wisdom in making a decision to buy, for example, a second hand car from a lay person or a painting from a side walk artist-seller.[45] Without too much inconvenience to herself, without too much skill, such a buyer could ascertain the actual condition of the car, the authenticity of the painting. . . . This type of fraud could be called "good fraud" or, in Latin, *"dolus bonus"* because it is expected and everyone capable of entering into a contract is put on notice that the law will not help those who are not willing to help themselves.

However, LSA-C.C. Art. 1954-2 excludes from the realm of application of the first paragraph contracts which are heavily based on a relationship of trust or confidence that prevails between some parties. Because of this kind of relationship, a first party may let her guard down, not question the integrity and honesty of the statements made to her by the second party to the contract. Even though the first party could have ascertained the truth without difficulty, inconvenience, or special skill, the second party did not act in "good faith," betrayed the trust or confidence of the first party and, therefore, ought not to derive a benefit from her wrong doing. Such relationships may (should?) exist in the context of a family, an employer-employee context. . . .

B.   Psychological/Moral.

The error made by the first party must have been "substantially" induced by the fraud committed by the second party and the fraud must have been committed by that second party or someone else but with the knowledge of that second party.

In the words of **LSA-C.C. Art. 1955: "Error induced by fraud need not concern the cause of the obligation to vitiate consent, but it must concern a circumstance that has substantially influenced that consent."**

As seen above, not every "fraud" or "dolus" should be taken into account; only if the fraud is "bad" or "malus." In addition, that required type of fraud,

---

creates a "duty to inform or disclose." On Good Faith, see Précis, Louisiana Law of Obligations in General, § 1.4.2.

[45] On Fraud and Hidden Vices in a contract of sale, see Précis, Louisiana Law of Sale and Lease, Chapter 4, § 4.1.1. In a contract of Lease, see same Précis at Chapter 3, Article 1.

which can be called "principal" as opposed to "incidental,"[46] must have led to such an error as to have "substantially influenced the consent" of the party in error.

What "fraud" adds to "error" is that in the case of fraud leading to an error, that error **"need not concern the cause of the obligation to vitiate consent. . . ."**[47] In other words, when "fraud" is established, the contract could be annulled for errors of consent other than when the **"error concerns a cause without which the obligation would not have been incurred and that cause was known or should have been known to the other party." (LSA-C.C. Art. 1949.)** More errors than an error as to "the cause" can become grounds for the relative nullity of the contract when those errors have been the outcome of fraud.[48]

A combined reading of LSA-C.C. Arts.1954-1 with 1955 suggests that the courts ought to appraise the degree of the error caused by fraud according to an *in concreto* standard. This means that the court ought to consider carefully the personal, physical, intellectual, psychological features of the party who, because of the fraud committed by the other party, made an error.[49] Such an appraisal of the degree of error is suggested by these words that not "every person" can ascertain **"the truth without difficulty, inconvenience, or special skill."**[50]

According to **LSA-C.C. Art. 1956: "Fraud committed by a third person vitiates the consent of a contracting party if the other party knew or should have known of the fraud."** There lies the second requirement for the moral component part of fraud to exist: fraud must be committed by one party when entering the contract with the other party who is the victim of the fraud. This requirement is somewhat puzzling because the error made by the party victim is exactly the same whether the author of the fraud is a party to the contract or not. One explanation for this rule of LSA-C.C. Art. 1956 is that in Roman law, "dolus" was considered to be a delict (tort) and not a vice of consent and the "exceptio doli" could be raised only against the party to the contract who committed fraud as personally liable. In addition, it would be somewhat illogical to penalize an innocent party, with the nullity of the contract because of the fraud committed by a "third person"in no way connected with the parties to the contract.[51] As a substitute to the nullity of the contract, the victim of the fraud

---

[46] "Incidental" when the contract would still have been entered into but on different terms which would have been more beneficial to the victim of the fraud. Damages, instead of the relative nullity of the contract, could be an alternative remedy available to the victim of the fraud.

[47] Excerpt from Art. 1955.

[48] On error as to the cause, see supra, Error, Conditions for an error to be a "vice of consent," Chapter 4, Article 1.

[49] LSA-C.C. Art. 1959-2 on Duress is very explicit in this respect: "Age, health, disposition, and other personal circumstances of a party must be taken into account in determining reasonableness of the fear." The criteria referred to here is that of an "in concreto" evaluation of the fear on the basis of the items listed: age, health. . . . The opposite criteria in the "in abstracto" criteria which takes as its standard of evaluation the "average person," this indefinite ordinary person around which are based most provisions of the civil Code.

[50] LSA-C.C. Art. 1954-1.

[51] Unless, as Art. 1956 states "the other party (other than the victim) knew or should have known

committed by a third person would have an action in damages[52] against that third person.

C. Proof of Fraud.

LSA-C.C. Art. 1957 states that **"Fraud need only be proved by a preponderance of the evidence and may be established by circumstantial evidence."** Art. 805 of the **LSA-C.C.P.** adds that "In pleading fraud or mistake, the circumstances constituting fraud or mistake shall be alleged with particularity. Malice, intent, knowledge, and other condition of mind of a person may be alleged generally."

§ 4.2.3. EFFECTS OF FRAUD.

Since "fraud" may lead to error as a vice of consent if fraud itself meets the requirements above and if it induces an error "substantial" enough but lesser than an error as to the principal cause of the contract, it is logical to grant to the party victim of the fraud and error the right to seek the relative nullity of the contract for lack of free and informed consent. Under **LSA-C.C. Art. 2031 "A contract is relatively null when it violates a rule intended for the protection of private parties, as when a party lacked capacity or did not give free consent at the time the contract was made. A contract that is only relatively null may be confirmed.**

"Relative nullity may be invoked only by those persons for whose interest the ground for nullity was established, and may not be declared by the court on its own initiative."[53] The effects of the relative nullity of the contract will be those prescribed in LSA-C.C. Art. 2033 in particular.[54]

In addition to, or in lieu of, the nullity of the contract, **"The party against whom rescission is granted because of fraud is liable for damages and attorney fees."(LSA-C.C. Art. 1958)**. It is worth pointing out that Art. 1958 uses the mandatory form of the verb "to be" where it states that "the party . . . *is* liable for damages and attorney's fees." Whenever a party to a contract is the victim of fraud and suffers a prejudice, the courts should remember that "fraud" or "dolus" was a delict (tort) in Roman law and that Louisiana law, as a recognized member jurisdiction of the civil law tradition, should look at fraud as an **"act . . . of man that causes damage to another"** and, therefore, **"obliges him by whose fault it happened to repair it."(LSA-C.C. Art. 2315)**.

---

of the fraud"; if one party to the contract is an accomplice of the third person committing fraud; or if the fraud was committed by a representative of a party to the contract." See also Principles of European contract law, Art. 4.111 and UNIDROIT Art. 3.11.2.

[52] LSA-C.C. Art. 2315-A would be the basis for such an action.

[53] See infra, Relative Nullity, § 9.2.1.

[54] See infra, Effects of Nullity, § 9.2.2.

ARTICLE 3
DURESS [VIOLENCE]

The third vice of consent listed in LSA-C.C. Art. 1948 is "duress."[55] When a party enters a contract under duress, that party is deprived of the "freedom" to express her consent rather than making an "error" when entering the contract. Therefore, duress should be looked upon as "an act of man" carried out with the intent to cause a prejudice to a party to a contract. Roman law treated "violence" or "duress" as a delict rather than as a vice of consent.[56]

Duress is made up of two component elements: a psychological element, the fear felt by a party to a contract, hence the vice of consent; and a material anti-social element consisting in the duress itself or the threats directed by the perpetrator against a party to a contract. These two component elements of duress make up its nature as described by **LSA-C.C. Art. 1959: "Consent is vitiated when it has been obtained by duress of such a nature as to cause a reasonable fear of unjust and considerable injury to a party's person, property, or reputation.**

"Age, health, disposition, and other personal circumstances of a party must be taken into account in determining reasonableness of the fear."

§ 4.3.1. THE CONSTITUTIVE ELEMENTS OF DURESS.

The vice of consent of duress is more the "reasonable fear" resulting from a threat than the act of violence itself. This threat can cause a fear of "injury to a party's person, property or reputation."

---

[55] "Duress" is the new name that was given in 1984 to the vice of consent that had always been known in the Louisiana civil Codes as "violence." "Violence" is still the name given to this vice of consent in the civil Codes of France (Arts. 1111 et seq.), Québec (Arts. 1402 et seq.) . . . Comment (b) to LSA-C.C. Art. 1959 justifies the change in names as follows: *"This article substitutes the term 'duress' for 'violence or threats,' the expression used in the source Articles . . . In sum, 'duress' is a word of art or technical word in the English language which expresses exactly what is meant by 'violence or threats' in C.C. Arts. 1850–1852 (1870)."* If the meaning of the two words "violence" and "duress" is the same, why make the change? Because "duress" is a "word of art or a technical word of the English language"? The Louisiana civil Code, the courts, and the bar of Louisiana appeared to have had no problem in using the "English" word *"violence"* which was *a term of art or a technical term in the civil law* of the State. So why the change? To "copy" the common law? Very likely, since the same Comment (b) refers to Black's Law Dictionary's definition of "duress" and the Restatement of Contracts. Our objection and our fear are that, as often happens in translating legal concepts of one legal tradition into concepts of another legal tradition, the substance of the old age Louisiana civil law understanding of violence will be lost to the common law meaning and interpretation of "duress" with the result that, at a click of a button, the whole caselaw of the common law states of the United States will also become the "Louisiana" understanding of "duress" under its many different common law forms. And, yet, we are told in Comment (a) to Art. 1959 that *"This Article is new. It does not change the law, however. It restates principles expressed in C.C. Arts. 1850 and 1851 (1870)."* So, if there is no change in the law and if there is only a substitution in words, why this change from "violence" to "duress"? We fear that much more was hidden behind a mere "substitution of words."

[56] Note, here, the similarity of treatment with "fraud."

A. Material Element of Duress.

A party can be coerced into a contract by fear of physical injury to her person, threats to one's health etc. . . . The threat can also be to one's patrimony, one's assets or "private things owned by individuals,"[57] including animals which would fall under the concept of "corporeal movables" which are "things, whether animate or inanimate, that normally move or can be moved from one place to another."[58] The fear can be, therefore, to one's economic and financial condition. The threat can also be to one's reputation, name, honor . . . as is often the case of blackmail. The fear of a danger compelling a party to enter a contract should be imminent or actual at the time the contract is entered into. A threat addressed in the distant past to a party to a contract entered into later on should not qualify as a vice of that party's consent.

B. The Psychological Element of Duress.

Since consent given under duress is a consent not "freely" given, and not one in error, that consent may have been given by a party to a contract when that party was not "free" of mind and spirit because another person, known of that party, was actually the target of the violence or duress, so much so that the party to the contract "feared" for that person's life, property or reputation. Therefore, **LSA-C.C. Art. 1960** states that **"Duress vitiates consent also when the threatened injury is directed against the spouse, an ascendant, or descendant of the contracting party.**

If the threatened injury is directed against other persons, the granting of relief is left to the discretion of the court."

The second paragraph of Art. 1960 vests much discretion in the Courts' willingness to interpret broadly or narrowly the degree of "reasonable fear" instilled in a party to a contract when the threatened injury is directed against someone else than that party. What if that person is a brother or sister (a collateral and not an ascendant or descendant)? A fiancé(e)? An uncle (therefore not an ascendant)? A paramour or a companion? When interpreting such an Article the courts should consider the spirit of that Article rather than its letter.

§ 4.3.2. CHARACTERISTICS OF DURESS: AUTHOR-PERPETRATOR, REASONABLENESS, UNLAWFULNESS.

As regards the author-perpetrator of the threat or duress directed against a party to a contract or somebody else as per Art. 1960, **LSA-C.C. Art. 1961** provides that **"Consent is vitiated even when duress has been exerted by a third person."** Indeed, what is of greater concern to the law on formation of contracts is the integrity of a party's consent, that party's freedom to contract or not to contract. Error on the part of that party cannot be required because that

---

[57] LSA-C.C. Art. 453.
[58] LSA-C.C. Art. 471.

party is fully aware of the reason or reasons why she is entering the contract and "error" is not one of the reasons. There lies a difference with "fraud" in which case it is the error made because of the fraud that may lead to the relative nullity of the contract. It follows logically that the law should not be concerned with restricting the source of the duress to the other party to the contract. The purpose of the law is to protect the party victim of duress and for that reason the court will have to appraise the degree of that party's fear: was the fear "reasonable"?

The determination of the "reasonableness" of the fear is made on the basis of two different standards: an *in abstracto standard* and an *in concreto standard.* The second paragraph of Art. 1959 invites the courts to make an application of these two standards. The same kind of threat to one's physical person will be felt differently by "the little old lady who lives alone with her cat" and by the "300 pound linebacker" or the "30 year old wrestling champion." Starting with the average reasonable person, or *in abstracto* standard, the courts will weigh the impact of a person's age, sex, health, disposition . . . on the degree of fear that that person should experience. The courts would resort to an *in concreto* standard by focusing on the "concrete" (real) factual situation placed before them.

The fear caused by the threat of duress must be the consequence of an unlawful threat. As *LSA-C.C. Art. 1854 of the Code of 1870* stated: *"The mere reverential fear of a relation in the ascending line, where no violence has been offered, nor threats made, will not invalidate a contract."* The reverential fear that Mom or Dad might cut off the money supply for their child's education if the child continues to thrive on failing grades will not be a ground for the relative nullity of a contract between child and parents whereby child would promise to spend more time studying than partying. Likewise, as **LSA-C.C. Art. 1962** states: **"A threat of doing a lawful act or a threat of exercising a right does not constitute duress.**

"A threat of doing an act that is lawful in appearance only may constitute duress." The first paragraph of this Article stands as a clear illustration of the difficulty of basing the theory of vices of consent either on "error" only or on the "freedom" to consent. In this first paragraph, the consent is not free despite the "threat" and it is not in error either! As regards the second paragraph of Art. 1962 we would recommend reading in it the words "or a threat of exercising a right" which appear in the first paragraph but not in the second. The parallelism in the structure and purpose of the two paragraphs justify such a reading. In addition, besides possibly giving a strict and literal meaning of the words "lawfulness or unlawfulness" of an act or exercise of a right, the courts should also resort to the theory of abuse of right[59] in their reading of "an act lawful in appearance only." Thereby the courts would give its full substantive value to the "nature" of duress as it is explained in Art. 1959, its second paragraph in particular. For example, a creditor (a lessor, for example) who would take advantage of the precarious situation of his debtor (his lessee) to gain an

---

[59] On Abuse of Right in Louisiana law, see 35 La. L. Rev. 965 (1975); 37 La. L. Rev. 747 (1977); 54 Tul. L. Rev. 1173 (1994); 32 Loy. L. Rev. 946 (1994).

advantage (damages, where none would be justified by the condition of the premises, or withholding the deposit) in excess of his due (rent) would be abusing his right to claim his due and could be considered as exerting duress against his lessee-debtor if he threatened the latter with his "right to take him to court"!

However, not all contracts entered into under duress are automatically relatively null. Under the circumstances described in **LSA-C.C. Art. 1963 "A contract made with a third person to secure the means of preventing threatened injury may not be rescinded for duress if that person is in good faith and not in collusion with the party exerting duress."** The example given in Comment (b) is to the effect that "a contract of loan made for the purpose of paying ransom cannot be rescinded for duress if the lender is in good faith," i.e. if the lender is not an accomplice of the kidnapper! Contracts entered into under a state of necessity, where the cause of the fear is to be found in exterior events in particular (being lost at sea and being saved by another ship under the conditions imposed by the captain of that rescue ship), **"may not be rescinded for duress if that person** (the captain) **is in good faith."**(LSA-C.C. Art. 1963). It remains that a court could be justified in "re-writing" the contract on account of its understanding of the meaning of "good faith" under the factual circumstances that surrounded the making of the contract.

§ 4.3.3. LEGAL CONSEQUENCES.

LSA-C.C. Art. 1964 states that **When rescission is granted because of duress exerted or known by a party to the contract, the other party may recover damages and attorney fees.**

When rescission is granted because of duress exerted by a third person, the parties to the contract who are innocent of the duress may recover damages and attorney fees from the third person." Since the Article reads "rescission is granted," it means that the party who entered the contract under duress can claim the relative nullity[60] of the contract as an affirmative defense.[61] In addition, that party may recover "damages and attorney fees" either from the other party to the contract who exerted duress or from the third person who exerted duress.

ARTICLE 4
LESION

For purposes of this Précis, Lesion does not require much attention. It has always been difficult to justify listing "lesion" under Vices of Consent as the concept of Lesion does not match well either error, or fraud or duress, although it could be argued that Lesion borrows a little from each one of these three vices of consent. It is the reason why **LSA-C.C. Art. 1965**, the only Code Article on Lesion in this Chapter on Vices of Consent (Arts. 1948-1965), does not give any definition of Lesion, nor does it provide for any legal regime of Lesion. For purposes of information only, we shall give the following two codal definitions of

---

[60] On the effects of nullity and relative nullity, see infra Chapter 9.
[61] See LSA-C.C.P. Art. 1005.

Lesion which will help explain why Lesion is a remedy available only, at this time, in a few institutions included in the Louisiana civil Code.

The following definition is taken from *LSA-C.C. Art. 1860* of the *Civil Code of 1870*: *"Lesion is the injury suffered by one who does not receive a full equivalent for what he gives in a commutative contract. The remedy given for this injury, is founded on its being the effect of implied error or imposition; for, in every commutative contract, equivalents are supposed to be given and received."*[62]

This second definition or description of Lesion is taken from the *Civil Code of Québec, Art. 1406*: *"Lesion results from the exploitation of one of the parties by the other, which creates a serious disproportion between the prestations of the parties; the fact that there is a serious disproportion creates a presumption of exploitation."*[63]

In the Louisiana civil Code, Lesion is a remedy available in some contracts of sale, in the contract of exchange, in some partitions of successions and of ownership in indivision.[64]

---

[62] Note the reference to "implied error or imposition": two vices of consent to which Lesion could be related, albeit "implied." Note also the reference to "commutative contract": Under the Civil Code of 1870 there existed a perfect harmony between that Code's definitions of "commutative contract" (see supra, Chapter 1, Article 3) and "lesion" (see supra). As stated above in this Précis (Chapter 1, Article 3), the now existing definition of commutative contract makes no sense when related to the existing instances of lesion included in the civil Code of today. Furthermore, there is absolutely no rational explanation for keeping LSA-C.C. Art. 1965 where it is. It rightfully belongs under "Nullity," Arts. 2029–2035.

[63] In this Article 1406 of the Québec Civil Code and in Art. 1860 of the Louisiana civil Code of 1870, we read the same idea that "lesion" is the objective outward manifestation of an implied or presumed vice of consent, "error, imposition, exploitation," consisting in an inequitable, disproportionate relationship in a commutative contract.

[64] On Lesion in: Sales, see LSA-C.C. Arts. 2589–2600 and Précis, Louisiana Law of Sale and Lease, Article 5 (LexisNexis 2007); Exchange, see LSA-C.C, Arts. 2664–2666; Partitions, see LSA-C.C. Arts. 814, 1406–1414.

Chapter 5

CAUSE
LSA-C.C. ARTS. 1966 TO 1970

Much has been written on the concept of cause and debates have taken place on the usefulness or not of this concept. It has been preserved in the 1984 revision of the Louisiana law of Conventional Obligations or Contracts. However, the legal regime of cause has been shortened from eight articles in the Civil Code of 1870 to five articles today. In addition, whereas in the Civil Code of 1870, *cause* appeared under the title "Of the Cause or Consideration of Contracts," the 1984 revision lists *cause* under the simple title of "Cause." These changes, in the title mainly, are not merely cosmetic; they have a profound meaning which aims at establishing *cause* as an essentially civil law concept and at distinguishing it from the common law concept of "consideration."[1]

The debates over the concept of cause justify presenting a survey of the historical developments of cause as a preliminary to a review of the contemporary theory of cause before describing the legal regime of cause which is still identified as a distinct feature of the civil law.

ARTICLE 1
BRIEF HISTORICAL SURVEY OF "CAUSE"

The word "causa" appears in some Roman law texts but it is clothed with many different meanings. The Roman jurists did not elaborate a theory of cause as we understand it today. The reason was that the Roman law of Obligations was essentially "formal" in the sense that it required that the will of parties to an obligation be manifested in particular forms. The word "causa" was actually identified with a particular "form," such as "specific words and phrases" or "the actual transfer of a thing" or "particular types of writings."[2] The closest connection between the Roman "causa" and our civil law concept of "cause" can be found in the Roman law "stipulatio," which was a "formal" contract but which could be annulled for lack of "causa" whenever the promisor, who had carried out his obligation, would not receive in return from the stipulator the performance the latter was committed to carry out. To prevent an enrichment of the stipulator, the contract could be annulled on the ground that the promisor's

---

[1] The preposition "or" in the title of the 1870 Civil Code was uncalled for and became the source of much confusion as to whether "cause" at civil law was the same thing as "consideration" at common law. It is worth pointing out that the title of Chapter 5 "CAUSE" [Title IV, Book III] of the 1984 revision of the law of Obligations reverts back to the same title "OF THE CAUSE" that existed in the Civil Code or Digest of 1808 [Section IV OF THE CAUSE, Chapter II, Title III, Book III].

[2] The Institutes of Justinian, Thomas Cooper, 1812 Lib. III. TIT. XIV De Obligationibus: "Let us first treat of those (obligations) which arise from contract; which are four fold: for obligations are contracted by the thing itself, by parol, by writing, or by consent of parties. . . ."

performance was "sine causa," without cause.[3]

The concept of cause was turned into a "theory of cause" when the canon law lawyers did away with the formalism of Roman law to substitute to it a mere agreement as an exchange of wills between parties based on the moral obligation to fulfill one's word. As a consequence, one would be at fault for not performing that moral duty. It was necessary, however, to find out if this obligation or commitment was properly justified by the "internal" reasons which may have prompted a party to feel bound in her conscience. The idea of a commutative justice became a justification for one's commitment but it was a "moral" concept of justice not a "material (economic) justice." The glossators and postglossators merged the canon law concept of cause with the Roman law exchange of wills to explain that the binding nature of an exchange of wills was due to the cause of the obligations created by the parties' wills. "Cause" was then the "end, goal, aim, purpose" (causa finalis) pursued by a party who binds herself to an obligation.

Domat brought some structure to this concept of cause which he incorporated into the three basic forms of contracts known in his days: synallagmatic, real and gratuitous contracts. Domat explains that in a synallagmatic contract, the obligation of one party has for its cause the commitment made by the other party. The two obligations support each other and each one serves as the foundation of the other. In a sale, the seller is willing to transfer the ownership of a thing be *cause* (!) he will receive the ownership of the price in exchange. For Domat, the intimate, internal reasons or motives that may prompt each party to enter the sale are not important, not essential to the validity of the sale.

As regards real contracts, such as a loan, the obligation of the lender to transfer or deliver the thing comes into existence at the time the thing is delivered or transferred to the borrower. It is that performance of delivering or transferring which is the foundation or cause of the lender's obligation. When the borrower has to return the thing borrowed, the cause of the borrower's obligation will be found in the actual return of the thing into the hands of the lender. Again, for Domat, the internal, intimate reasons that may have prompted the parties to enter the loan are not important, not essential to the validity of the loan.

In gratuitous contracts, the "cause" can only be the liberal intent, the generous intent of the donor who gives away something and who will not receive anything in return for his performance. Why did the donor make a donation, why this generous intent? Again the motives, reasons . . . are not important.

All in all, Domat's theory of cause was that of an abstract and objective cause: the very kind of contract entered into was sufficient to disclose the cause of that contract. Thus, all contracts of sale had the same objective cause, i.e. the acquisition of ownership; all gratuitous contracts had the same objective cause, i.e. the generous altruistic intent of the donor; all real contracts had the same

---

[3] An interesting analogy can be made here with Article 2298 of the civil Code which states in its first two sentences that "A person who has been enriched without cause at the expense of another person is bound to compensate that person. The term 'without cause' is used in this context to exclude cases in which the enrichment results from a valid juridical act or the law. . . ."

§ 5.1.1. CONTEMPORARY THEORY OF CAUSE & ITS LEGAL REGIME 57

objective cause, i.e. the actual transfer or delivery of a thing into someone else's hands.

Pothier restated Domat's theory of cause which, through Pothier's writings, found its way in the French Civil Code of 1804 and the Louisiana Civil Code or Digest of 1808.

Pretermitting here the debates on the usefulness or uselessness of Domat's theory of cause, we will consider now the contemporary theory of cause and outline its legal regime.

§ 5.1.1. CONTEMPORARY THEORY OF CAUSE AND ITS LEGAL REGIME.

A. Contemporary Theory of Cause.

One may have noticed that the "history" of cause ties or relates that concept to an obligation rather than to a contract. In a unilateral contract the "one sided" obligation that is created, in a donation for example, has for its objective cause the gratuitous intent of the donor. In a bilateral or synallagmatic contract each obligation has for its objective cause the other obligation which is its objective counterpart. It could be said, at this point, that it is a misnomer to speak of the cause of a contract since the validity of a contract is contingent upon the validity of the obligations created by the parties and these obligations by their legal nature will give its name to the contract of which they are component parts. For example, when an obligation is to give gratuitously it may give rise to a donation between living persons, in which case we have a bilateral juridical act under the form of a unilateral contract. The same gratuitous obligation may consist in a legacy if it is a component part of a testament in which case we have a unilateral juridical act but no contract.[4] If one wants to acquire the ownership of some thing as a result of an obligation to give, one may choose to give a price in money or to give a thing for another thing to be received; in the first case, the obligation to give will give rise to a contract of sale whereas, in the second case, the parties enter into a contract of exchange. In both instances the cause (objective cause) of each obligation is the same: acquire the ownership of either a price or a thing. On the other hand, the objects of these two obligations are different and it is the object here that will give its name to the contract: the name will be "sale" in one case because of the price[5] and "exchange"[6] in the other case because a thing is exchanged for another thing.

Thus "cause" is a component part of a contractual obligation as is clearly stated in **LSA-C.C Art. 1966** according to which: **"An obligation cannot exist**

---

[4] On Unilateral and Bilateral Juridical Acts, see Précis, Louisiana Law of Obligations in General, § 1.1.2.; for Unilateral and Bilateral Contracts, see above Chapter 1, Article 1.

[5] A sale is defined as ". . . a contract whereby a person transfers ownership of a thing to another for a price in money." Art. 2439, Précis, Louisiana Law of Sale and Lease, Chapter 1.

[6] Exchange is defined in Art. 2660 as ". . . a contract, by which the parties to the contract give to one another, one thing for another, whatever it be, except money; for in that case it would be a sale."

without a lawful cause." One will have noticed, in this Article, the connection between the "obligation" and the necessary requirement of its "cause" The same can be said about **LSA-C.C. Art. 1969: "An obligation may be valid even though the cause is not expressed."**[7]

These two Articles lead us to investigate further this concept of cause. Indeed, if "an obligation cannot exist without a lawful cause," that "cause" has to be something more than an objective cause: how can an obligation to acquire the ownership of a thing be unlawful on account of its objective cause which is to acquire the ownership of something?[8] There is nothing illegal, per se, with the acquisition of ownership. Likewise, there is nothing illegal with the intent to be generous unless one digs a little deeper in the minds and hearts of the parties to bring forth the internal, intimate reason or reasons that may have actually motivated them (in the case of a bilateral contract) or one party only (in the case of unilateral gratuitous contract) to enter into a contractual relationship. The two Code Articles cited above will be of use only if the concept of cause encompasses a subjective element besides or in addition to a merely objective element. Hence the very broad definition of cause in the first paragraph of **LSA-C.C. Art. 1967: "Cause is the reason why a party obligates himself."**[9] Here again the connection is made between "cause" and "obligates."[10] Thus, looking beyond the objective cause which is characteristic of any donation, one should be asking the question: why did the donor really make that donation? What was his personal motive, his true intimate reason to "donate"? Could it have been an immoral reason, such as to make the donee a "dependent" or an "abused" person in an immoral relationship with the donor? Likewise, in a sale, why did the seller intend to sell a particular item? To deprive his family or a third person of their right to that item by selling it in a hurry at a low price? Was it to discriminate against another potential buyer?

The contemporary theory of cause provides a justification for the binding effect of a person's will and the duty to perform legally entered into obligations; it also sets the limits of the binding effect of the will by declaring invalid obligations which have an illegal or immoral cause; it further provides some sort of guarantee to parties who are told that **"Contracts have the effect of law for the parties and may be dissolved only through the consent of the parties or on grounds provided by law. Contracts must be performed in good**

---

[7] The verb used is "expressed"; thus, reasoning a *contrario sensu* or *expressio unius, exclusio alterius*, one must read Art. 1969 as considering an obligation with an "implied" "implicit" "presumed" cause as a valid obligation. Consider a "check" which bears no indication of its purpose but only the amount and the name of the beneficiary: what is the check for? A donation? A payment of a price for a thing bought? A refund? The "cause" of the obligation to transfer, gratuitously or onerously, the amount of money stated on the check is not given and, yet, the check is valid; its "cause" may not be expressed without endangering its validity.

[8] Leaving aside the issues of "capacity" (see supra Chapter 2), "object" (see infra Chapter 6).

[9] The absence of an adjective before "cause" should lead to a broad understanding of the concept of "cause." An *a generali sensu* interpretation ought to be given of the concept since such an interpretation is not restricted, limited, or confined by any adjective of any kind (such as "objective," "moral," "natural," or "sentimental").

[10] The word "contract" does not appear in this whole Art. 1967; see this Art., Cause, § 5.1.1.A.

faith."(LSA-C.C. Art. 1983). The courts, therefore, are not free to modify the obligations lawfully created by parties to a contract for "reasons" other than those that have motivated the parties.

But there lies the problem with the subjective cause and the selection of the parameters of its legal regime. Indeed, one needs to ask the question: which reason out of the many reasons which could be attributed to a party or the parties to a contract is to become the principal and determinant reason and, therefore, *the cause* of the contract? The wording of **LSA-C.C. Art. 1966** refers to *"Cause"* as being, in *the singular form*, **"the reason why a party obligates himself."** What if one can identify several reasons prompting a party to be bound: which one of these reasons will be "the cause" of the obligation and, beyond, the cause of the contract?

§ 5.1.2. LEGAL REGIME OF CAUSE.

The legal regime of cause comprises three requirements: (a) a cause must exist and (b) it must be "common" or "shared" (LSA-C.C. Arts. 1966, 1967, 1969, 1970); in addition (c) that cause must be lawful (LSA-C.C. Art. 1968).

A. Existence of "the" Cause.

For a *reason* to become *"the cause"* of an obligation which, in turn, will become *the cause* of the contract, it is necessary, as a first step, to identify one reason from all other reasons as being the "determinant-prevailing" reason[11] so that it could become the cause of the contract if it is "common" and if it is lawful. It can then be said that the two parties have "agreed" to raise that reason or cause from its original status as the cause of an obligation to the status of "the cause of the contract," thus a cause common to both parties. It explains why that determinant-prevailing reason or cause must exist at the time of formation of the contract and still be in existence at the moment the obligation or the obligations must be performed. The "cause" has become a component part, a requirement essential to the existence and validity of the contract. As **LSA-C.C. Art. 2300** states very clearly: **"A thing is not owed when it is paid or delivered for the discharge of an obligation that does not exist."**

Let us illustrate, with two examples, this requirement of the existence of the cause at the time of formation and during the existence of the contract.

Suppose a contract of sale which requires the seller to sell a particular car to the buyer. The car is the object of the seller's obligation to transfer or deliver. The buyer is motivated by the desire to buy that particular car and such is the cause of his obligation. Thus, at the time of formation of the sale, the buyer's obligation has a cause which is shared with the seller and the object of the latter's own obligation to deliver the car does exist at that same time. Let us

---

[11] The second step will consist in establishing that the determinant reason was common or shared by both parties (in a bilateral contract) so that it will become the cause of the contract.

assume that before the ownership of the car is transferred to the buyer[12] and unbeknownst to both parties the car is seriously damaged by a fortuitous event. Since the object of the seller's obligation (the car) is no longer what it was at the time of formation of the contract of sale, the cause or reason that prompted the buyer to buy that particular car is no longer what it was when the sale was entered into and before the ownership was ever transferred to that buyer. There occurred a partial or total subsequent failure of cause such that the buyer should not be compelled to pay the price of the now damaged car. The contract of sale should be annulled for lack of one of its essential requirements: the existence of a cause.[13]

Suppose that a buyer has bought some bricks of a certain color coating to build an exterior wall of his house. After the wall has been built a heavy storm washed away the very color of the coating that the buyer wanted the bricks to show for several years. It can be said that the buyer made an error as to the cause or reason for his buying these particular bricks which, in turn, were the object of the seller's obligation to deliver. In this particular case, error as to the quality of the bricks would probably not lead to the nullity of the contract because the parties could not be returned to the situation they were in before the contract was entered into.[14] The buyer will have to accept a financial compensation in lieu of the "special color coating" of the bricks. In such contracts of sale, the obligation of warranty owed by the seller to his buyer is a legal device meant to maintain an even balance between the integrity and value of the object sold by the seller and the cause of the obligation that made the buyer want to buy that object for a price of an amount considered equivalent to the value of that object.[15]

That a "cause" must exist does not mean that the cause must be expressly stated in the contract. Since many contracts are valid and binding when entered into orally only, it follows that the subjective cause of those oral contracts cannot be written down or expressed for all to see.[16] Even when a contract is in writing, it is not necessary that the cause be expressed as is stated in **LSA-C.C. Art. 1969: "An obligation may be valid even though its cause is not expressed."** As long as there is an exchange of consent between parties and an obligation created as a result, we must presume that the obligation was created for "a reason" common to the parties. Thus a check issued by A to B for x

---

[12] See Précis, Louisiana Law of Sale and Lease, transfer of ownership of movable things by consent, Chapter 2, Article 2, § 2.2.1.

[13] It can also be argued that because there is no longer an object to the seller's obligation, the synallagmatic feature of the contract of sale (a thing for a price) can no longer be fulfilled for lack of object. See infra Object, Chapter 6.

[14] On Nullity, see infra Chapter 9, Article 2. As Art. 2029 states clearly, that nullity (and not dissolution or rescission) occurs when a contract lacks one of the requirements for its formation. Art. 2033 states, in part, that "if it is impossible or impracticable to make restoration in kind, it may be made through an award of damages. . . ."

[15] On Warranty, see Précis, Louisiana Law of Sale and Lease, Chapter 4, § 4.1.2. et seq. On Price, see same Précis Chapter 2, Article 4.

[16] For example, the transfer of the ownership of movable things. Art. 2456 does not require a writing : "Ownership is transferred between the parties as soon as there is agreement on the thing and the price is fixed, even though the thing sold is not yet delivered nor the price paid."

amount of money without any written statement on the check as to the reason for it will be a valid check. It could be a loan, a donation, the payment of a price. Furthermore, if a court should determine that the cause expressed in a contract **"is untrue, the obligation is still effective if a valid cause can be shown."**[17] For example, a court could rule that the expressed cause, whether objective or subjective, of an apparent contract of lease is "untrue" and that the "true" cause of that contract is actually that of a contract of sale. A court can re-write a contract either if it considers that the re-written contract reflects more accurately the intent of the parties and the true cause of the contract, or if the re-written contract should have been the contract that the law required the parties to select.

B. The Cause of the Contract Is a "Common or Shared" Reason/Cause.

In a donation, which is a unilateral contract, the donor-obligor is usually motivated by a gratuitous intent which is to provide a benefit to the donee-obligee. However, the donor's reason for making a donation can be other than the mere intent to donate. It could be an intent to deprive somebody else from her due; or it could a reason with an immoral or unlawful purpose. Is it sufficient for that unlawful or immoral reason to exist in the mind or heart of the donor for that donation to be annulled? How secured or safe would any and all donations be? Can there be a cause of the donation only if donor and donee share in that unlawful or immoral cause? More will be presented, below, on this matter under the requirement of "lawfulness" of the cause.[18]

If we turn to the contract of sale, which is a bilateral contract, the buyer is motivated by some reason (or reasons) to buy, whereas the seller is motivated by his own reason (or reasons) to sell. Suppose a buyer of a car wants to buy from a dealer a car which is absolutely identical to the car owned by someone whom he wishes to kill with an explosive hidden under the hood. Such evil reason is the subjective and determinant cause that motivates the buyer. Should that subjective reason of the buyer's obligation become the cause of the contract of sale with the seller? What if the buyer does not disclose this highly personal and unlawful reason to his seller? Suppose, on the other hand, that the seller knew of the deep hostility that the buyer had vis-à-vis the third person; would that knowledge by the seller be sufficient to make the buyer's personal reason become the cause of the contract? What if the buyer does actually share with the seller "his reason" for buying the car?[19]

In the example given above of the bricks with a special color coating, what if the buyer did communicate to the seller the subjective and determinant reason why he wanted to buy these special bricks? What if the buyer did not give the seller any hint, any indication of his reason for buying these bricks? Suppose that these bricks are very well known for their particular coating: can one

---

[17] LSA-C.C. Art. 1970: "When the expression of a cause in a contractual obligation is untrue, the obligation is still effective if a valid cause can be shown."

[18] On Lawfulness of the Cause, see infra § 5.1.2.C.

[19] See further, infra, Lawfulness of the Cause § 5.1.2.C.

assume then that the seller should have either presumed or known that the cause of the contract was that special color coating on these particular bricks because it was the only possible reason for the buyer to buy those bricks?

In such instances, the courts will be called upon to exercise some judicial discretion in their construction of the facts of a particular case and in their appraisal of the individual position or situation of the parties involved (a professional v. a layman; two professionals; two laymen . . .). Most importantly, the courts should be guided by the fundamental principle stated in **LSA-C.C. Art. 1759** according to which **"Good faith shall govern the conduct of the obligor and the obligee in whatever pertains to the obligation."**[20]

Good faith,[21] "Offenses and Quasi-Offenses"[22] as well as the binding nature of a will or intent lawfully communicated, either expressly or implicitly, provide legal justifications for the expanded, but questionable, definition of cause which appears in the second paragraph of **Art. 1967: "A party may be obligated by a promise when he knew or should have known that the promise would induce the other party to rely on it to his detriment and the other party was reasonable in so relying. Recovery may be limited to the expenses incurred or the damages suffered as a result of the promisee's reliance on the promise. Reliance on a gratuitous promise made without required formalities is not reasonable."** Thus a "reasonable" promise made by a promisor either to another person or to other persons, such as a promise of sale[23] or of a reward, should bind the promisor to carry out his obligation, in totality or in part, vis-à-vis the promisee-other person who acted reasonably relying on the reasonable promise made and who, as a consequence, suffered a detriment or prejudice quantifiable in money.[24]

We believe that it is relatively easy to explain Art. 1967-2 as suggesting that a contract has been created between the promisor and the person who acted, in

---

[20] On Good Faith and Art. 1759 in general, see Précis, Louisiana Law of Obligations in General. See also footnote 22 below.

[21] LSA-C.C. Art. 1759. See Précis, Louisiana Law of Obligations in General, § 1.4.2.

[22] LSA-C.C. Art. 2315-A. can be used as a foundation for Art. 1967-2.

[23] On Promise of Sale, Promise to Sell, see Précis, Louisiana Law of Sale and Lease, § 1.1.1. On "Option," see same Précis § 1.1.3. et seq.

[24] Comment (a) to Art. 1967 states that the Article "incorporates detrimental reliance as an *additional* ground for enforceability." We take issue with this comment for two reasons: First, "comments"are not part of the Code articles themselves and, thus, these comments are not part of the law; in addition, the Titles to the Code articles are not part of the law either (see R.S. 1:13). It follows that the reference to "detrimental reliance" in the Title of Art. 1967 and in comment (a) should be disregarded and not be used even in an attempt to describe or elaborate on the contents of Art. 1967 which should be interpreted on a different ground than that of "detrimental reliance." It is true, however, that in the text of Art. 1967-2 one can read the words "rely" and "detriment." To the word "detriment" we would have preferred to read the words "prejudice" or "damage," so as to avoid the surreptitious or clandestine insertion of the common law concept of "detrimental reliance" in the Louisiana civil Code. Our second reason for taking issue with comment (a) and for rejecting "detrimental reliance" as an "additional ground for enforceability" is that, as explained above, Art. 1759 on Good Faith, Art. 2315-A on Offenses and Quasi-Offenses, and Arts. 1941 and 1944, provide the necessary legal (they are Code Articles) grounds for an action (not any additional remedy) on the part of the promisee against the promisor for breach of the duty or principle of good faith, or for breach of a juridical act or, still, for having caused a damage to another.

good faith,[25] on the basis of the promise and suffered a prejudice as a result. Indeed, when that person is aware of the promise made, as is suggested by the text of Art. 1967-2, and acts upon it, whether or not the promisor himself is aware of it, it can be said that an "acceptance" by the promisee has been manifested by the latter's expected reasonable action. That acceptance has been made "tacitly" by the promisee. Is it not what we read in **LSA-C.C. Art. 1941**: **"When commencement of the performance either constitutes acceptance or makes the offer irrevocable, the offeree must give prompt notice of that commencement unless the offeror knows or should know that the offeree has begun to perform. . . ."**? Furthermore, a very strong argument, *a fortiori ratione*, can be made on the legal ground of the binding nature of the "will" on the basis of **Art. 1944: "An offer of a reward made to the public is binding upon the offeror even if the one who performs the requested act does not know of the offer."**

C. Lawfulness of Cause.

If among the reasons that prompted the parties to enter into a contract there happens to be one reason of an immoral or unlawful nature, it is very likely that a court would "pick" that reason, from among many others, as the cause of the contract even though that reason may not have been the determinant or prevailing reason for the parties. It is the courts' duty to preserve and maintain public order and good morals in the performance of contracts in particular. To that effect the courts will take into account both the objective theory of cause and, most often, the subjective theory of cause.

LSA-C.C. Art. 1968 states that **"The cause of an obligation is unlawful when the enforcement of the obligation would produce a result prohibited by law or against public policy."** The objective theory of cause cannot find much room for application to bilateral or synallagmatic contracts under this Article. Only if the "object" of an obligation is illegal, immoral, or out of commerce can such a contract be annulled . . . for unlawful object. Otherwise, there is nothing "objectively" illegal or immoral in wanting to partake of a bilateral-synallagmatic contract be it a sale, an exchange, a lease. Much more likely, the illegality or immorality of the cause of a contract will concern the subjective cause, the personal reason(s) which entice parties to enter into a contractual relationship. The contract can be either unilateral or bilateral since all contracts must have a cause to fit the requirements of a contract under the Civil Code. The question which has to be addressed is whether the immoral or illegal cause must be shared by both parties to the contract (donor and donee; seller and buyer) for the contract to be declared null by the courts, or whether it should suffice that one party only be motivated by an unlawful or immoral cause for, if that cause can be proven, the courts to declare the contract null? Which one of these two concerns should prevail over the other: good morals and public order on the one hand or the private interests of two or a few individual parties on the other hand? We believe that the Louisiana civil Code has taken a

---

[25] On Good faith and Offer, see Consent, Chapter 3, Offer and Acceptance, A. Features and characteristics of an "offer" § 3.1.1. On Art. 1941, see Acceptance, § 3.1.2.2. On Art. 1944, see supra Chapter 3, Article 3.

very clear and definite side where it states that **"Persons may not by their juridical acts derogate from laws enacted for the protection of the public interest. Any act in derogation of such laws is an absolute nullity." (LSA-C.C. Art. 7).** One should understand the words "Any act" in as broad a sense as possible since "Any" sets neither a limit nor a restriction to the scope of application of "act."[26] Furthermore, the connection between "the protection of the public interest" and the "absolute nullity" of "any act" sends a message to the courts to enforce the protection of the public interest in absolute preference to the "private" interest of parties to an "act." Whether shared, common or not, any unlawful or immoral reason should carry with it the absolute nullity of the act of which it meant to be the "cause."

---

[26] On the notion of "act" see Précis, Louisiana Law of Obligations in General, § 1.1.2.

Chapter 6

OBJECT AND MATTER OF CONTRACTS
LSA-C.C. ARTS. 1971 TO 1977

This heading is somewhat ambiguous as it relates "Object" to "Contracts" and includes the additional word "Matter" as relating also to "Contracts." Are "Object" and "Matter" different concepts and, therefore, two different requirements for a contract to exist and create obligations? Since "titles" should not have any substantial "legal" import or significance, suffice it to say that this title embodies an ambiguity which resides, for example, in the following two articles: 1) **LSA-C.C. Art. 1906**: "**A contract is an agreement by two or more parties whereby obligations are created, modified, or extinguished**"; 2) LSA-C.C. Art. 1971: "**Parties are free to contract for any object that is lawful, possible, and determined or determinable.**"

Art. 1906 relates or associates "a contract" to "an obligation" (created, modified or extinguished) which "obligation," according to Art. 1756, binds an obligor "to render a performance in favor of another . . . [which] performance may consist in giving, doing, or not doing something." The "something" mentioned in Art. 1756 is an all encompassing word meant to refer to the infinite kinds of "objects" which will be "given," "done" or "not done" as a result of an existing obligation. For example, an obligation to give "something" is created by a donation; the donation will bear on "the thing" (money, for example) to be transferred gratuitously by the donor to the donee;[1] in a sale, the seller is under the obligation to "give," i.e. transfer the ownership of the thing sold to the buyer.[2] In a contract of mandate, the mandatary binds himself "to do" something "transact one or more affairs for the principal."[3]

Art. 1971 states that "**Parties are free to contract for any object that is lawful, possible, and determined or determinable.**" This Article, and others, relates or associates a "contract" with an "object" and that "object [must be] lawful, possible, and determined or determinable."

The question is then the following: is the Civil Code requiring that a "contract" have an "object" or that an "obligation" have an "object"? If we opt for the first alternative, we are then facing a dilemma when a contract is bilateral since such a contract will have "two objects," one for each of the two obligations

---

[1] LSA-C.C. Art. 1468: "A donation inter vivos (between living persons) is an act by which the donor divests himself, at present and irrevocably, of the thing given, in favor of the donee who accepts it."

[2] LSA-C.C. Art. 2439-1: "Sale is a contract whereby a person transfers ownership of a thing to another for a price in money. . . ."

[3] LSA-C.C. Art. 2989: "A mandate is a contract by which a person, the principal, confers authority on another person, the mandatary, to transact one or more affairs for the principal."

created, as in a contract of sale: the thing and the price.

This example of a sale provides us with the answer to the ambiguity raised by the wording of the Code Articles 1906 and 1971 quoted above. The answer, as we see it, is the following: a contract, as an agreement, has for its purpose to "create, modify or extinguish" obligations; such obligations are, then, to "give" something, [an object movable or immovable], or to do something, [a service for example] or to abstain from doing something [drinking, for example]. So, strictly speaking, a contract has no object, whereas an obligation has an object. There are, therefore, two "objects" in a contract of sale: one owed by the seller who must transfer the thing he sold to the buyer, and one owed by the buyer who must transfer the "price" to the seller. Why should the thing sold by the seller be considered as "the object of the contract of sale"? Why couldn't the price paid by the buyer be that "object" of the contract of sale? Likewise, in a contract of "mandate" there are two objects, if the mandate is onerous: the principal must "pay" "compensate" ("give") the mandatary for his services ("do"). Which object of one obligation or the other is the object of the contract of mandate?

In conclusion, whenever we will use the expression "the object of the contract" we will subsume and actually intend to write about the "object of the obligation" created by a unilateral contract or the "object" of one or of the other obligation created by a bilateral contract. In most instances the "object of the contract" will be identified with the object of the principal obligation created by the contract because it is that principal obligation which will give its name to the contract. For example, in a donation which creates only one obligation on the part of the donor, it will be the object of that obligation which will become the object of the contract of donation. In a sale, it is the object of the seller's obligation to "give," to transfer the ownership of a thing which will be identified with the "object of the contract of sale" because without that obligation of the seller there would be no "price" and, therefore, no sale.

For a contract to be valid, its object must meet certain features or characteristics. The 1984 legislative revision of the Law of Obligations has given a formal existence to an object of a contract which, until then, had been recognized by the Louisiana jurisprudence under its civil law name of "promesse de porte-fort."

ARTICLE 1
LEGAL CHARACTERISTICS or FEATURES OF AN OBJECT

LSA-C.C. Art. 1971 lists the three characteristics which must be met by an object to be the object of a contract: **"Parties are free to contract for any object that is lawful, possible, and determined or determinable."**

§ 6.1.1. LAWFULNESS OF THE OBJECT.

Laws for the preservation of public order prohibit parties from entering a contract which would have an unlawful object or an immoral object. In the words of **LSA-C.C. Art. 7:** **"Persons may not by their juridical acts derogate from laws enacted for the protection of the public interest. Any act in derogation of such laws is an absolute nullity."** Thus contractual obligations to give something unlawful (narcotics, . . .) and contractual obligations to do something unlawful (crime against a person . . .) will be absolutely null. No right of action will be available to the parties to such contracts. As stated in **LSA-C.C. Art. 2030** "**A contract is absolutely null when it violates a rule of public order, as when the object of a contract is illicit or immoral. A contract that is absolutely null may not be confirmed.**

Absolute nullity may be invoked by any person or may be declared by the court on its own initiative."[4] Furthermore, "a performance rendered under a contract that is absolutely null because its object or its cause is illicit or immoral may not be recovered by a party who knew or should have known of the defect that makes the contract null. The performance may be recovered, however, when that party invokes the nullity to withdraw from the contract before its purpose is achieved and also in exceptional situations when, in the discretion of the court, that recovery would further the interest of justice." (LSA-C.C. Art. 2033-2)[5]

§ 6.1.2. DETERMINATION OF THE OBJECT: KIND, QUANTITY, QUALITY.

LSA-C.C. Art. 1973 makes the determination of the object of a contract conditional upon the parties agreeing on the "kind" of object and the "quantity" of that object. Nothing is said of the "quality" of the same contractual object. In this respect, one has to refer to LSA-C.C. Art. 1860 listed in the civil Code under "Extinction of Obligations" and "Performance."[6]

A. Kind.

What is a "kind"? In the absence of a definition in the Civil Code, we are told by **LSA-C.C. Art. 11** that "**The words of a law must be given their generally prevailing meaning. Words of art and technical terms must be given their technical meaning when the law involves a technical matter.**" In this instance, the general meaning of the word "kind" can be found in a dictionary as referring to "a class that is defined by the common attribute or attributes possessed by all of its members <flowers of all kinds>, <the kind of person who gets angry easily>."[7] Should someone who orders "a dozen flowers" have sufficiently identified the object by its "kind" for the seller to know which "flowers" the buyer ordered? Should a caller order, on the phone, two cases of "beer" for a reception, will the owner of the liquor store know what "kind" of beer the buyer wants? Is it sufficient to say that the seller "**need not give one of the best quality but he may not tender one of the worst.**"?[8] Most likely not. As regards obligations to do, would an ad seeking "a secretary" be a sufficient description of the "kind" of personal services sought? Most likely not. Thus, the

---

[4] See infra Nullity, Chapter 9, Article 2.
[5] See infra Effects of Nullity, § 9.2.2.
[6] See Précis, Louisiana Law of Obligations in General, § 7.1.1.B.
[7] Webster's II New College Dictionary, 1999, at p. 607.
[8] LSA-C.C. Art. 1860, in part.

word "kind", in these general articles on Object and Matter of Contracts, should be read as demanding a more focused meaning so that there would be little doubt in the minds of the parties as regards the "identity" of the object of their contract. The parties must have come to agree, at least, on a group of services or things that share common traits or characteristics and, thus, single them out as an identifiable group or type of services or things. Ordering twelve "roses" should be preferred to twelve "flowers", ordering "a Louisiana civil Code" should be preferred to "a Civil Code," and so on.

Still parties to a contract bearing on a thing or services that need to be ultimately "determined" when performance is to take place should be as precise as possible in their determination of the "object" of their contract or agreement. Anticipating that parties to a contract of sale might fail to adequately "determine" the object of their contract [the thing to be sold by the seller], the civil Code fills the "gaps" in the agreement of the parties with a series of Articles on objects "that have to be individualized from a mass of things" or things that have to tried, tested and tasted, and viewed.[9] So, the whole purpose of the process of determining the object of a contract is to single out, individualize, identify the object of the principal obligation in such a manner that it can become the object of "the contract" the parties want to enter into.

B. Quantity.

A second facet of the determination of an object can be its quantity. **"The quantity of a contractual object may be undetermined"** at the time the parties enter their contract **"provided it is determinable"**[10] at the time performance is due. Buying one half or one third of a harvest of oranges is buying a determinable quantity out of a whole mass; likewise, buying one hundred pounds of oranges from a whole harvest is buying a determinable quantity of "pounds" of oranges.[11]

The determination of the quantity of an object can be left, as per the intent of the parties, to a third person. **"If the determination of the quantity of the object has been left to the discretion of a third person, the quantity of an object is determinable.**

If the parties fail to name a person, or if the person named is unable or unwilling to make the determination, the quantity may be determined by the court."(LSA-C.C. Art. 1974). At least two situations can be fitted under this Article. On the one hand, parties to a contract may have left to a third person to determine the quantity of the object of their contract without making the decision of that person a 'suspensive condition' of their contract. What the parties wanted was someone else than themselves to determine the quantity but the same parties were actually more concerned with their contract and their obligations coming into existence than with the services of a "particular" person making the decision as to the quantity. Should that "any" third person fail to

---

[9] See Précis, Louisiana Law of Sale and Lease, § 3.1.2. LSA-C.C. Arts. 2457 et seq.

[10] LSA-C.C. Art 1973-2.

[11] Id. note 9.

§ 6.1.2. DETERMINATION OF THE OBJECT: KIND, QUANTITY, QUALITY   69

make the required decision, the court will step in and takeover from that failing third person. On the other hand, the parties to a contract may have identified or named a particular person to make that decision. In this instance the parties have "suspended" the existence of their contract on the decision of a named person on account of the trust they have in that person and that person only, or on account of a particular relationship they have with that person, etc. In such an instance where the parties to a contract have made the *strictly personal* obligation owed by the third person a *suspensive condition*[12] of their agreement, the court will not be allowed to substitute itself to the intent of the parties.

Another mode of determining the quantity of an object of a contract is to take into account **"the output of one party or the requirements of the other. In such a case, output or requirements must be measured in good faith."** (LSA-C.C. Art. 1975). The quantity of our monthly consumption of electricity will be determined at the end of the month by the greater or lesser extent of our requirement for electricity. The quantity of paintings bought in a year by a gallery from a particular artist will depend on the output of paintings by the artist.

In order to deter any party from taking advantage of the other, the duty of good faith on the part of that party setting the quantity of the object will give the court an opportunity to ensure a proper balance in the obligations of the parties.

C.   Quality.

As far as the quality of an object or a thing might be important, even essential, to its determination, the civil Code includes a suppletive rule of law in Article 1860. As this Article states, it is concerned with the performance of an obligation which has been created by a contract suggesting, therefore, that at the time of formation of their contract the parties had failed to agree on the quality of that object or thing.[13] It follows that an agreement on the quality of an object/thing is not essential to the actual determination of the object at the time of formation of the contract. The law will feel the gap of "quality" of the thing when the parties fail to agree. Still, it is highly advised and recommended that parties to a contract express their consent on the quality of the object to make it, for example, a subjective cause of their contract.[14] **LSA-C.C. Art. 2529** should

---

[12] On Personal Obligations, see Précis, Louisiana Law of Obligations in General, § 2.1.2; on Condition and Suspensive Condition, see the same Précis, § 2.2-B.1.

[13] An agreement on the quality of the thing/object of a unilateral contract is not of much concern since such a contract creates only one obligation and are usually gratuitous. In a donation, only the donor is concerned with the quality of the thing he/she "donates" to the donee. The latter would be ill advised (and most likely ungrateful) to question the quality of a "gift."

[14] This is particularly true in synallagmatic commutative contracts, such as a sale, where one obligation (the obligation of the seller, for example) is considered to be the equivalent of the other (the obligation of the buyer). A buyer will want to adjust the price he pays to the quality of the thing he buys. Otherwise the buyer would likely bring an action for "error as to the quality of the object." See in this respect, Précis, Louisiana Law of Sale and Lease, § 4.1.4. A2. Not of the Kind, Not of the Quality; Not Conforming.

be a warning to parties to a synallagmatic contract where it states that **"When the thing the seller has delivered, though in itself free from redhibitory defects, is not of the kind or quality specified in the contract or represented by the seller, the rights of the buyer are governed by other rules of sale and conventional obligations."**

§ 6.1.3. POSSIBILITY OR IMPOSSIBILITY OF THE OBJECT.

A third legal requirement that must be met by the object of a contract is that the object be "possible."[15] The issue is between objects which are possible of performance and those which are impossible of performance.

Only an object/thing that is absolutely impossible of ever existing or that existed at one time but no longer exists leads to the absolute nullity of the contract. "To the impossible no one can be held." Swimming non-stop across the Pacific Ocean, touching the moon from the earth, not drinking water for several months in a row, etc., are objects that no human being can do or not do; an obligation that would have such an object could not exist because it would have no "possible" object to do or not to do. As regards an obligation to give, if at the time parties enter a contract of sale of a house not knowing that the house had been destroyed by fortuitous event a few days before, that contract of sale would have no object and the seller would not be entitled to the price of a thing which he could not transfer to the buyer. There would be impossibility to transfer, i.e. to deliver, the house.

In all the above instances, nobody could give, do, or not do the object of the obligation entered into.

On the other hand, the impossibility could be "relative," in the sense that for personal reason(s) the obligor himself could not carry out his performance although somebody else could. For example, if an obligor agrees to swim across the English Channel for a certain amount of money when he can barely swim thirty yards in a pool, the performance he bound himself to carry out will be impossible for him to do but many other persons have proven that it can be done. The impossibility of performance is "relative" in the sense that it is "personal" to that obligor and not "absolutely" impossible for someone else. Such an obligor will be validly bound by the contract; he will be in breach of a "possible" object of an obligation and, thus, liable to pay compensatory damages for breach of an obligation to do something.

Are "future things," things that will come into existence in the future, "determined or determinable," "possible or impossible" things/objects? **LSA-C.C. Art. 1976** states that **"Future things may be the object of a contract.**

"Beers" are not all of the same quality. "Pearls" are not all of the same quality. "Roofers' services" are not all of the same quality. Should any buyer of beer or pearls be satisfied with "not one of the best, but not one of the worst"?

[15] LSA-C.C. Art. 1971. See supra Chapter 6, Introduction.

The succession of a living person may not be the object of a contract other than an antenuptial agreement. Such a succession may not be renounced." A farmer can sell his "future" crop; a painter can sell a painting that he will do next year; a singer can schedule to sing in an opera two years from the day of the contract. Aren't "futures. Commodities or stocks bought or sold upon agreement of delivery in time to come"?[16] **LSA-C.C. Art. 2450** states: **"When more than one thing are sold together as a whole so that the buyer would not have bought one thing without the other or others, a redhibitory defect in one of such things gives rise to redhibition for the whole."**[17] A hope, as contrasted with a future thing, is a thing that exists at the time the "hope" is purchased; the "hope" is a thing in existence when it is "given."[18]

ARTICLE 2
PROMESSE DE PORTE-FORT

In the 1984 revision of the Code Articles on Conventional Obligations, former Article 1889 of the Code of 1870 was rewritten to focus more precisely on the civil law institution of "promesse de porte-fort" as is its French name. Such an institution can be the single object of a contract or one of several objects of a contract. Its purpose is to "possibly" involve a third person in a contractual obligation entered into between the two contracting parties. Since, as a general rule and as will be explained below, a contract can **have the effect of law for the parties**[19] only, for a third person to be involved in an existing contractual relationship not of her making it is reasonable to expect that third person to express, somehow, her willingness or consent before becoming a party to that pre-existing contract. Hence, in the words of **LSA-C.C. Art. 1977: "The object of a contract may be that a third person will incur an obligation or render a performance.**

The party who promised that obligation or performance is liable for damages if the third person does not bind himself or does not perform." What is this institution of a "promesse de porte-fort" and what are its effects?

§ 6.2.1. PROMESSE DE PORTE-FORT: DESCRIPTION AND NATURE.

Suppose a representative, such as a mandatary,[20] conducts some business for his principal, such as purchasing the works of French legal writers like Pothier, Cujas, and Toullier. While conducting his business, the mandatary comes across a great collection of Blackstone's works. Not "mandated" to buy legal works

---

[16] Webster's II New College Dictionary, p. 455.

[17] See Précis, Louisiana Law of Sale and Lease § 2.3.2. Existence of Things, and § 2.3.3. Future Thing.

[18] See, LSA-C.C. Art. 2451 and Précis, Louisiana Law of Sale and Lease, § 2.3.4. Hope.

[19] Excerpt from Art. 1983; on Effects of Contracts, see infra Chapter 8, particularly Art. 1985. Former Code Art. 1889 stated in its first sentence that "No one can, by a contract in his own name, bind any one but himself or his representatives. . . ."

[20] On Representation, see LSA-C.C. Arts. 2985 to 2988; on Mandate, see LSA-C.C. Arts. 2989 to 3034.

other than French legal works, our mandatary could be in a quandary: to buy or not to buy Blackstone's? What if the principal would absolutely refuse to consider the purchase of Blackstone's works to be within even the broadest description of his mandatary's duties? If the mandatary bought Blackstone's works he could be saddled with his expensive purchase and, yet, there exists this ray of hope that the principal might want to acquire works of authors other than French authors.

This is where the promesse de porte-fort comes in as a possible option for the mandatary to act for the benefit of his principal. The mandatary, acting beyond the scope of his duties, could enter into a contract with the seller of Blackstone's works, and this is the promesse de porte-fort, with the commitment that he, the mandatary, would seek and obtain the ratification or approval of his purchase by his principal. In fact, the mandatary is telling the seller that the ultimate buyer will be the principal and not himself, that he would drop out of the picture once the principal would have ratified the purchase. The mandatary is binding himself towards the seller by an obligation of result, i.e. obtain the principal's consent. What if the principal refuses his consent? We will consider the effects of a promesse de porte-fort below.

We have chosen to illustrate this mechanism of a promesse de porte-fort with the case of a mandatary or representative because only someone who knows well the person (principal) for whose benefit he is willing to bind himself towards another (a seller, for example) would be willing to stand as a porte-fort in the place of the person-principal. Such instances of promesse de porte-fort are more likely to occur within a family or between close friends, that is, whenever there exist some close ties between the porte-fort and the person whom he wants to benefit by his actions.

One must focus very specifically on the behavior of the porte-fort to distinguish that legal relationship from that of a mandate particularly where a mandatary would **"contract in his own name without disclosing his status as a mandatary."** Such a mandatary would **"bind himself personally for the performance of the contract."**[21] However, ultimately, **"the principal is bound to perform the contract that the mandatary, acting within the limits of his authority, makes with a third person."**[22] This is not the case in a promesse de porte-fort; the principal or third person is not bound to perform the contract entered into by the porte-fort with his co-contracting party. In a triangular porte-fort situation, the principal-third person is not aware that someone may be acting for his benefit since the porte-fort has received no instruction from "anyone" to act for a third person-principal. On the contrary, in the case of a mandate, **"the principal is bound to the mandatary to perform the obligations that the mandatary contracted within the limits of his authority. . . ."**[23] If a mandatary has exceeded the limits of his authority, **"the principal is not bound to the mandatary to perform the obligations that the mandatary contracted" "unless the principal ratifies those acts."**[24] Any

---

[21] LSA-C.C. Art. 3017.
[22] LSA-C.C. Art. 3020.
[23] LSA-C.C. Art. 3010.
[24] Id.

altruistic motivation and behavior on the part of a "porte-fort" may be costly to that porte-fort but that is not sufficient a reason to reject the existence of such an institution proper to the civil law.

§ 6.2.2. EFFECTS OF A PROMESSE DE PORTE-FORT.

Two opposite situations must be considered: in one instance, the third person-principal may have ratified the contract entered into by the porte-fort whereas, in a second situation, that third person-principal may have refused to ratify the contract.

A. Ratification by the Principal-Third Person.

Two effects flow from a ratification by the principal-third person of the juridical act or contract entered into between the porte-fort and the co-contracting party.

One first effect is that the third person-principal is now "bound to perform the contract that the porte-fort has made with his co-contracting party."[25] The relationship now created is exactly as if a "mandatary" had exceeded his powers in contracting with "another," but where the principal would have ratified the contract entered into by his mandatary with "another."[26] Ratification by the principal means that the porte-fort has fulfilled the obligation of result he entered into with "another," the co-contracting party. The "ratifying" principal is substituted to the porte-fort. If the porte-fort had bought Blackstone's works and because of ratification, those works "became" the ownership of the principal retroactively to the time when the porte-fort entered the contract of sale of those works.

A second important effect of ratification is that it releases the porte-fort of any subsequent obligation; he is now out of the picture so much so that he is not liable for any breach, by the principal, of the obligations created by the ratified contract. A porte-fort is not an accessory contract like a suretyship contract is since a "surety" must stand by the obligor as long as the principal obligation has not been performed.[27] A porte-fort owes one "principal obligation," an obligation of result, obtain the consent, approval, ratification of the principal and once this obligation has been fulfilled, the porte-fort owes nothing else.

B. Refusal by the Principal to Ratify.

The principal is free not to ratify the contract entered into by the porte-fort with a third person. The principal cannot be compelled "to do" something, i.e. "ratify," against his will. Since the porte-fort failed to perform his own

---

[25] The words in between quotes are an "adaptation" of Art. 3020 on "mandate" to the relationship created by a promesse de porte-fort. This is done in order to show the similarity between a mandate and a promesse de porte-fort.

[26] See LSA-C.C. Art. 3019 on ratification in a mandate relationship.

[27] LSA-C.C. Art. 3035 states: "Suretyship is an accessory contract by which a person binds himself to a creditor to fulfill the obligation of another upon the failure of the latter to do so."

obligation of result to do something — obtain the principal's ratification — the porte-fort is now required to pay damages to "his" co-contracting party because the contract did not come into existence as the porte-fort had "promised" his co-contracting party.[28]

---

[28] LSA-C.C. Art. 1994: "Upon an obligor's failure to perform an obligation to deliver a thing, or not to do an act, or to execute an instrument, the court shall grant specific performance plus damages for delay if the obligee so demands. If specific performance is impracticable, the court may allow damages to the obligee.

Upon a failure to perform an obligation that has another object, such as an obligation to do, the granting of specific performance is at the discretion of the court." LSA-C.C. Art. 1986. "An obligor is liable for the damages caused by his failure to perform a conventional obligation.

A failure to perform results from nonperformance, defective performance, or delay in performance."

Chapter 7

THIRD PARTY BENEFICIARY — STIPULATION POUR AUTRUI
LSA-C.C. ARTS. 1978 TO 1982

This institution of the civil Code stands at the crossroad of the formation of a contract, on the one hand, and the effects of a contract, on the other hand. It can, therefore, be considered under either subject matter as long as a cross reference is made from the subject matter under which this institution of a third party beneficiary is included to the other subject matter.[1] Thus, just as a promesse de porte-fort can be the object of a contract, we have chosen to describe the legal regime of the "stipulation pour autrui" under the title of formation of a contract and, more specifically, as an object of a contract. **Article 1978 (1)** is very clear in this respect: "**A contracting party may stipulate a benefit for a third person called a third party beneficiary.**" The "benefit" referred to in this article can be "the" single object of a contract, or "one" of the objects of a contract as, for example, in a conjunctive obligation or an alternative obligation. We could, therefore, re-write Art. 1978 (1) to read like Art. 1977 (1) on the promesse de porte-fort, as follows: *"The object of a contract may be that a benefit is stipulated for a third person. . . ."*

We will consider successively the notion of a stipulation (A), the conditions for the valid existence of a stipulation (B) to be followed by the legal regime of a stipulation (C).

ARTICLE 1
NOTION OF A STIPULATION FOR THE BENEFIT OF ANOTHER

A stipulation pour autrui is a legal device bringing together three parties: one of them is called "stipulator", another "promisor", and the third "beneficiary". The interplay among these parties is such that the stipulator receives the commitment of the promisor that the latter will render a performance to the beneficiary. Thus, the beneficiary becomes an obligee, a creditor, as a consequence of the obligation created by the contract between the stipulator and the promisor. The beneficiary is, therefore, a "third party" to that contract. Yet, although a "non-party" to the contract and not represented[2] in the contract, the beneficiary will receive "the benefit of the effects" of that contract. In a word, a stipulation for the benefit of another is "bilateral" in its creation but "triangular" in its effects. Indeed, a third party beneficiary stipulation is one of the few illustrations of the principles stated in **Art. 1983** that "**Contracts have the effect of law for the parties. . . .**" (bilateral formation) and in **Art. 1985** which states

---

[1] See infra on effects of contracts vis-à-vis third parties, Chapter 8.

[2] On representation, see LCC Arts. 2985–2988.

that "**Contracts may produce effects _for_ third parties only when provided by law.**"[3] (triangular effects) For example, a donation by X to Y may include a "charge'" on Y for the benefit of Z.[4] A loan between a bank and a borrower may actually be for the benefit of the borrower's child.

The mechanism of a third party beneficiary stipulation is such that it creates a right of its own nature, the "benefit", in the sense that neither the stipulator nor the promisor ever had this right in their patrimonies to transfer it to the beneficiary. This right vested in the beneficiary is created, therefore, by a contract between the stipulator and the promisor out of their own bilateral legal relationship. Therefore, the actual vesting of this right into the patrimony of the beneficiary is contingent not only on the validity of the contract between stipulator and promisor but also on the performance of their obligations by these two parties.

ARTICLE 2
CONDITIONS FOR A VALID STIPULATION

A "stipulation" being a clause in a contract, that contract must meet all the requirements for a valid contract.[5] The requirement of cause is the one of greater concern because the stipulator cannot use the device of a stipulation to transfer "indirectly" to the beneficiary and via the promisor a right which he, the stipulator, could not have transferred "directly" by a contract with the beneficiary himself.[6]

§ 7.2.1. CONDITIONS PERTAINING TO THE CONTRACT BETWEEN STIPULATOR AND PROMISOR.

The contract between the stipulator and the promisor must be binding between the parties as the "principal contract" which includes an accessory stipulation.[7] Thus a stipulation pour autrui could not exist in the absence of a supporting-principal contract. This contract, whether onerous or gratuitous, must meet the requirements for the validity of any contract[8] in addition to meeting the specific requirements of the nominate contract the parties may have intended to enter into, like a sale or a donation. This fundamental requirement of a valid principal contract explains why the subsequent enforcement by the "beneficiary" of the accessory stipulation for his benefit will depend on the performance of their obligations by the parties to the principal contract.

---

[3] See infra Chapter 8, our emphasis of "for." Contracts cannot be intentionally detrimental to third parties but third parties may be beneficiaries without expressing their consent for the benefit to be created. For example, in a life insurance contract, the future beneficiary of the contract may be unaware that he/she is a beneficiary until the time of the death of the stipulator.

[4] See LCC Art. 1527.

[5] See supra Formation of Contracts, Chapters 2 to 7.

[6] See, e.g., LCC Arts. 1475 and 1519.

[7] On Principal and Accessory Contracts, see supra Chapter 1, Article 4.

[8] On the Requirements for a Contract, see supra Chapter 2.

§ 7.2.2. CONDITIONS PERTAINING TO THE STIPULATION ITSELF.

A stipulation being a juridical act, that act must meet the requirements for any valid juridical act. Of major concern should be the "free" intent of the stipulator and a lawful "cause" for the stipulation. A stipulator cannot do indirectly, by way of a stipulation pour autrui, what he cannot do directly in a contract with the beneficiary.

Must a stipulation pour autrui be for an identified or named person or can it be for an "identifiable person" or, still, can it be for a future person?

Obviously there is no question that a stipulation can be provided for an identified third party. Such is the case of many life insurance contracts. However, it is not an essential requirement for a valid stipulation that the third party beneficiary be identified at the time the stipulator "stipulates for the benefit of another." The stipulator may stipulate for the benefit of a party who will be "identifiable" at the time the performance of the stipulation can be demanded from the promisor. Such would be the case of an insurance contract entered into by a seller for the benefit of that party who will be in possession of the goods at the time the goods would perish. A father or a mother could have a life insurance contract for the benefit of his/her children born or to be born.[9]

ARTICLE 3
EFFECTS OF A STIPULATION FOR THE BENEFIT OF ANOTHER

Because of the triangular effect of a stipulation, three sets of effects must be considered.

§ 7.3.1. EFFECTS BETWEEN STIPULATOR AND PROMISOR.

These effects, and there are two sets of effects in this relationship, must be considered first because they concern the principal contract. A first set of effects is created by the principal contractual relationship between the stipulator and the promisor. These effects are those of the contract these parties entered into. If that contract is a sale, then each party must fulfill its obligations vis-à-vis the other as in any bilateral commutative contract of sale.[10]

The second set of effects bears on the accessory clause, the stipulation created by the contract. The stipulator has, obviously, an interest that the stipulation be carried out by the promisor for the benefit of the third party. As stated in **Art. 1981 (2): "Also the stipulator, for the benefit of the third party, may demand performance from the promisor."** Should the promisor breach his obligation vis-à-vis the third party, the stipulator may either seek the dissolution of the

---

[9] Art. 26 is a good example of a stipulation for the benefit of an "identifiable" person: "An unborn child shall be considered as a natural person for whatever relates to its interests from the moment of conception. If the child is born dead, it shall be considered never to have existed as a person, except for purposes of actions resulting from its wrongful death."

[10] On the Effects of a Contract of Sale, see Précis, Louisiana Law of Sale and Lease, Chapter 3.

contract[11] or, if possible, the performance of the stipulation on behalf of the third party beneficiary.[12]

§ 7.3.2. EFFECTS BETWEEN THE STIPULATOR AND THE THIRD PARTY BENEFICIARY.

A. Consent and Revocation.

The relationship between the stipulator and the third party beneficiary is not a direct "effect" of the stipulation. It is only indirectly, through the promisor, that the stipulator is in a legal relationship with the third party. Thus the cause that prompted the creation of the stipulation is to be found in the interest or reason the stipulator has in having the promisor carry out a performance for the benefit of the third party. That same reason or cause explains why the consent expressed by the third party to the stipulation in his favor vests rights in that party against both the stipulator and the promisor. As **Art. 1978(2)** states: **"Once the third party has manifested his intention to avail himself of the benefit, the parties may not dissolve the contract by mutual consent without the beneficiary's agreement."** Since the stipulator's interest or reason for stipulating for the benefit of a third party justifies the validity of the stipulation, it follows that **"The stipulation may be revoked only by the stipulator and only before the third party has manifested his intention of availing himself of the benefit."** Art. 1979(1). However, the primary relationship between the stipulator and the promisor and the obligations thereby created between them makes the promisor a party to the stipulation: he is 'the obligor' of that stipulation and he may have a reason to want to perform. Thus, **"If the promisor has an interest in performing, however, the stipulation may not be revoked without his consent."** Art. 1979(2).[13]

Should the stipulation pour autrui be lawfully revoked, the principal contract between stipulator and promisor remains in existence and the latter will owe the performance of what was the stipulation to the former.[14] Art. 1980: **"In case of revocation or refusal of the stipulation, the promisor shall render performance to the stipulator."**

---

[11] On dissolution of contracts, see infra Chapter 9, Article 1.

[12] There is, in this case, a situation analogous to the Management of the Affairs of Another, Negotiorum Gestio, Arts. 2292–2297.

[13] With respect to this right of revocation, one may ask a question about the legal nature of that right: Is the right to revoke strictly personal to the stipulator or can this right be heritable and accessible to the stipulator's creditors by way of a revocatory action or an oblique action? See Précis, Louisiana Law of Obligations in General, § 2.1.2. On Revocatory and Oblique actions, see infra Chapter 11.

[14] This is an application of the principle according to which the nullity or failure of an accessory contract necessarily part of a principal contract has no impact on that principal contract. The validity of the principal is not contingent on the validity of the accessory. A contrario, an invalid principal contract carries with it the invalidity of an accessory contract whose existence is conditional on the existence of the principal contract. See this Précis, Chapter 1, Article 4.

B. Onerous or Gratuitous Stipulation.

A stipulation may be for a stipulator a means of performance of an obligation he owes the third party. A seller, S1, entitled to receive a payment from his buyer, B1, may instruct that buyer to pay the price to a third party, TP, who could be an obligee, a creditor, of the seller, S1, on account of a prior contract of sale. That third party, TP, could have been a seller to S1, entitled therefore to payment of a price from S1, his purchaser. Since S1 is entitled to receive payment of a price from B1, his buyer, S1, can then instruct B1, by way of a stipulation pour autrui, to pay that price to TP to whom S1 is indebted. By means of the stipulation, S1 will extinguish, in whole or in part, his 'onerous' obligation towards TP and B1, in turn, will extinguish his own obligation to pay S1. Two onerous obligations are extinguished by one stipulation for the benefit of another.

A stipulation pour autrui can also be "gratuitous" when the stipulator wishes to make a donation to the third party through the promisor's performance. A seller, instead of accepting payment of the price from his buyer, could instruct that buyer, by way of a stipulation, to become a promisor and "donate" the price to a third party such as a charitable organization. Life insurance contracts are a possible means for the stipulator to make donations to third parties. Such 'indirect' donations must obviously be lawful, particularly with respect to their cause, although the requirement of the "form" of the donation will be dispensed with.

§ 7.3.3. EFFECTS BETWEEN THE PROMISOR AND THE THIRD PARTY BENEFICIARY.

Once the third party has "**manifested his intention to avail himself of the benefit,**"(Art. 1978), she is vested with "**the right to demand performance from the promisor.**" (Art. 1981).

The third party beneficiary does not have the right to demand the dissolution of the principal contract between the stipulator and the promisor. That right belongs only to the parties to the principal contract. However, besides the right to demand performance of his obligation from the promisor, the third party should have the "alternative" right to seek the payment of compensatory damages from that promisor in case of breach of his obligation. It follows that the third party receives the "benefit" of the performance directly from the promisor and not from the stipulator. That performance comes out of the promisor's patrimony. Hence, the creditors of the stipulator have no right over the performance owed by the promisor whether the third party is a "gratuitous obligee" or an "onerous obligee" as a consequence of the stipulation[15]. Because the right of the third party is a "direct" right against the promisor, that right is acquired by the third party as soon as the stipulation has been created, even unbeknownst to that third party, and that right is "affirmed" and made irrevocable once the third party has manifested his intent to avail himself of the

---

[15] See infra Chapter 11, however, on the possible availability of a pauliana or oblique action..

benefit. Thus the "affirmation"[16] by the third party does not create her right to the stipulation since that right existed already in the principal contract between the stipulator and the promisor.

The stipulation being "accessory" to the principal contract to which the third party is not a "contractual party," the obligations created by that principal contract cannot take second rank to the stipulation. The promisor has a primary interest in the performance of the obligations created by the principal contract. Thus, if an insured, as stipulator, does not make his monthly payments to the insurer, the latter as **"The promisor may raise against the beneficiary such defenses based on the contract as he may have raised against the stipulator." Art. 1982.** If a seller is in breach of his obligation of warranty against eviction or his warranty against defects, his buyer, as promisor of the obligation to pay the price to the third party beneficiary, may raise these same "defenses" against the third party beneficiary that he could have raised against his seller-stipulator.[17]

---

[16] One could look at this affirmation as a kind of ratification. See Précis, Louisiana Law of Obligations in General, Ratification § 6.1.1.

[17] One may point to an anomaly, here, between the "direct" right vested in the third party against the promisor, and the right of that promisor to raise defenses arising from a contract to which the third party is not a contractual party. The right of the third party is thus contingent upon the performance of obligations which are outside his control. However, considerations of equity in favor of the promisor justify the soundness of Art. 1982.

Chapter 8

EFFECTS OF CONVENTIONAL OBLIGATIONS OR CONTRACTS
LSA-C.C. ARTS. 1983 TO 2012

Whenever parties enter into a contract it is with the expectation that the obligation(s) thereby created will be carried out, performed, in such a manner that each party will receive her 'contractual' due. This expectation, by each party, is supported and justified by two sets of effects created by any contract.

First of all, all contracts, regardless of their specific nature (unilateral or bilateral, onerous or gratuitous, for example[1]), are subject to the control of two fundamental principles which are laid down in **LSA-C.C. Art. 1983: "Contracts have the effect of law for the parties and may be dissolved only through the consent of the parties or on grounds provided by law. Contracts must be performed in good faith."** These two principles are, first, the 'effect of law' of any contract and, second, the 'performance in good faith' of the obligations created by the contract.

The second set of effects triggered by a contract will depend on the kind or kinds of obligations which bind the parties. These obligations may bind one or both parties to **"render a performance . . . [which] . . . may consist of giving, doing, or not doing something." Art. 1756.** This second set of effects of a contract will be determined, therefore, by the 'giving' something, the 'doing' something or the 'not doing' something.[2]

ARTICLE 1
GENERAL EFFECTS OF ALL CONTRACTS:
EFFECT OF LAW-GOOD FAITH

§ 8.1.1. EFFECT OF LAW.

This principle that a contract has the **"effect of law for the parties"** means that the parties, and the parties only, are bound by their intent. This principle is known as the "principle of the relative effect of contracts". This is so whether the contract, as seen by all, evidences the true intent of the parties to that open contract, or whether that open contract visible to all can "lawfully" hide the true intent of the parties when there exists an undisclosed or hidden contract between them. In this second situation, the question to be addressed is that of "simulation."

---

[1] On the distinction between Unilateral-Bilateral/Synallagmatic Contracts, Onerous and Gratuitous Contracts, and other distinctions, see supra Chapter 1.

[2] See infra Specific Performance-Damages, Chapter 8, Articles 2 and 3.

A. That a Contract has the Effect of Law for the Parties Leads to Three Sub-Effects or Consequences.

First, only the parties themselves are bound by their contract; their contract is their "law". A contract, being the *expression of the wills* of two parties, is as binding between them as "legislation", which is itself the *"expression of the legislative will,"*[3] is binding on and between the citizens. This first sub-effect has traditionally been stated in its Latin form *"Pacta Sunt Servanda."*[4] In a sense, the legislator delegates "its will" to private persons when they negotiate, frame, shape, or draft their own "legislation" under the form of a contract governing their own interests. It means also that parties cannot enter into a contract that would be in violation of the legislative will.[5] There are limitations to the freedom of contract whenever a greater interest, good order for example, must prevail over the individual wills of parties to a contract. This binding effect of a contract can be explained either by vesting in the parties' wills the power to make their own law for themselves or in the trust, in the sense of good faith,[6] that motivates each party to enter into a contract with the other and to perform her obligations because the other party is 'expected', in good faith, to perform her own obligations.[7]

Second, whether we explain the binding force of a contract by the "power of the will" of a party to make her own law, or by the trust/good faith of each party in the other, it is easy to understand why **Art. 1985** states that **"Contracts may produce effects for third parties only when provided by law."** In other words, a contract between parties A and B cannot have effects *"against"* a third person C who is not a "party" to that contract. On the other hand, what Article 1985 is also saying, *a contrario sensu*, is that by their contract, A and B can provide *"for"* a third party, such as provide some benefit to C. Since one is presumed not to want to turn down a benefit, one's consent can be presumed. Such is the effect, for example, of a "stipulation *for* the benefit of another."[8]

Third parties, heirs in particular, can be brought into the contract between A and B and incur obligations if they agree and if the obligations are transferable by inheritance, assignment, subrogation, or other modes of transfer of obligations.[9] According to **Art. 1984 "Rights and obligations arising from a contract are heritable and assignable unless the law, the terms of the contract or its nature preclude such effects."**

---

[3] Emphasis ours.

[4] General maxim coined by canon lawyers. "The maxim appears as an official heading to the first chapter of the De pactis title of the Decretals of Gregory IX." See Alain A. Levasseur, Comparative Law of Contracts: Cases and Materials 127 (Carolina Academic Press 2008).

[5] See infra Nullity of Contracts, Chapter 9, Article 2.

[6] This "trust" is analogous to "reliance" in the common law.

[7] See supra Cause, Chapter 5, § 5.1.2.B. "The cause of the contract is a "common or shared reason/cause."

[8] Emphasis ours. On Stipulation for the Benefit of Another, see supra Chapter 7.

[9] On Assignment, see Précis, Louisiana Law of Sale and Lease, § 2.3.5. On Transfer of Obligations, see Précis, Louisiana Law of Obligations in General, Article 1. On Inheritance, see civil Code Arts. 947 et seq.

Third, a corollary of the principle that a contract is the law of the parties is stated in Art. 1983 in these words: "Contracts . . . may be dissolved only through the consent of the parties . . . or on grounds provided by law." A contract cannot be revoked unilaterally by one party when that party had to have the consent of the other to be bound by the contract. Only the parties together can "undo" what they have "done"; mutual consent is therefore necessary to revoke a contract which had been created by mutual consent. By the same token, because of the exchange of their wills, parties can, in "their" contract, provide that each one will have the right to denounce unilaterally, their contract in the future. Thus parties may "anticipate" on their future consent to undo the contract. Such an anticipation can be called *"mutuus dissensus"*, a consent to mutually disagree in the future.

On the other hand, if one party fails to perform her obligations in violation of either the trust placed in her by the other party or the duty of good faith in the performance of obligations, then the "aggrieved" party "**has a right to the judicial dissolution of the contract or, according to the circumstances, to regard the contract as dissolved** . . ."Art. 2013 (1). In some justified circumstances a party may, therefore, unilaterally, and lawfully, consider the contract as dissolved without, obviously, seeking the consent of the party who failed to perform without any lawful reason.

The legal regime of some contracts may allow one party to "unilaterally" dissolve a contract. For example "**A lease with an indeterminate term . . . terminates by notice to that effect given to the other party by the party desiring to terminate the lease . . .**"Art. 2727.[10] Under Art. 2901 ". . . **In case of urgent and unforeseen need, the lender may demand the return of the thing at any time.**" Another example can be found in **Art. 3025** which gives the principal the right to "**terminate the mandate and the authority of the mandatary at any time. . . .**" In these contracts, it is the law which provides for a right to "exit" a contract.

Another legal ground for the "undoing" or dissolution of a contract is an "impossibility of performance" under **Art. 1876: "When the entire performance owed by one party has become impossible because of a fortuitous event, the contract is dissolved.**" In this respect, we are referring to the topic of "**Impossibility of Performance**" discussed elsewhere.[11]

B.   Open or Simulated Contract and Counterletter.

1.   *Simulation and Third Parties.*

Parties to a contract can, for lawful reasons, hide their true intent in a hidden contract, called **counterletter** because the letter and the intent of that hidden contract go against or counter to the intent of the open contract which is called a simulated contract. LSA-C.C. Art. 2025 states that "**A contract is a simulation when, by mutual agreement, it does not express the true intent**

---

[10] On Lease, see Précis, Louisiana Law of Sale and Lease Chapter 5, Article 6.

[11] See Précis, Louisiana Law of Obligations in General, Chapter 7, Article 2.

of the parties. **If the true intent of the parties is expressed in a separate writing, that writing is a counterletter."**[12]

The existence of such an Article in the civil Code emphasizes the freedom to enter into any lawful contract and the role given to the intent or will of parties to a contract. They are free, within the boundaries of the law, to contract as they wish. For example, two parties to an open but simulated contract of sale could enter into a hidden contract or counterletter to stipulate that the seller will remain owner of the thing "fictitiously transferred by the simulated contract" and that no price will be paid by the so-called buyer. In such an instance of simulation there is a total or absolute disguise regarding the nature of the contract: the sale is apparent only — in reality, there is no sale at all. The civil Code would describe this type of simulation as "absolute": **"A simulation is absolute when the parties intend that their contract shall produce no effects between them. That simulation, therefore, can have no effects between the parties." Art. 2026.**

Instead of a counterletter amounting to "no sale" and no contract at all, the counterletter could provide that the party who, in the simulated contract is the "named" seller, is actually a donor of a thing to the other party who is a donee. The simulated sale is actually a donation.

A simulation can be relative: **"A simulation is relative when the parties intend that their contract shall produce effects between them though different from those recited in their contract. A relative simulation produces between the parties the effects they intended if all requirements for those effects have not been met." Art. 2027.** The price of the open contract of "sale" could be higher or lower than the price agreed upon in the counterletter, which latter price would prevail between the parties.

One could see a kind of simulation of 'persons' in **Art. 3017** whenever **"A mandatary who contracts in his own name without disclosing his status as a mandatary binds himself personally for the performance of the contract."** Should that mandatary fail to perform, the third person with whom the mandatary contracted could claim the benefit of the counterletter and have an action against the principal. As **Art. 3020** states **"The principal is bound to perform the contract that the mandatary, acting within the limits of his authority, makes with a third person."** The reason why the third person could bring an action against the principal is because **"counterletters can have no effects against third persons in good faith"** and **"any simulation, either absolute or relative, may have effects as to third persons." Art. 2028.**[13] In other words, in application of the principle of the relative effect of a contract, a counterletter cannot impose obligations or be detrimental towards someone who is not a party to that counterletter. But, *a contrario*, a counterletter may be of benefit to a third person. Such would be the case of an "open" donation from A

---

[12] But see R.S. 9:2712 prohibiting counterletters affecting any public property.

[13] For a third person to rely on the benefit created by a counterletter so that she can bring an action for the enforcement of the counterletter, the third person will have to prove the existence of the counterletter as she would have to prove the existence of a contract. See Précis, Louisiana Law of Obligations in General, Proof of Obligations, Chapter 6.

to B to which a hidden counterletter would be attached instructing B, the "apparent donee", to actually transfer gratuitously to C the thing object of the donation. A's reason or motive for the hidden counterletter with B could be that A wants to remain an anonymous donor to C when hiding behind B who would be the "apparent" donor.

2. *Counterletter and Third Parties.*

A third party who wishes to receive the benefit created in her favor by a counterletter may have to prove the existence of that counterletter should a controversy arise. Assuming that the third party can establish the existence of the counterletter to claim a benefit, what would then be the fate of the rights of those third parties who relied on the open contract?

Suppose, in this very much simplified example, that in an open and written contract of sale a seller "S" is to receive a price of 10,000 from his buyer "B". Suppose that in a counterletter the seller is to receive a price of only 5,000 from B. It is obvious that the buyer B is saving 5,000. But what if a creditor "C" of the seller S is claiming to have a right to be paid 10,000 by S who happens to have no liquidity to pay that debt. Whose right should prevail? Should B have the right to tell C that he, B, will pay only 5,000 because that is the amount he has agreed to pay in the counterletter with S? Should C have the right to rely on the "open-simulated" contract which states that S is to receive 10,000 from B? Since the counterletter can have no effect against a third party who has a legitimate right of action, C has the right to rely on the contract which is open to him, the sale for 10,000, and which is simulated only for S and B.

Suppose now that both S and B are indebted: S to his creditors "Sc" and B to his creditors "Bc". Suppose that the amount claimed by both sets of creditors is 5,000. It will be in the interest of Sc's creditors to rely on the open contract of sale since S is to receive 10,000 from B. On the other hand, it would be in the interest of Bc's creditors that B pay only 5,000 as the counterletter gives B the right to do. The conflict between the two sets of creditors is staged by the fact that S and B are "bound" by two contracts; hence the question: which set of creditors should prevail? One set of creditors, Sc's creditors, has an easy burden of proof: the open contract is there for them to rely on. B's creditors, on the other hand, will have to prove the counterletter to be able to rely on it.[14] If they do prove that S and B had entered into a counterletter, B's creditors will then be pitted directly against S's creditors: the counterletter v. the open-simulated contract.

Since one principle governing simulation is that **"counterletters can have no effects against third persons in good faith,"**[15] the creditors who rely on the open/simulated contract, should prevail. The seller S's creditors will have the

---

[14] Since they are third parties to the counterletter, because they did not take part in the writing of the counterletter, if there is a writing, then B's creditors should not be required to prove the written existence of the counterletter but only that the parties to the simulated-open contract did intend to be bound by a counterletter.

[15] Art. 2028.

advantage as long as they are **in good faith.**[16] The free flow of trade and the security of transactions so require.

§ 8.1.2. GOOD FAITH.

Art. 1983 states, in part, that "**contracts must be performed in good faith.**" This Article is to the Effects of Contracts or Conventional Obligations what Art. 1759 is to the whole subject matter of Obligations. Actually, Art. 1983 is merely a specific application to the performance of contracts of the general principle formulated in **Art. 1759** according to which **"good faith shall govern the conduct of the obligor and the obligee in whatever pertains to the obligation."** What pertains to "the" obligation is, besides the formation of a contract, the performance of their obligations in good faith by parties to a contract.[17]

"Good faith, in the execution as well as in the formation of a contract, amounts to each party not betraying the confidence created by the willingness to enter into a contract;[18] such an expectation is at the heart of the contract particularly when the contractual relationship is to last over a period of time. It is the embodiment of the general duty of honest and fair behavior. . . . Good faith is the mere extension of the binding force of a contract, rather than a limitation imposed on the creditor; the latter is not required to waive his right or interest in the name of some vague juridical solidarity but, instead, to give the contract its full force to an extent compatible with his own personal interest. . . ."[19]

ARTICLE 2
SPECIFIC PERFORMANCE AND PUTTING IN DEFAULT

§ 8.2.1. SPECIFIC PERFORMANCE.

"Voluntary" performance of obligations is discussed in the Précis on the Louisiana Law of Obligations in General particularly with respect to the parties to the performance and the object of the performance.[20]

Under the topic of Effects of Conventional Obligations the type of "performance" to be discussed is, actually, the nonperformance by the obligor of his obligation and, therefore, the possibility or not for the obligee to obtain "specific performance" of the obligation owed to him by the recalcitrant obligor. **Art. 1986** states that "**Upon an obligor's failure to perform an obligation to deliver a thing, or not to do an act, or to execute an instrument, the court shall grant specific performance plus damages for delay if the obligee so demands. If specific performance is impracticable, the court may allow damages to the obligee.**

---

[16] See infra, The Revocatory Action and The Oblique Action, Chapter 11.

[17] See supra Formation of Contracts, Chapters 2-7. See Précis, Louisiana Law of Obligations in General, Good Faith § 1.4.2.

[18] See supra Confidence, Trust, Reliance, Cause, Chapter 5.

[19] Alain A. Levasseur, Comparative Law of Contracts: Cases and Materials 104, #764 (2008).

[20] Précis, Louisiana Law of Obligations in General, Article 1.

Upon a failure to perform an obligation that has another object, such as an obligation to do, the granting of specific performance is at the discretion of the court."

And Art. 1987 adds that "**The obligor may be restrained from doing anything in violation of an obligation not to do.**" In this latter case, the law is very clear: an obligee may be allowed to "restrain" his obligor **"from doing anything in violation of an obligation not to do."**[21] Under the Code of civil procedure, "an injunction [could] be issued in cases where irreparable injury, loss or damage may otherwise result to the applicant . . ." (Art. 3601) or "a temporary restraining order [could] be granted . . ." (Art. 3603). Thus, in general, obligations not to do can be specifically enforced.

With respect to obligations to give and obligations to do, Article 1986 of the civil Code is clear in the distinction therein made between these two kinds of obligations.

With respect to an obligation to give, i.e. the transfer of a real right over a thing, such as the ownership of a thing to someone, specific performance may be obtained by constraint. The Code of civil procedure provides for some remedies such as: "executory proceedings used to effect the seizure and sale of property . . ." (Art. 2631); or "if the plaintiff is entitled thereto, the court shall order the issuance of a writ of seizure and sale . . . of the property affected by the mortgage or privilege . . ." (Art. 2638); or "a writ of attachment or of sequestration shall issue when . . ." (Art. 3501); or "a judgment for the payment of money may be executed by a writ of fieri facias directing the seizure and sale of property of the judgment debtor" (Art. 2291); still, "a party in whose favor a judgment of possession has been rendered may obtain from the clerk a writ of possession directing the sheriff to seize and deliver the property to him if it is movable property, or to compel the party in possession to vacate the property by use of force, if necessary, if it is immovable." (Art. 2501) . . . In addition, **Article 1988** of the civil Code gives an **"obligee the right to a judgment that shall stand for the act"** or instrument that the obligor failed to execute. So, in general, under the civil Code and the Code of civil procedure, obligations to give are susceptible of being specifically enforced.

The specific enforcement of an obligation to do is quite another matter.[22] As Art. 1986 states in fine, "**the granting of specific performance is at the discretion of the court.**" In reality it is impossible to have an obligation to do specifically enforced for fear of infringing, a little or excessively, upon the individual freedom of the obligor. If a storyteller does not want to tell stories, whatever the reason, the obligee has no means available to "force" the storyteller to perform. If a house painter fails to perform his obligation to paint a house, the owner of the house cannot resort to force to make the painter paint his house. One can state that if the element of *"intuitu personae"*[23] is dominant in the kind of obligation to do under consideration, then specific performance will not be available.

---

[21] See Précis, Louisiana Law of Obligations in General, § 1.2.1.C.

[22] Précis, Louisiana Law of Obligations in General, Obligations to Do § 1.2.1.B.

[23] On Intuitu Personae, see supra Chapter 1, Article 2, Gratuitous cContract.

On the other hand there are obligations to do which ought to be specifically enforceable. Such a specific performance is contemplated in Art. 4733 of the Code of civil procedure: "If the lessee or occupant does not comply with the judgment of eviction . . . the court shall issue immediately a warrant directed to and commanding its sheriff . . . to deliver possession of the premises to the lessor or owner." We have seen Article 2501 of the Code of civil procedure which allows the use of force against someone who refuses to vacate an immovable property. Thus, as **Art. 1986** of the civil Code expresses in a wise statement, the use of force amounting to specific performance of an obligation to do **"is at the discretion of the court."**

§ 8.2.2. DEFAULT; PUTTING IN DEFAULT; EFFECTS AND MANNERS.

As seen above, because a contract is the law between the parties the obligee is entitled to receive the performance the obligor owes him. As long as the obligor can perform, the obligee has the right to expect that his obligor will carry out his performance as expected and on time. Should the obligor fail, without any lawful excuse such as an impossibility of performance,[24] to carry out his obligation, the obligee can either demand specific performance if performance is still possible[25] or, in the alternative, seek the payment of compensatory damages.[26]

An obligor is not bound merely to carry out his performance of the principal object of his obligation. That principal performance must also be carried out on time. It stands to reason that the obligor may not delay indefinitely the actual performance of his obligation without the obligee becoming somewhat impatient and anxious to obtain his "due" from his obligor. There exists, therefore, in every obligation an element of "time", actually an obligation to perform "on time". This is so either because the parties explicitly or implicitly agreed on a "term" for the performance of an obligation by one of them,[27] or because of the nature of the contract (a lease, for example), the kind of object of the performance (e.g., perishable goods), or simply because one must assume the existence of **"a reasonable time"**[28]. This obligation to perform on time by one party, obligor, gives the other party, obligee, the right to **"put the obligor in default"(Art. 1991)** so that **"damages for delay in the performance** [will be] **owed"** by the obligor to the obligee**"from the time the obligor is put in default"** Art. 1989.

---

[24] On Impossibility of Performance, see Précis, Louisiana Law of Obligations in General, Chapter 7, Article 2.

[25] See supra.

[26] See infra Chapter 8, Article 3.

[27] On Term, see Précis, Louisiana Law of Obligations in General, Chapter 2, Article 2, Part A.

[28] LCC- Art. 1778; see supra note 25.

A. Purpose of Putting in Default.

As the Code Articles on "Putting in Default" state very clearly,[29] the purpose of putting an obligor in default is to inform him that the obligee cannot wait any longer for the obligor to perform his obligation. In a sense, the obligee has "had it". The delay in the obligor's performing on time is causing a prejudice to the obligee in the same way that **"every act whatever of man that causes damage to another obliges him by whose fault it happened to repair it."** Art. 2315-A. The fault of the obligor is in not performing on time and, as a consequence, in causing a damage to the obligee. The damage caused to the obligee will entitle him to receive *"moratory damages"*, that is to say **"damages for delay in perform[ing]..."** Art. 1989. One need think only of the interest one must pay a credit card lender when not making a payment on time, i.e. by a due date. Paying the interest will not exempt the holder of the credit card from making a payment towards the principal debt which is the "principal obligation" of the performance owed the lender. In other words, a putting in default has for its target the timing of the performance of an obligation and not the performance of the principal obligation itself. **"Other damages"** than moratory damages **"are owed from the time the obligor has failed to perform"** (Art. 1989) the principal obligation. These other damages are called *"compensatory damages"* because they are **"damages caused by"** the obligor's **"failure to perform a conventional obligation"** (Art. 1994) and these damages will be **"measured by the loss sustained by the obligee and the profit of which he has been deprived."** Art. 1995.[30]

The requirement of putting an obligor in default is justified as long as the obligor could still perform and the performance would still be of benefit to the obligee. "When a delayed performance is due to an impossibility of performing, neither a putting in default nor a notice of dissolution would be justified under such circumstances."[31]

B. Manners of Putting in Default.

There is an "automatic" and efficient way to put an obligor in default and there are ways or manners which require the obligee to do something, i.e. to act.

The relationship between a 'term' and 'putting in default' is natural since both concepts are concerned with 'time', time for the performance of an obligation. **LCC-Art. 1778** states that: **"A term for the performance of an obligation is a period of time either certain or uncertain. It is certain when it is fixed. It is uncertain when it is not fixed but is determinable either by the intent of the parties or by the occurrence of a future and certain event. It is also uncertain when it is not determinable, in which case the obligation must be performed within a reasonable time"**. Art. 1778 stresses that **"a term... is a period of time."**

---

[29] LCC-Arts. 1989-1993.

[30] On Compensatory Damages, see infra Chapter 8, Article 3.

[31] On impossibility of performance, see Précis, Louisiana Law of Obligations in General, Chapter 7, Article 2.

Since the concept of "Term" is addressed extensively in the Précis on Louisiana Law of Obligations[32] it will not be necessary to repeat here what is said in that Précis. Suffice to say that whenever a term is fixed or clearly determinable, the mere arrival of the term will automatically put the obligor in default: **"When a term for the performance of an obligation is either fixed or clearly determinable by the circumstances, the obligor is put in default by the mere arrival of that term. In other cases, the obligor must be put in default by the obligee, but not before performance is due." Art. 1990.** In this respect, the Louisiana civil Code has adopted the Roman law maxim *"Dies interpellat pro homine"*, i.e. "the occurrence of the day makes its own demand." It is therefore in the interest of an obligee to have a term fixed, or determinable at least, in a contract since he will not be required to 'act', to do something to put his obligor in default; the putting in default will occur automatically without his demand.

Where there is no term, fixed or determinable, attached to the timing of performance of his obligation by an obligor, the obligee, if he has the right to demand performance from his obligor, will have to **". . . put the obligor in default by written request of performance, or by an oral request of performance made before two witnesses, or by filing suit for performance, or by a specific provision of the contract." Art. 1991.**

C. Effects of Putting in Default.

One first effect of putting in default is, as seen above, that from that time on **"Damages are owed for delay in the performance . . ." Art. 1989(1).**

A second effect which may affect an obligation to give when it simultaneously transfers the risk of loss of a thing to the obligee and imposes on the obligor the obligation to deliver that same thing in his possession to the obligee, is that **"If an obligee bears the risk of the thing that is the object of the performance, the risk devolves upon the obligor who has been put in default for failure to deliver that thing." Art. 1992.**

D. Defenses Raised by the Obligor.

According to **Art. 1993, "In case of reciprocal obligations, the obligor of one may not be put in default unless the obligor of the other has performed or is ready to perform his own obligation."** In a sense, an obligor X of a reciprocal or bilateral onerous obligation created by a synallagmatic contract with Y, may raise as a defense to his being put in default by the obligee Y, that when Y is looked at in his situation as an obligor of a reciprocal obligation owed to X, Y himself has not performed his own obligation or is unable of performing that obligation for the benefit of X. Because of what has now become a lack of 'reciprocity', X can raise the defense of the *exceptio non adimpleti contractus* or exception of nonperformance so that X cannot be compelled to perform or pay damages for breach of contract. A good illustration of the mechanism of the *exceptio* can be found in **Art. 2487** which gives a seller the right to **"refuse to**

---

[32] On Term, see Précis, Louisiana Law of Obligations in General, § 2.2.A.

deliver the thing sold until the buyer tenders payment of the price, unless the seller has granted the buyer a term for such payment."

ARTICLE 3
DAMAGES

The word "damages", without any adjective in front of the word, refers usually to "compensatory damages" i.e. damages meant to compensate an obligee for the loss he suffered from the non performance of his obligation by the obligor.[33] In the law of delicts or torts, the obligation to pay damages to the victim is the primary obligation the tortfeasor owes the victim. When a contract exists, each party to a bilateral contract is to perform his obligation or obligations as agreed. The parties know that, under the law of the civil Code, failure to perform an obligation will result in the **"obligor [being] liable for the damages caused by his failure to perform a conventional obligation." Art. 1994(1).** That obligation to pay damages comes into existence if the obligor fails to perform without any lawful excuse, or if there is defective performance or delay in performance. **Art. 1994(2).** In other words, an obligation to pay damages is neither an alternative obligation[34] nor a facultative obligation since the obligor does not have the choice either to perform the contractual obligation or to pay damages; he cannot choose one over the other. An obligee has the right to refuse the payment of damages instead of the performance of his obligation by the obligor since such was agreed 'in good faith' when both parties entered into their contract and as long as the obligor could still perform.

Contractual damages are due by an obligor to an obligee when, under the law, the obligor can be held liable because of **"his failure to perform a conventional obligation"** or when his **"failure to perform results from nonperformance, defective performance, or delay in performance."** Art. 1994. We can refer to these compensatory damages as conventional or contractual damages to distinguish them from "delictual" damages. Such delictual damages find their source of law in **Arts. 2315 et seq.**[35] On the basis of these Articles, a court can oblige a tortfeasor to repair the damage caused by his act. This 'repair' takes the form of compensatory pecuniary damages. Those **"damages may include loss of consortium, service, and society . . ."** (Art. 2315-B) and **"in addition to general and special damages, exemplary damages may be awarded . . ."** Art. 2315.4. Furthermore, **"In the assessment**

---

[33] "Compensatory" in contrast with "moratory" damages due for the failure to perform on time.

[34] On Alternative and Facultative Obligations, see Précis, Louisiana Law of Obligations in General, Chapter 4. In this respect, we consider that Article 2007 is either extremely poorly written or that its "legal" statement is in direct conflict with the law of contracts which ranks the obligation of the obligor to perform his obligation as the principal and primary obligation and the payment of damages as a *secondary*, but absolutely not alternative, obligation in case of nonperformance of the primary obligation. In Art. 2007, *performance of the principal obligation should be listed first,* "*or*" should be deleted, and the payment of stipulated damages described as a *consequence* of the nonperformance of the principal obligation. The obligor has the "right" to perform his "principal" obligation if he can and is willing, and he can be held to pay the stipulated damages only "in lieu of" his failure to perform his principal obligation. For more discussion, see infra LSA-C.C. Art 2007 at § 3.3.1.

[35] Arts. 2315 et seq. are listed under the title "Offenses and Quasi-Offenses."

of damages in cases of offenses, quasi-offenses, and quasi-contracts, much discretion must be left to the judge or jury." Art. 2324.1.

By contrast with "delictual damages" which are due as a consequence of a juridical fact, conventional damages find their justification in a juridical act, a contract. In a contractual relationship, the intent of the parties could be either to provide or stipulate in advance an amount of damages that should be paid by that party to the contract who fails to perform, or the parties may simply decide, expressly or implicitly, to give a court the authority to assess the amount of damages that will be paid by the party in breach of her contractual obligation.

§ 8.3.1. STIPULATED DAMAGES.

Since we are focusing, here, on conventional obligations or contract, the parties to a contract may, at the time of formation of the contract and in anticipation of a party not performing, "**stipulate the damages to be recovered in case of nonperformance . . .**" Art. 2005. The parties may so provide so as to leave as little discretion as possible to 'the judge or the jury' in determining the amount of 'compensatory damages'. Indeed, if the parties have not so stipulated in advance, the damages to be recovered in case of nonperformance if they **"are insusceptible of precise measurement . . . shall be left to the court** [for their] **reasonable assessment"** Art. 1999. And **Art. 1995** gives this instruction to the court that the **"Damages are measured by the loss sustained by the obligee and the profit of which he has been deprived."**

Who better than the parties themselves can determine by anticipation the amount of damages which one party ought to receive for the loss she sustained and the profit of which she was deprived in case of breach of her primary obligation by the other party or even in case of breach of that party's secondary obligation to perform on time?

The contractual clause stipulating for damages creates an *accessory* or *secondary* obligation which will come into existence only in case of non performance by an obligor of his principal obligation. It follows that the invalidity or nullity of the principal obligation will carry with it the invalidity or nullity of the stipulated damages clause. **"Nullity of the principal obligation renders the stipulated damages clause null."** But the converse is not true: **"Nullity of the stipulated clause does not render the principal obligation null."** Art. 2006.[36] Basically, an *"accessory"* obligation cannot have an existence of its own; it will exist only if a principal and valid obligation pre-exists.[37] Should the performance of the principal obligation be impossible, the **"obligor whose failure to perform the principal obligation is justified by a valid excuse is also relieved of liability for stipulated damages."** Art. 2008.

Since a stipulated damages clause is included in a contract, the obligor knows in advance that his failure to perform will vest in the obligee the right to demand

---

[36] Such is the outcome dictated by the maxim *accessorium sequitur naturam rei principalis* (the accessory follows the nature of the principal thing). See Pothier, Inst. Coutum. 2,1, reg. 14.

[37] In a contract of sale, for example, the seller does not owe warranty to his buyer unless there exists a valid contract of sale.

the payment of the stipulated damages. When **"An obligee . . . avail[s] himself of a stipulated damages clause [he] need not prove the actual damage caused by the obligor's nonperformance, defective performance, or delay in performance."** Art. 2009. In order to prevent one party taking advantage of the other at the time of formation of a contract and in order to ensure that the parties act in good faith **"in whatever pertains to [their] obligation"** (Art. 1759) and in compliance with public order, the legislature felt compelled to provide for some control over the freedom of the parties to include a stipulated damages clause of their choice in their contract. As **Art. 2012** states: **"Stipulated damages may not be modified by the court unless they are so manifestly unreasonable as to be contrary to public policy."** Furthermore, **"Stipulated damages for nonperformance may be reduced in proportion to the benefit derived by the obligee from any partial performance rendered by the obligor."** Art. 2011.

In the event a clause in a contract stipulates that the obligor will owe 'delay damages', **Art. 2010** states that the **"obligee may not avail himself"** of the clause **"stipulating damages for delay unless the obligor has been put in default."** This Art. 2010 is, to some extent, a restatement of **Art. 1989(1)**. We believe that the third paragraph of this **Art. 1989** should apply, to-wit, that the obligor of the obligation to pay delay damages could be **"put in default by the mere arrival of the term"**, which is the general and now standard legal rule. In addition, **Art. 1990** emphasizes the same rule where it states that **"When a term for the performance of an obligation is either fixed, or is clearly determinable by the circumstances, the obligor is put in default by the mere arrival of the term . . ."**.[38]

There remains to place **Art. 2007** in the context of "stipulated damages", where it is located, but also in the broader context of damages in general. If we bring into our analysis **Art. 1994** which explains why and when "damages" are due, we are told that **"An obligor is liable for the damages caused by his failure to perform a conventional obligation."** In other words, "*damages*" are owed by an obligor only when he has failed to perform the principal conventional obligation which he was bound to perform under the contract. It means also that the obligee has to wait until the obligor fails to perform (or performed poorly) before that same obligee can seek the payment of "*damages*". There is absolutely no "legal" reason or ground for treating "*stipulated damages*" differently from "*damages*". Thus, we believe, the problem raised by the wording of **Art. 2007**. It states that **"An obligee *may demand either* the stipulated damages *or* performance of the principal obligation, but he may not demand both unless the damages have been stipulated for mere delay."**[39] One will have noticed the parallelism created by "*either*" followed by "*or*". Such a parallelism is of the essence of an "*alternative obligation*" which we have described as placing "two (or more) items of performance on the same plane so that they are all principal items. No single item is an accessory to another."[40] It suffices to read **Art. 2005**, particularly its second paragraph, to understand, as we explained above, that a clause stipulating damages creates a 'secondary or accessory obligation'. It

---

[38] See supra Putting in Default, § 8.2.2.

[39] Emphasis in *italics* ours.

[40] On Alternative Obligations, see Précis, Louisiana Law of Obligations in General, § 4.2.

suffices also to read **Art. 2008** which refers to the obligor's failure to perform the 'principal obligation' to understand that, once again, the stipulated damages clause creates a secondary obligation and not a principal obligation. In other words, the poor wording of **Art. 2007** leaves one with the impression that, in this Article and this Article only, the obligee is given a choice, as in an alternative obligation, to **"demand either the stipulated damages or performance of the principal obligation."** Strangely, this same Art. 2007 expressly refers to the existence of a *"principal obligation"* suggesting, therefore, that the other is *"secondary or accessory"* as is also expressly stated in the second paragraph of **Art. 2005:**[41] **"That stipulation gives rise to a secondary obligation for the purpose of enforcing the principal one."**

In conclusion, we must read **Art. 2007** to mean that the obligee must first demand the performance of the "principal" obligation as long as the obligor is deemed capable of performing that principal obligation which he bound himself to perform and which he has the right to perform under his contract with the obligee who cannot, unilaterally, take that right away from him. Only if the obligor does not perform and cannot perform under specific performance or only if the obligor's performance is defective can the obligee claim "the stipulated damages" which are meant to compensate him for the loss he suffers and the profit of which he has been deprived because of the obligor's nonperformance or defective performance of the principal obligation.

This is not meant to say that the parties to a contract cannot enter into an "alternative obligation", one of which would consist in a sum of money (obligation to give) and the other in performing services (obligation to do). In this instance the parties would place the two obligations on the same level, the two obligations would be equally demandable, the validity of one would not be contingent on the validity of the other. . . .[42]

§ 8.3.2. COURT ASSESSED DAMAGES.

Whenever an obligor fails to perform his obligation it is likely that he will be **"liable for the damages caused by his failure . . ."** which may result **"from nonperformance, defective performance, or delay in performance." Art. 1994.** The contractual obligation of the obligor to perform the principal obligation, first and foremost, and his accessory obligation to pay damages as a "back up" obligation are of such a paramount importance that the law issues, in **Art. 2004**, a stern warning to both parties to a contract: **"Any clause is null that, in advance, excludes or limits the liability of one party for intentional or gross fault that causes damage to the other party.**

---

[41] Another illustration of the poor drafting of this Art. 2007 is that it places the secondary obligation to pay the stipulated damages in "first place" before the performance of the "principal obligation" so as to give the impression that the obligee is advised to demand the stipulated damages in preference to the performance of the principal obligation. It is legal nonsense. Art. 2007 should be re-written and refer to the performance of the principal obligation first, and refer to the payment of the stipulated damages second as a consequence of the breach of the principal obligation.

[42] On Alternative Obligations, see Précis, Louisiana Law of Obligations in General, § 4.2.

Any clause is null that, in advance, excludes or limits the liability of one party for causing physical injury to the other party."

A principle built on two qualifications provides a general scheme for the granting of damages. There are, also, two special types of damages which have their own legal regime.

A. Principle and Its Qualifications.

The principle stated in **Art. 1995** applies, as a general proposition, to obligations to give, to do and not to do: "**Damages are measured by the loss sustained by the obligee and the profit of which he has been deprived.**" Since these concepts of loss sustained (*damnum emergens*) and deprivation of profit (*lucrum cessans*) which are the two component parts of the damages owed by the obligor are often not susceptible of precise measurement in advance, i.e. at the time the parties enter into their contract, the court will be given "**much discretion . . . for the reasonable assessment of these damages.**" Art. 1999.

One important first qualification is dictated by the obligor's good or bad faith. Any party to a contract should be guided by the "general principle" of good faith[43] which stands as a warning issued by the law to the parties to the effect that their rights and obligations as planned in their contract will be under the constant correcting or enhancing control of their **conduct** from the very beginning to the very end of their contractual relationship.

Good faith in the formation and the execution of a contract means that each party should not betray the confidence and trust established on both sides of the contract as a consequence of their "free" willingness to enter into a contractual relationship. This is even more important when the obligations created by the contract will spread over a period of time. Good faith is, in a sense, the "moral" justification for the binding force of contracts. It follows that "**An obligor in good faith is liable only for the damages that were foreseeable at the time the contract was made.**" Art. 1996. *A contrario*, "**An obligor in bad faith is liable for all the damages, foreseeable or not, that are a direct consequence of his failure to perform.**" Art. 1997. What damages are "foreseeable or not" and what damages "are a direct consequence" of the obligor's failure to perform will be for a court to determine following a "**reasonable assessment of these damages.**" Art. 1999.

A second qualification attached to the principle takes into consideration the behavior of the other party to the contract, the obligee. Good faith is required of both parties. Thus "**An obligee may not recover damages when his own bad faith has caused the obligor's failure to perform or when, at the time of the contract, he has concealed from the obligor facts that he knew or should have known would cause a failure.**

If the obligee's negligence contributes to the obligor's failure to perform, the damages are reduced in proportion to that negligence." Art. 2003.

---

[43] Art. 1759: "Good faith shall govern the conduct of the obligor and the obligee in whatever pertains to the obligation." See Précis, Louisiana Law of Obligations in General, § 1.4.2.

Good faith and a corollary duty of loyalty explain also why "**An obligee must make reasonable efforts to mitigate the damage caused by the obligor's failure to perform. When an obligee fails to make these efforts, the obligor may demand that the damages be accordingly reduced.**" Art. 2002[44].

B. Special Regimes: Non-Pecuniary Loss and Sums of Money.

1. *Non-pecuniary Loss.*

Art. 1998 of the civil Code amended and revised former Art. 1934 of the civil Code of 1870 which had given rise to much uncertainty and controversy in the jurisprudence. **Art. 1998** applies to "non-pecuniary loss" or "*dommage/préjudice moral*" as are the legal expressions in French and Québec civil law. As a nonpecuniary loss, it affects a "value, a feeling, a belief" which has no patrimonial content or monetary value and which, therefore, is very personal to the party affected by the loss. A party may suffer a loss should her name be misused, her reputation tarnished, her credit endangered, her feelings hurt, her hope crushed, her feelings humiliated. Such non-patrimonial losses can be compensated under **Art. 1998**: "**Damages for non pecuniary loss may be recovered when the contract, because of its nature, is intended to gratify a nonpecuniary interest and, because of the circumstances surrounding the formation or the nonperformance of the contract, the obligor knew, or should have known, that his failure to perform would cause that kind of loss.**

Regardless of the nature of the contract, these damages may be recovered also when the obligor intended, through his failure, to aggrieve the feelings of the obligee."

It is to this kind of loss, a non pecuniary loss, that **Art. 1999** will be applied in most instances since such a loss will be difficult to evaluate. Therefore, the damages themselves will be difficult to measure precisely. That measurement will have to be given a **reasonable assessment** by a court exercising **much discretion**. (Art. 1999).

2. *Obligations in Money.*

"Compensatory" damages are meant to re-establish an equilibrium between two patrimonies whenever that planned and negotiated equilibrium has been broken by a party failing to perform her expected principal obligation. The "monetary" object of the secondary obligation to pay damages has, for its purpose, to re-establish the broken equilibrium. However, when the object of the principal obligation is, itself, the payment of an amount of money and the obligor fails to "deliver" that amount of money, it is impossible to substitute to

---

[44] It is possible to justify this obligation of the obligee to mitigate the damage caused by the obligor's failure to perform by applying the principle of the management of the affairs of another (negotiorum gestio), Arts. 2292–2297. An obligee, acting in good faith, manages the affairs of the obligor when he attempts to mitigate his loss or damage that could be caused by the obligor's failure to perform. The obligee would be the "manager" and the obligor, the "owner".

the principal performance of paying "money" a secondary obligation to pay "money". The remedy available to the obligee will be to attempt to obtain performance by "constraint" as it is explained above under "Specific Performance" of obligations to give.[45]

Nevertheless, if the obligee is willing to "wait it out'" in the hope that in the long run the obligor will be able to pay the principal amount of money, he may call on **Art. 2001** which allows him to add interest to the principal or capital of the debt: **"Interest on accrued interest may be recovered as damages only when it is added to the principal by a new agreement of the parties made after the interest has accrued."**[46]

Instead of seeking to specifically enforce the principal obligation to pay money, the obligee may simply seek "moratory damages", i.e. damages for the delay in carrying out the principal performance.[47] Hence the statement in **Art. 2000** to the effect that **"When the object of the performance is a sum of money, damages for delay in performance are measured by the interest on that sum from the time it is due, at the rate agreed by the parties or, in the absence of agreement, at the rate of legal interest as fixed by Article 2924. The obligee may recover these damages without having to prove any loss, and whatever loss he may have suffered he can recover no more. If the parties, by written contract, have expressly agreed that the obligor shall also be liable for the obligee's attorney fees in a fixed or determinable amount, the obligee is entitled to that amount as well."**

---

[45] See Specific Performance § 8.2.1.

[46] Such a financial operation is known as "anatocism" or compound interest.

[47] See supra Moratory Damages, § 8.3.2.B.2.

Chapter 9

DISSOLUTION AND NULLITY
LSA-C.C. ARTS. 2013-2024

ARTICLE 1
DISSOLUTION

"Dissolution", in the civil Code, is the "undoing" of an existing bond of law such as a contract, for example. The essence of the word "dissolution" means that something that exists or has existed is or was "dissolved" and, thus, ceases or has ceased to exist.

The word "dissolution" is not the only one used in the civil Code to convey the same meaning that the word "dissolution," in a legal sense, carries. There is in the Code a whole Chapter on Conventional Obligations or Contracts that bears the title "Dissolution" [Chapter 9]. The word dissolution is found, earlier in the civil Code, in **Art. 246** which states that **"The minor not emancipated is placed under the authority of a tutor after the dissolution of the marriage of his father and mother. . . . "** Strangely enough, the words 'dissolution of the marriage' are not used in the Code articles on Marriage itself. It is the word "Termination" of the Marriage which is used[1]. **We find the verb "dissolved" in Art. 1876.**[2] We are told in **Art. 1559** that **"Donation [Donations] inter vivos are liable to be revoked or dissolved on account of . . ."** and the word 'dissolution' appears in the title of the same Article. As seen above, **"Once the third party has manifested his intention to avail himself of the benefit, the parties may not dissolve the contract by mutual consent . . ." Art 1978.**[3]

Words such as "termination", "extinction", or "rescission" are also often used in the place of 'dissolution' to mean the same thing as dissolution. Actually, **Chapter 4** of **Lease** combines, in its title, the words "**Termination and Dissolution**" and the Code Articles use interchangeably "termination" and "dissolution"[4]. **Art. 159** states that **"A judgment of divorce terminates a community property regime retroactively to the date of filing . . .".** A whole **Chapter** bears the title "**Extinction of Obligations.**'[5] In Art. 751 one can read that '**A predial servitude is extinguished by . . . ";** under "**Assignment of Rights**", **Art. 2644** reads that "**such performance extinguishes the obligation . . . ".** Other titles in the civil Code Articles use the word "rescission", such as

---

[1] Art. 101.

[2] Art. 1876: "When the entire performance owed by one party has become impossible because of a fortuitous event, the contract is dissolved. The other party may then recover any performance he has already rendered."

[3] On Third Party Beneficiary, see supra Chapter 7.

[4] Art. 2715 uses "dissolution"; Article 2716 uses "termination."

[5] Chapter 6 Extinction of Obligations, Arts. 1854–1905.

Section 7 "Of the Rescission of Partition"[6] **or Chapter 12 "Rescission for Lesion Beyond Moiety".**[7]

All this to say that a variety of words are used, unfortunately not consistently, in the civil Code to instruct us that some existing legal relationships come to an end for reasons provided by law or as per the intent of parties. What is essential and most important to state here is that these different words, whichever one is selected, are all to be contrasted with, and differentiated from, the concept and word "nullity". As will be discussed below, "nullity" prevents the coming into existence of a juridical act because an essential requirement for that act is lacking or because the act is against public order.

The concept of 'dissolution' and, therefore, the legal meaning of the word itself is that a legal bond has been created and has been in existence and that, most likely, it has had effects or could have had effects. However, because of circumstances that have occurred during the existence of the bond of law, the latter must now be dissolved or considered as having been dissolved. For example, **Art. 2013** provides that **"When the obligor fails to perform, the obligee has a right to the judicial dissolution of the contract . . ."** Obviously a contract was in existence, it created obligations on the obligor but, while the contract was in existence, the obligor failed to carry out his obligation. As a consequence of this breach of his obligation by the obligor, the obligee now "has the right to" ask the court to "dissolve" the contract.

§ 9.1.1. GROUNDS FOR DISSOLUTION.

One can identify two different sets of grounds that justify the dissolution of a contract. One set includes grounds which are outside the control of the obligor to bring about or not and the other set includes grounds which are within the control of the obligor to bring about or not. Obviously, the consequences of a dissolution resulting from one set of grounds will be different from the consequences resulting from the other set of grounds.

A. Grounds Outside the Control of the Obligor.

If the obligor is prevented from performing his obligation because of some circumstance or reason outside his control, he cannot be considered at fault and, therefore, he should not be required to carry out any other secondary obligation, the payment of compensatory damages in particular. In the words of **Art. 1876: "When the entire performance owed by one party has become impossible because of a fortuitous event, the contract is dissolved. The other party may then recover any performance he has already rendered."**[8] In the event an obligation is alternative and "the two items which were contemplated as potential objects of the performances of the alternative obligation have been destroyed by fortuitous event before the obligor was put in default to exercise

---

[6] Arts. 1397–1414.

[7] Arts. 2589–2600.

[8] See Impossibility of Performance in Précis, Louisiana Law of Obligations in General, § 7.2.1.

his choice and in the absence of any fault on his part, the whole alternative obligation is extinguished regardless of which party has been granted the choice."[9]

So, an obligor who cannot perform his contractual obligation because of some circumstance outside his control, will be relieved of any performance because of the dissolution of the contract; the contract has ceased to exist.

B. Grounds Within the Greater or Lesser Control of the Obligor.

The legal nature or identity of a contract may give either party the right, when exercised in good faith, to 'terminate' the contract. **Art. 2024** provides: "**A contract of unspecified duration may be terminated at the will of either party by giving notice, reasonable in time and form to the other party.**" The nature and foundation of a contract for the "hiring of servants and laborers" are such that "**A man is at liberty to dismiss a hired servant attached to his person or family, without assigning any reason for so doing. The servant is also free to depart without assigning any cause.**" Art. 2747. Likewise, "**The principal may terminate the mandate and the authority of the mandatary at any time. A mandate in the interest of the principal, and also of the mandatary or of a third party, may be irrevocable, if the parties so agree, for as long as the object of the contract may require.**" Art. 3025.

The fact that the obligor may have contributed to the breach of his own principal obligation will have consequences for that obligor. As **Art. 2013** states: "**When the obligor fails to perform, the obligee has a right to the judicial dissolution of the contract or, according to the circumstances, to regard the contract as dissolved. In either case, the obligee may recover damages. In an action involving judicial dissolution, the obligor who failed to perform may be granted, according to the circumstances, an additional time to perform.**"

However, a failure to perform by the obligor may also result from the breach of performance of a secondary obligation in such a manner that the future performance of the principal obligation will be endangered. Fearful of the future, an obligee may take some preventive measure as mentioned in **Art. 2023 (1)**: "**If the situation of a party, financial or otherwise, has become such as to clearly endanger his ability to perform an obligation, the other party may demand in writing that adequate security be given and, upon failure to give that security, that party may withhold or discontinue his own performance.**" This Article is reminiscent of **Art. 1771** under conditional obligations or **Art. 1783** under obligations with a term.[10]

Performance of the principal obligation on time may be of the "essence" of the contract. Thus "When a delayed performance would no longer be of

---

[9] See Alternative Obligations in Précis, Louisiana Law of Obligations in General, § 4.2.1.

[10] See Précis, Louisiana Law of Obligations in General, §§ 2.2-A.3 and 2.2-B.2.

value to the obligee or when it is evident that the obligor will not perform, the obligee may regard the contract as dissolved without any notice to the obligor." Art. 2016

An obligor who fails to perform, besides being granted, may be, an additional time to perform, may have a lawful reason not to perform at all as explained in **Art. 2022: "Either party to a commutative contract may refuse to perform his obligation if the other has failed to perform or does not offer to perform his own at the same time, if the performances are due simultaneously".**[11]

Should a court rule that an obligor has rendered a substantial performance but not the full performance, the obligor should have to pay some compensatory damages to the obligee in an amount equivalent in value to the "partial non performance". Such is necessary not only to serve as a warning to obligors but also to make sure that obligors perform their obligation to the fullest extent, when they can. Thus a **"substantial performance," as determined by a court,** maintains the contract in existence but must lead to the payment of some damages to the obligee even though **"the part not rendered does not substantially impair the interest of the obligee." Art. 2014.** In other words, obligors should not be encouraged to "substantially perform". Not only the contract will not be dissolved but that same contract will empower the court to grant some compensatory damages to the obligee.

Where **Art. 2020** makes use of the words ". . . **performance . . . essential to the contract**", it calls for a distinction between the words 'substantial' and 'essential'. **"When a contract has been made by more than two parties, one party's failure to perform may not cause dissolution of the contract for the other parties, unless the performance that failed was essential to the contract."** The adjective "essential" tells us that a party's performance was of the "essence" of the contract, whereas the other parties' performances were 'secondary'. A performance is of the 'essence' of a contract when it is the raison d'être of the contract, to the point, possibly, of giving the contract its legal identity or name. Such would be the case of a contract entered into between a client and a law firm because of the exclusive reputation of one particular lawyer in the firm. It could also be the case of a contract between a "charitable organization" and a band whose leader is the 'essential' reason for hiring the band. If that lawyer or that band leader cannot or will not perform, the whole contract should be dissolved since the other lawyers in the firm or the other members of the band were only 'secondary parties' to the contracts. It remains that, under the guise of interpretation and in order to maintain the contract in existence because of the 'circumstances', a court may rule that a partial performance was 'nevertheless' *substantial*, under Art. 2014, because the interest of the obligee was *not substantially impaired.*

§ 9.1.2. MECHANISM OF DISSOLUTION.

Dissolution can be "judicial" when declared by a court of law, or it can be left to the parties to a contract.

---

[11] On Commutative Contracts, see supra Chapter 1, Article 3.

Judicial dissolution may be declared by a court "when the obligor fails to perform" because "the obligee has a right to the judicial dissolution of the contract . . ." and he "may recover damages." Art. 2013(1). However, the fact that the obligee has a right to a judicial dissolution does not mean that the court has no discretion in the matter. As seen above, a court may give the obligor "**an additional time to perform**" (Art. 2013(2))[12] or the court may consider that "**the obligor has rendered a substantial part of the performance. . . .**" (Art. 2014.) A court asked to declare an obligation dissolved because of non performance or partial performance by an obligor, will take into account "the circumstances" and the good or bad faith of the parties involved, the obligor's good or bad faith in particular.[13]

Dissolution can be claimed by the obligee to have occurred "automatically", "of right", where, "according to the circumstances" he may "**regard the contract as dissolved.**" Art. 2013. This same Article goes on to say that "**the obligee may recover damages.**" It is obvious that the obligor will be somewhat reticent to pay, willingly, 'damages' to the obligee in addition to having to accept that the contract "is" dissolved. It is most likely that only a court will be in a position to grant damages to the obligee.[14] The likelihood of Art. 2017 applying without a court being ever involved is very slight: "**The parties may expressly agree that the contract shall be dissolved for the failure to perform a particular obligation. In that case, the contract is deemed dissolved at the time it provides for or, in the absence of such a provision, at the time the obligee gives notice to the obligor that he avails himself of the dissolution clause.**" In most instances, despite the occurrence of dissolution being 'automatic', one party or the other will feel that she was aggrieved in one way or another and litigation will be the only door open to solve the conflict. Thus, we are going back to Art. 2013 and the involvement of a court.

The situation that is most likely to occur is described in **Art. 2015**: "**Upon a party's failure to perform, the other may serve him a notice to perform within a certain time, with a warning that, unless performance is rendered within that time, the contract shall be deemed dissolved. The time allowed for that purpose must be reasonable according to the circumstances. The notice to perform is subject to the requirements governing a putting of the obligor in default and, for the recovery of damages for delay, shall have the same effect as a putting of the obligor in default.**"[15] Just as a Putting in Default may have become useless because it is clear that the obligor will not or cannot perform, likewise "**When a delayed performance would no longer be of value to the obligee or when it is evident that the obligor will not perform, the obligee may regard the contract as dissolved without any notice to the obligor.**" Art. 2016.

---

[12] On this kind of Term, or Term of Grace, see Précis, Louisiana Law of Obligations in General, § 2.2-A.1.

[13] See Good Faith, Précis, Louisiana Law of Obligations in General, § 1.4.2.

[14] On Damages, see this Précis, Chapter 8, Article 3.

[15] On Putting in Default and Its Effects, see this Précis, § 8.2.2.

§ 9.1.3. EFFECTS OF DISSOLUTION.

The effects of dissolution of a contract must be looked at in the framework of the relationship between the parties but also with respect to the relationship between these parties and third parties.[16]

A. Between the Parties.

The effects of dissolution between the parties are governed by one principle and some exceptions to that principle.

The principle is that the parties must be returned to the situation they were in before the contract was entered into. To state the principle otherwise, the parties must be returned to the *status quo ante*. There are exceptions to that principle on account of an impossibility or impracticability to restore the parties to their pre-contract situation.

The principle is stated in the first sentence of **Art. 2018 "Upon dissolution of a contract, the parties shall be restored to the situation that existed before the contract was made. . . ."** It follows that the contract is 'retroactively' undone, erased, as if it had never existed. It is the same principle which is also stated in Art. 1775 with respect to the retroactive effect of the occurrence of a condition.[17] It is also the same principle we will be discussing under Nullity of Contracts and Art. 2033 in the next Chapter.[18]

The second sentence of this first paragraph of Art. 2018 takes into consideration the fact that the 'restoration in kind' is not always, actually very seldom, possible. Damages will be awarded by the court to prevent one party from being enriched at the expense of the other. Moreover, the court will have to decide whether additional damages should be paid by the party in bad faith or at fault in bringing about the dissolution of the contract.

To return the parties to the *statu quo ante*, i.e. the situation they were in before they contracted, is most often a 'fiction' and in reality an impossibility. Hence the exceptions or limitations to the retroactive effect of a dissolution as stated in the second paragraph of **Art. 2018 "If partial performance has been rendered and that performance is of value to the party seeking to dissolve the contract, the dissolution does not preclude recovery for that performance, whether in contract or quasi-contract."**

Here again, it will not be necessary to restate what was written about the "exceptions or limitations" to the retroactive effect of the occurrence of a condition.[19] Suffice it to say that the situation contemplated in the second paragraph of Art. 2018 is fully justified by the principle of unjust enrichment or "enrichment without cause" as it is found in Art. 2298.[20] That party who, in good

---

[16] Many of the same effects of Nullity can be transposed to Dissolution.

[17] See The Condition in Précis, Louisiana Law of Obligations in General, § 2,2-B.1.

[18] See infra Nullity, Chapter 9, Article 2.

[19] See The Condition in Précis, Louisiana Law of Obligations in General, § 2.2-B.2.(b).

[20] Art. 2298: "A person who has been enriched without cause at the expense of another person is

faith, has partially performed and who is facing an impossibility to recover her partial performance should have the right to recover the 'value' of that partial performance to the extent that it has enriched the other party.

As regards **Art. 2019**, it addresses another situation in which 'restoration' is impossible, impractical or simply useless. **"In contracts providing for continuous or periodic performance, the effect of the dissolution shall not be extended to any performance already rendered."** It is obvious that a party who has performed 'personal services' cannot actually recover, later on, these services. A reference can then be made to **Art. 1776** to the effect that **"In a contract for continuous or periodic performance, fulfillment of a resolutory condition does not affect the validity of acts of performance rendered before fulfillment of the condition."**[21]

B. Vis-à-vis Third Persons/Parties.

The rights of third persons against parties to a contract depend on the onerous or gratuitous nature of the juridical act which created these rights and on the type of thing, movable or immovable, on which those rights may bear.

Article 2021 stands as the lone Article dealing with the impact of the dissolution of a contract on the rights that third parties may have acquired from a party to that contract. It states that **"Dissolution of a contract does not impair the rights acquired through an onerous contract by a third party in good faith. If the contract involves immovable property, the principles of recordation apply to a third person acquiring an interest in the property, whether by onerous or gratuitous title."**

The requirement of "good faith" on the part of the third party is 'essential' to the preservation of the rights that the third party acquired by an onerous juridical act.[22] Although **Art. 522** is concerned with the "nullity" of a title, since the retroactive effects of the "dissolution" of a contract are the same as those of nullity, **Art. 522** can be used as an illustration of Art. 2021(1) regarding the effect of the dissolution of a contract on the rights acquired "for fair value" and on movables by third parties. **"A transferee of a corporeal movable in good faith and for fair value retains the ownership of the thing even though the title of the transferor is annulled on account of a vice of consent."** An application of **Art. 522** can also be found in **Art. 3229** which provides that **"If the sale was not made on credit, the seller may even claim back the things in kind, which were thus sold, as long as they are in possession of the purchaser, and prevent the resale of them; provided the claim for**

---

bound to compensate that person. The term 'without cause' is used in this context to exclude cases in which the enrichment results from a valid juridical act or the law. The remedy declared here is subsidiary and shall not be available if the law provides another remedy for the impoverishment or declares a contrary rule. The amount of compensation due is measured by the extent to which one has been enriched or the other has been impoverished, whichever is less. The extent of the enrichment or impoverishment is measured as of the time the suit is brought or, according to the circumstances, as of the time the judgement is rendered."

[21] See specifically : (c) Exceptions (i) p. 53, The Condition, note 17 supra.

[22] On Onerous and Gratuitous Juridical Acts, see Précis, Louisiana Law of Obligations in General, § 1.1.2.

restitution be made within eight days of the delivery at farthest, and that the identity of the objects be established."

As far as the rights acquired by onerous title by third persons may bear on immovables, **Art. 2021(2)** states the rule in these words: **"If the contract involves immovable property, the principles of recordation apply to a third person acquiring an interest in the property whether by onerous or gratuitous title."** It corroborates a statement made in **Art. 517** to the effect that **"the transfer of ownership (of an immovable) . . . is not effective against third persons until the contract is filed for registry in the conveyance records . . ."**[23]

Since Art. 2021 deals with the effects of onerous juridical acts, *a contrario sensu* gratuitous juridical acts must have the opposite effects. Since a third person who received "gratuitously" did not carry out an onerous performance for the benefit of either one of the parties to a contract, the third person should be required to return the benefit she received if demanded, for example, by a creditor of a party to the contract. Such is the meaning of **Art. 2039** on the revocatory action: **"An obligee may attack a gratuitous contract made by the obligor whether or not the other party knew that the contract would cause or increase the obligor's insolvency."**[24] However, if the third person received in good faith she should not suffer any prejudice and, because of her good faith, should not have to return more than the amount of her enrichment. It can be said **"the amount of compensation due is measured by the extent to which one has been enriched or the other has been impoverished, whichever is less." Art. 2298(2).**[25]

ARTICLE 2
NULLITY

Nullity, caducity, dissolution, rescission: what do these concepts have in common if anything at all?

Nullity of a juridical act is the sanction resulting from the non existence or the failure in the integrity of an essential requirement at the time the juridical act is entered into. As **Art. 2029** states very clearly: **"A contract is null when the requirements for its formation have not been met."** As an example, a juridical act will be null if the consent given by one party is the result of a fraudulent action by the other party. Consent, as described above, is essential to the existence of a juridical act and there can be no contract without a free and enlightened consent of the parties. If, before the nullity is declared to have occurred, the juridical act led the parties to carry out some performance, that performance will have to be *retroactively* "erased" because it had no legal ground on which to stand.

There lies the distinction between "*nullity*" and "*caducity*". This latter word is used in the titles given to two civil Code articles by the editors of the Code.

---

[23] See also Art. 3338.

[24] On the Revocatory Action, see infra Chapter 11, Article 1.

[25] Art. 2298 under Enrichment Without Cause; see supra § 9.1.3.

Thus the "editorial title" to Art. 1741 is: *Caducity:* causes and effects, and the "editorial title" to Art. 1749 is: Donation of property to be left at death; *caducity.* Nowhere in the texts of these two Articles, in the law therefore, is the word "caducity" used. What we read, however, is that a donation is in existence, thus valid, but that, later on, an event occurs as a result of which *"the donation becomes of no effect at all"* (1741) or the donation *"becomes of no effect . . ."* (Art. 1749). In other words, a valid donation will cease to have effects in the future when an event described in the Articles occurs. *"Caducity"*, therefore, operates only in the future, it *has no retroactive* effect; it does not erase the past of a juridical act.[26] The consequences of "caducity" are simply that the legacy or donation will have no effect in the future.

Dissolution, as stated above,[27] is the legal consequence of the breach of the performance of an obligation or of the occurrence of a cause or ground exterior to the contract.

Rescission[28] is a legal word used in lieu of nullity in some specific instances of juridical acts such as a compromise (Art. 3082), in the case of lesion in a sale (Art. 2589 et seq.),[29] in an exchange (Art. 2664 et seq.), in a partition (Art.814).

There are two broad kinds of Nullity, absolute or relative, depending on the type of cause or ground that justifies the nullity of a juridical act. Whether absolute or relative, a nullity has a retroactive effect which is the "identifying" feature of any nullity. However, because of the difference in the degree of condemnation in the cause of a nullity or another, some effects will vary in one kind of nullity and the other.

§ 9.2.1. KINDS OF NULLITY AND EXTENT OF NULLITY: ABSOLUTE AND RELATIVE.

A. Nullity of the Whole Contract: Absolute and Relative Nullity.

LCC Art. 2030 describes an absolute nullity in these words: **"A contract is absolutely null when it violates a rule of public order, as when the object of a contract is illicit or immoral. A contract that is absolutely null may not be confirmed. Absolute nullity may be invoked by any person or may be declared by the court on its own initiative."** Article 2031 describes a relative nullity as follows: **"A contract is relatively null when it violates a rule intended for the protection of private parties, as when a party lacked**

---

[26] In the 1870 original version of civil Code Articles 1700 et seq., before the 1997 revision, the verb used for "becomes of no effect" was "fall(s)", e.g., "The legacy falls . . ." (1700); "It likewise falls if . . ." (1701). In 1997 the verb "lapse(s)" has been substituted; see, e.g., Arts. 1589 or 1591. It is our firm opinion that the expression or verbs "becomes of no effect" or "falls" much better convey the idea of "caducité" than the common law tainted verb "lapse." In addition, the French translation of "fall or falls" was under the form of the adjective "caduc" in French.

[27] See this Précis, Dissolution, supra Article 1.

[28] See more hereunder.

[29] See Précis, Louisiana Law of Sale and Lease, § 2.5.1.

capacity or did not give free consent at the time the contract was made. A contract that is only relatively null may be confirmed. Relative nullity may be invoked only by those persons for whose interest the ground for nullity was established, and may not be declared by the court on its own initiative."

Article 2030 suggests that a juridical act is absolutely null when the violation of the law is of great concern and so major that it is "absolutely" necessary to protect, by the absolute nullity of the juridical act, the general interest or public order of the societal group at the expense of the private interest of the parties involved in the unlawful juridical act. Since drawing an ideal and imaginary line between the "general interest or public order" on one side and the "private interest" of the parties on the other side is a quasi impossibility, in most instances the courts will have to assume the responsibility of drawing that line whenever they will be confronted with this issue. In other words, although a nullity is absolute and *de jure*, as a matter of law, so that a court should have no discretion in the matter but to declare the nullity, still, because a court will have to be called upon to declare the nullity, the *de jure* nullity of a juridical act is in the hands of the court.

The lesser effects of relative nullity are explained by the fact that the 'nullity' of the juridical act occurs in the relation between the parties because only their private interest, as opposed to 'public', is at stake; that private interest of the parties deserves some degree of protection. It follows that, because of the private nature of this kind of nullity, the relative nullity of a juridical act can be 'waved' by the party or parties or it can be 'cured' by the party protected by the nullity. In addition, whereas an action to have a juridical act declared absolutely null does not prescribe, an action in relative nullity does prescribe.[30]

In some instances, the courts are guided in their evaluation of the nature of a nullity and, therefore, in the amount of discretion they may have. For example, Art. 94 states that **"a marriage is absolutely null when contracted without a marriage ceremony. . . ."**. Since the nullity is absolute, the Court has no discretion in the matter, so much so that **"a judicial declaration of nullity is not required."** In such an instance, a court will have to "declare" the absolute nullity of the marriage.

Art. 1965 states that "A contract may be annulled on grounds of lesion only in those cases provided by law." Strangely enough, none of the Articles on Lesion beyond Moiety[31] uses the verb "annul" or the word "nullity". The words used in the Articles are to the effect that such a **"sale of an immovable may be rescinded for lesion . . ."** Art. 2589. Is 'rescission' suggesting that the sale is 'null'? Rescission in the Louisiana civil Code is actually the equivalent of 'relative nullity' since the nullity must be asked from the court and the court, in its discretion and according to the circumstances, will have to determine whether there is 'lesion' or not[32]

---

[30] On Prescription of the Actions, see infra § 4.2.2.B.

[31] Arts. 2589–2600.

[32] Rescission at civil law is not a contract as it is at common law where it consists in an agreement between parties to a contract to terminate their contract.

We read in **Art. 3072** that "a compromise shall be made in writing or recited in open court, in which case the recitation shall be susceptible of being transcribed from the record of the proceedings." Does 'shall', the imperative form of the verb to be, suggest that in the absence of a writing, the compromise cannot exist and, actually, has never existed because of an absolute nullity? Is the legal consequence for a compromise the same as is the case of a marriage without a ceremony? Art. 3082 states that **"A compromise may be rescinded for error, fraud, and other grounds for the annulment of contracts. Nevertheless, a compromise cannot be rescinded on grounds of error of law or lesion."** Where this Article refers to "grounds for the annulment of contracts" as leading to "rescission" or "'relative nullity" of contracts, a compromise can be "relatively null".[33] However, the contract of compromise is also a formal or solemn contract and must, therefore, be in writing. Reasoning *a contrario* on Art. 3082 and on account of the reasons behind the requirement of a writing for a valid compromise, plus the use of "shall", it should be said that the absence of a writing prevents a compromise from existing so that the nullity should be absolute.

What kind of nullity affects **"a donation in favor of a person who is incapable of receiving"**? Art. 1475 states only that such a donation **"is null."** Whose interest is being protected by the nullity? Art. 1478 is a little more explicit: **"A donation inter vivos or mortis causa shall be declared null upon proof that it is the product of fraud or duress."** Since the nullity has to be declared, it means that a court will be called upon to weigh the interests protected and, therefore, the nullity should be considered as "relative." Can the same be said about Article 1475 despite the absence of "declared" but, on the other hand, the use of the present tense in "is null"?[34] **Art. 1520** uses the present tense in *"is null"* but it adds that **"a disposition that is not in trust . . . is null with regard to both the institute and the substitute."** The addition of the words 'with regard to both the institute and the substitute' suggests that the nullity is in relation to these two parties, so that the nullity should be looked upon as 'relative'.[35]

B. Nullity of a Provision: Relative Nullity.

Art. 2034 limits the "presumptive" nullity of a contract to one provision of a contract: **"Nullity of a provision does not render the whole contract null unless from the nature of the provision or the intention of the parties, it can be presumed that the contract would not have been made without the null provision."** We find, here, an application of the concepts of "cause" and "confirmation".[36] If only the private interest of the parties to the null contract is

---

[33] See Vices of Consent, supra Chapter 4.

[34] See other Articles: 1479, 1480.

[35] Art. 1520: "A disposition that is not in trust by which a thing is donated in full ownership to a first donee, called the institute, with a charge to preserve the thing and deliver it to a second donee, called the substitute, at the death of the institute, is null with regard to both the institute and the substitute."

[36] On Cause, see supra Chapter 5; on Confirmation, see Précis, Louisiana Law of Obligations in General, § 6.1.1.C.1.

at stake, it may be possible to preserve the contract but read the contractual provision which is relatively null out of the contract. **Art. 1480** offers a good example of such a "selective and relative nullity": "**When a donation inter vivos or mortis causa is declared null because of undue influence or because of fraud or duress, it is not necessary that the entire act of donation or testament be nullified. If any provision contained in it is not the product of such means, that provision shall be given effect, unless it is otherwise invalid.**"[37] Likewise, **Art. 1519** provides that "In all dispositions inter vivos and mortis causa impossible conditions, those which are contrary to the laws or to morals, are reputed not written."

§ 9.2.2. EFFECTS OF NULLITY.

A. Right of Action.

With respect to the vesting of the "right" of action in a plaintiff, the examples of relative nullity given above clearly lead to say that a relative nullity can be claimed only by that party whose interest is meant to be protected. Such is the case in the most common instance of relative nullity, i.e. vices of consent in the formation of a contract.[38] Because a private interest is at stake, the party protected by the relative nullity can "cure" the ground of nullity by such juridical acts as "confirmation" and "novation". It is worth stating again that "**Confirmation is a declaration whereby a person cures the relative nullity of an obligation. An express act of confirmation must contain or identify the substance of the obligation and evidence the intention to cure its relative nullity. Tacit confirmation may result from voluntary performance of the obligation.**" Art. 1842. Likewise "**. . . If the obligation is only relatively null, the novation is valid, provided the obligor or the new one knew of the defect of the extinguished obligation.**" Art. 1883(2).[39]

It may happen in a few instances that a person other than the 'protected' party be allowed to claim the benefit of a relative nullity meant to protect somebody else. It is the case, for example, of the representative of an incapable person.[40] Under civil Code **Art. 28**, and reasoning *a contrario*, a person who has not reached the age of majority has no capacity to make any kind "**of juridical act, unless otherwise provided by legislation.**" **Art. 221** therefore states that "**The father is, during the marriage, administrator of the estate of his minor children. . . .**" The same is true of Art. 395 on the "incapacity" of an interdict to make a juridical act. The father or the curator are representatives charged with the responsibility to represent the incapable person and act on his or her behalf.

---

[37] One will note that this Article 1480 makes a clear distinction between "undue influence" and "duress"; these concepts are not the same. See our discussion, and criticism, of duress under Vices of Consent, supra Chapter 4.

[38] See this Précis, supra Integrity of Consent, Chapter 3, Article 4.

[39] Confirmation is to be distinguished from ratification in Art. 1843. On Ratification, see Précis, Louisiana Law of Obligations in General, § 6.1.1.

[40] See Representation, Code Arts. 2985–2988.

Art. 1844 suggests that some third persons may have the right to "benefit" from the relative nullity of a juridical act and object to the retroactive effect of the nullity when the confirmation or ratification of that juridical act would impair their rights acquired in good faith under the "annullable" juridical act: "**The effects of confirmation and ratification are retroactive to the date of the confirmed or ratified obligation. Neither confirmation nor ratification may impair the rights of third persons.**"

Under **Art. 2044**, a creditor should have the right to claim the relative nullity of a juridical act entered into by his debtor that "causes or increases" the insolvency of that debtor. The action available to the creditor is the "oblique action" described below.[41]

As regards the absolute nullity of a juridical act, it is obvious that more plaintiffs should be granted the right of action than only those who may seek the relative nullity of a juridical act. The protection of the public interest needs for the circle of potential plaintiffs to be enlarged to include anyone who has a "legitimate interest" because of some legal relationship he or she has with the parties to the absolutely null juridical act. It could be relatives, creditors, the parties themselves, or their representatives, but also, where appropriate the official representative of the societal group in charge of enforcing the law.

B. Prescription.

Art. 2032 speaks for itself: "**Action for annulment of an absolutely null contract does not prescribe.**

Action of annulment of a relatively null contract must be brought within five years from the time the ground for nullity either ceased, as in the case of incapacity or duress, or was discovered, as in the case of error or fraud.

Nullity may be raised at any time as a defense against an action on the contract, even after the action for annulment has prescribed."

So, an action for the relative nullity of a juridical act prescribes in five years, whereas the right of action for an absolute nullity never prescribes. It is important to point out here that if an action may prescribe, particularly for a relative nullity, the defense or exception of nullity itself never prescribes. Such is the meaning of the third paragraph of Art. 2032. This exception which goes back to the Digest of Justinian is known in civil law jurisdictions under this form: *Quae temporalia sunt ad agendum perpetua sunt ad excipiendum.*[42]

The same is true of the third paragraph of **Art. 2033** which provides that "**Nullity may be raised at any time as a defense against an action on the contract, even after the action for annulment has prescribed.**"

---

[41] See Oblique Action, infra Chapter 11, Article 2.

[42] "Whatever one has a certain time to demand, one is always allowed to raise as an exception." A form of such an exception can be found in the Louisiana Code of Civil Procedure, Art. 424.

C. Retroactivity.

A principle common to both kinds of nullity is that of the retroactive effect of the nullity.[43] The first sentence of the first paragraph of **Art. 2033** is very clear: "**An absolutely null contract, or a relatively null contract that has been declared null by the court, is deemed never to have existed. . . .**" If the contract is *deemed never to have existed*, it follows that anything that has been done "in the past", any of the performances that have been carried out by a party or the parties have to be erased, wiped out, as if nothing had ever occurred. The problem is practical: how to restore the past to what it was before the parties entered their contract and performed, in toto or in part, their obligations. Somewhat of an answer is given in Arts. 2033 and 2035 which draw a distinction between the effects of retroactivity between the parties themselves, on the one hand, and vis-à-vis third persons, on the other hand.

1. *Retroactivity and the Parties.*

The principle that applies in the relationship between the parties is stated in these terms in the second sentence of **Art. 2033**: "**The parties must be restored to the situation that existed before the contract was made. If it is impossible or impracticable to make restoration in kind, it may be made through an award of damages.**" An exception to that principle is stated in the second paragraph of **Art. 2033**: "**Nevertheless, a performance rendered under a contract that is absolutely null because its object or its cause is illicit or immoral may not be recovered by a party who knew or should have known of the defect that makes the contract null. The performance may be recovered, however, when that party invokes the nullity to withdraw from the contract before its purpose is achieved and also in exceptional situations when, in the discretion of the court, that recovery would further the interest of justice.**"

As regards the principle of the retroactive effect of nullity, whether relative or absolute, it has the same effects as the retroactivity of a resolutory condition the purpose of which is to wipe out the effects of whatever performance may have occurred.[44] Thus, each party must return to the other the performance received because that performance has become "undue". As **Art. 2299** states: "**A person who has received a payment or a thing not owed to him is bound to restore it to the person from whom he received it.**" And as **Art. 2304** further states: "**When the thing not owed is an immovable or a corporeal movable, the person who received it is bound to restore the thing itself, it exits. If the thing has been destroyed, damaged, or cannot be returned, a person who received the thing in good faith is bound to restore its value if the loss was caused by his fault. A person who received the thing in bad faith is bound to restore its value even if the loss was not caused by his fault.**" The good or bad faith of a party will further determine the amount of the restoration owed to the other party as indicated in **Art. 2305**: "**A person who in good faith

---

[43] On the Principle of Retroactivity, see Précis, Louisiana Law of Obligations in General, § 2.2-B.2.

[44] See footnote 17, supra.

alienated a thing not owed to him is only bound to restore whatever he obtained from the alienation. If he received the thing in bad faith, he owes, in addition, damages to the person to whom restoration is due."[45]

The exception described in **Art. 2033-2**,[46] is a standard application of the civil law maxim: *Nemo auditur suam propriam turpitudinem allegans*. This maxim is somewhat equivalent to the common law maxim of "clean hands". A court will not listen to someone who relies on her/his turpitude in order to claim the recovery of her/his performance. The violation of the law or good morals is such that a court cannot possibly encourage this kind of transaction by allowing the party or parties to recover their "illicit or immoral" performance. The best way to discourage individuals from entering this kind of contracts is to make it clear that the courts will not allow them to recover their performance.

The second sentence of this same second paragraph of **Art. 2033** gives a court some discretion in light of the circumstances of a particular case so as to allow recovery in the **"interest of justice"**.

2. *Retroactivity and Third Parties.*

We have seen above that a contract between two parties is *res inter alios acta*, that it is the law between the parties and that it cannot cause detrimental effects to third persons.[47] It is therefore easy to understand that, likewise, the nullity of a contract between two parties should not have detrimental effects against good faith third persons, i.e. persons who did not know and could not have known of the ground of nullity of a contract to which they were not parties. "Good faith" once again will protect those third persons who can claim its benefit. Hence **Art. 2035**: **"Nullity of a contract does not impair the rights acquired through an onerous contract by a third party in good faith. If the contract involves immovable property, the principles of recordation apply to a third person acquiring an interest in the property whether by onerous or gratuitous title."**

The civil Code offers many illustrations of an application of the principle of good faith on the part of a third person whose rights acquired by onerous title might be affected by the nullity of a contract. Such is the case, for example, of Articles 522, 1281(1), 3480-3481-3482[48] etc. . . . On the other hand, if the third person, in good faith, acquired her rights by gratuitous title, a reasoning *a contrario* on the above Articles would lead to requiring that person to return whatever she acquired gratuitously. Having acquired gratuitously, in the sense that the third person did not transfer anything of value to her "donor", a party to the null contract, to require that third person to return whatever she received gratuitously would not impoverish her patrimony. We find a justification for this

---

[45] To the exception stated in the second paragraph of Art. 2033 quoted above, we can add another exception on account of the incapacity of one party to contract. With respect to this second exception it will be sufficient to refer back to Capacity as a requirement for a valid contract and, in particular, to Arts. 1919 and 1923. See supra Chapter 2.

[46] See supra page 42.

[47] See supra § 9.1.3.B.

[48] See these articles in the Louisiana Pocket Civil Code.

reasoning in **Art. 2039: "An obligee may attack a gratuitous contract made by the obligor whether or not the other party knew that the contract would cause or increase the obligor's insolvency.**[49]

---

[49] See infra the Revocatory Action, Chapter 11, Article 1.

Chapter 10

INTERPRETATION OF CONTRACTS
LSA-C.C. ARTS. 2045 TO 2057

A contract being, presumably, the outward manifestation of the parties' intent, the Code Articles which lay down the "rules" of interpretation of contracts can only have for their purpose to provide guidelines to ascertain and extract the intent of the parties out of the contract. This is the whole meaning of Art. 2045: "**Interpretation of a contract is the determination of the common intent of the parties.**"

The courts whose responsibility it is to ascertain that common intent of the parties are given, first of all, the words of a contract to read; they are, then, confronted with the task of uncovering the intent of the parties through the words they used. However, because parties to a contract are often unable to incorporate fully and accurately their common intent in the words of their contract, they will shift to the court the responsibility of ascertaining that common intent which may have existed at some point in the past or which, in most instances, may have to be "presumed" as having been the "common intent" of the parties. Although the civil Code lays down a certain number of rules of interpretation to guide the courts, the latter will necessarily have to exercise some discretion in their own "interpretation" of these rules of interpretation.[1]

ARTICLE 1
RULES OF INTERPRETATION

The majority of the Code Articles on this issue of interpretation focus on the words of the contract and the provisions of the contract. Art. 2046 invites the Courts to consider that "**When the words of a contract are clear and explicit and lead to no absurd consequences, no further interpretation may be made in search of the parties' intent.**" In addition, "**The words of a contract must be given their generally prevailing meaning. Words of art and technical terms must be given their technical meaning when the contract involves a technical matter.**" Art. 2047. If the meaning of the words used is somewhat ambiguous, uncertain, then "**Words susceptible of different meanings must be interpreted as having the meaning that best conforms to the object of the contract.**" Art. 2048.

The words of a contract must be read also within the context of the provisions of the contract. Four Code Articles look at the provisions of a contract as a whole so that one provision can possibly help interpret other provisions. So state

---

[1] LSA-C.C. Arts. 2045 to 2057. There is in this matter some analogy with the Code Articles on Interpretation of Laws, LSA-C.C. Arts. 9–13.

Articles 2049, 2050, 2051 and 2052[2]. This latter **Art. 2052** is particularly instructive. It states, basically, that when the parties to a contract written in broad or general terms happen to include in their contract a **"special reference to a specific situation,"** that specific reference should not be read as restricting the **"general scope"** of the contract. The "general" should not lose to the "special." For example, if parties to a contract of sale have made one reference to a particular mode of determining the price of the sale, it should not mean that other modes of determining the price are to be excluded. As long as it appears clearly that the scope of the contract or "common intent" of the parties was to have a sale with a price determined somehow, then the single mode of determining the price mentioned in the contract cannot be meant to restrict the scope of that contract which was intended by the parties to be a "sale." The "specific" mode of determining the price should be looked at as an "illustration" of the need to have a price for the sale to exist, i.e. the scope of the contract, and not as the "exclusive mode" of setting that price which is only one component part of the contract of sale.

It remains however, that in relating a provision of a contract to another provision in the same contract the courts must strive to **"determine the common intent of the parties."** Art. 2045. Ascertaining that "common intent" should be the goal to reach.

This is particularly important in those instances where one party to a contract is in a weaker bargaining position than the other party. The civil Code gives the courts two special rules to use for the purpose of protecting that party presumed to be the weaker of the two in any one of two situations contemplated in Articles 2056 and 2057.

Article 2056 is concerned with a type of contract which is more and more common, particularly in dealings with legal entities. This type of contract, usually in a typewritten form with blanks to be filled in, is the standard-form contract. A special rule was necessary to provide some guidance in the interpretation of such a contract: **"In case of doubt that cannot be otherwise resolved, a provision in a contract must be interpreted against the party who furnished its text. A contract executed in a standard form of one party must be interpreted, in case of doubt, in favor of the other party."** In most instances, "the party who furnished the text" is the "stronger" of the two parties, the one with more bargaining power and, most likely, also the "offeror" even though there may have been some negotiations back and forth with the offeree. To reinstate some balance in the different level of the bargaining powers between the two parties, the "law" invites the court to interpret such "standard-form contracts" "in favor of the other party", the weaker party, to the contract.

Article 2057 lays down a special rule or "starting guide" to interpret contracts which may raise some doubt as to the meaning of one or more their provisions. **Art. 2057** states that **"In case of doubt that cannot be otherwise resolved, a contract must be interpreted against the obligee and in favor of the obligor of a particular obligation. Yet, if the doubt arises from lack of a necessary explanation that one party should have given, or from negligence or fault of**

---

[2] See LSA-C.C. Arts. 2049 to 2052 in Appendix I.

one party, the contract must be interpreted in a manner favorable to the other party whether obligee or obligor." This rule is but an application to the interpretation of contracts of a general approach exhibited all through the civil Code to the effect that whenever a choice has to be made between a party who is under a burden or "onus" (hence onerous obligation) and one who is to receive the benefit of that "onus," the first one, the obligor, ought to be "favored." We have seen, for example, that **"When an obligation is alternative, the choice of the item of performance belongs to the obligor unless . . ." Art. 1809.** We read in **Art. 1779** that **"A term is presumed to benefit the obligor unless. . . ."** This **Art. 2057** takes the same approach in its first sentence. The second sentence addresses a somewhat different situation which is that the principle of "good faith" is called upon to help interpret a contract in favor of one party or the other regardless of whether one party is the obligor and the other is the obligee.

ARTICLE 2
BENDING THE RULES: INTERPRETATION IS NOT REVISION

§ 10.2.1. BENDING THE RULES.

It is an easy statement to make that to interpret a contract is to ascertain the true common intent of the parties. It is quite another task to be able to claim to have actually ascertained, with some degree of certainty, what "was" or "is" the common intent of the parties. If a court is called upon to "interpret" a contract, it is obviously because the parties disagree as to this concept of their common intent. In a sense, the court will be acting as a "third party" to the contract and will be asked to determine the "common intent" of the parties as if it had participated in the formation of the contract between plaintiff and defendant. Because of that "fiction", a court can only somewhat "bend" or "accommodate" the rules of interpretation seen above which are grounded in the contract as the "personal" involvement and contribution of the parties themselves.

The tools given to a court are listed in Articles 2053 to 2055[3]. One will note the particular reference to "Equity" and to "Usage" (or Usages) as sources of the presumed common intent of the parties. Indeed, all parties to contracts are presumed to be "reasonable persons", thus motivated by the same sense of Equity or the same common reference to "Usages". These "extra contractual" sources of the "law" of parties to a contract are somewhat reminiscent of **Art. 4** of the civil Code which invites the courts to **"proceed according to equity . . . and prevailing usages" "when no rule for a particular situation can be derived from legislation or custom. . . ."** The "contract" being the law between the parties, a parallel is then made with "legislation" being the law for all who are under its control.

---

[3] See LSA-C.C. Arts. 2053 to 2055 in Appendix I.

§ 10.2.2. INTERPRETATION IS NOT REVISION.

Whenever the performance of the obligations created by a contract spreads over any length of time there exists the risk that the actual performance of the obligations may not match the performance as expected or as anticipated by the common intent of the parties when they entered their contract. The many different kinds of "surrounding circumstances" that prevailed at the time the contract was entered into may or, rather, are likely to be different from the circumstances that will surround the actual performance of the obligations created by the contract. For example, the supply of a particular component part necessary to the manufacturing of a product may dry out for all sorts of reasons, political, financial, environmental, etc.; the value of a currency is bound to be affected over a period of time; an economic or financial crisis can occur overnight; etc. The question then raised is: what of the situation of the party negatively affected by a subsequent change in the circumstances? Can a court "re-write" the contract to adapt it to present day surroundings and claim, still, to "interpret" the contract as per the presumed "common intent" of the parties as it was at the time of formation of their contract? Can a court simply say: this is what the parties would have wanted had they been able to "foresee," on the day of their contract, the change, in the course of time, of the surrounding circumstances so as to make that change a part of their contract? It is obvious that the party to the contract who is "favored" by the change in circumstances will argue that the "common intent" of the parties was to "stick" to *rebus sic stantibus* (things remaining as they are). That "favored" party will argue that the parties have contracted in light of the then existing circumstances, as the circumstances were at the time of the contract with no contemplation of the now existing and changed circumstances. Otherwise, that same favored party would argue, we would have planned in our contract for ways to adapt and modulate our obligations to circumstances changing over a period of time.[4]

A few specific Articles in the civil Code invite the judge to "re-write" a contract in specific circumstances. Such is the case of Art. 1861(2), Art. 1877, Articles 1951 and 1952.[5] However, in all other circumstances, a contract being the "law" between the parties it should not be revised by a court under the guise of "interpretation". The civil Code instructs a court to resort to **"interpretation of a contract** [to determine] **the common intent of the parties"**[6] and nothing more. If a party's consent was "free" and "informed" when given,[7] the fact that "her" contract turns out to be "hard" and "tough" on her should be no "legal" reason for a court to rewrite the contract to make it more "equitable" for that "complaining" party while "imposing" a new contract on the other party.

---

[4] For example, a clause in the contract inviting the parties to revise the contract every six months, once a year, etc., or an indexation clause. See Précis, Louisiana Law of Obligations in General, Impossibility of Performance § 7.2.1.

[5] See LSA-C.C. Arts. 1867 and 1877 in Appendix I. See Précis, Louisiana Law of Obligations in General § 7.2.2. on Partial Impossibility; LSA-C.C. Arts. 1951-1952 in Appendix I; see also this Precis, Cause, supra Chapter 5.

[6] LSA-C.C. Art. 2045.

[7] See this Précis, Consent, Chapter 3, supra.

Chapter 11

REVOCATORY AND OBLIQUE ACTIONS
LSA-C.C. ARTS. 2036 TO 2044

An obligor's patrimony is made up of rights and obligations which have a monetary value and, for that reason, an obligor is "**obliged to fulfill his engagements out of all his property, movable or immovable, present and future.**" Art. 3182. Whenever that obligor acts or fails to act in such a way as to cause his own insolvency or increase his already established insolvency, that obligor's immediate creditor-obligee could have legitimate reasons to fear for his own right to obtain the performance of the obligations owed him by his obligor.

An obligee who watches over his own interest has two actions available to him to protect "indirectly" his right to obtain some form performance from his obligor. One action is known as the "Revocatory Action" and the other is the "Oblique Action". Each action is triggered into existence by different sets of conditions.

ARTICLE 1
THE REVOCATORY ACTION

The action, named *revocatory* in the Louisiana civil Code, is also known in civil law jurisdictions as the "paulian action" or "pauliana action".[1] It is described in **LSA-CC. Art. 2036** in the following terms: "**An obligee has a right to annul an act of the obligor, or the result of a failure to act of the obligor, made or effected after the right of the obligee arose, that causes or increases the obligor's insolvency.**" The legal regime of the revocatory action is defined by the conditions under which it can be brought and the effects flowing from its successful outcome.

§ 11.1.1. CONDITIONS[2] FOR THE EXISTENCE OF A REVOCATORY ACTION.

Art. 2036 suggests that two sets of conditions must be met: one set of conditions concerns the obligee's right against his obligor and the second set focuses on the obligor's act or failure to act.

As regards the obligee's right, it is necessary that this right be either in existence and vested in the obligee or that this right be at least 'potential' before

---

[1] Some have written that the action has been named after the Roman legal scholar Paulus.

[2] Under the civil Code of 1870 and until the revision of 1984, "fraud" was one of the requirements or conditions for the availability of a revocatory action. Such a condition of fraud is no longer required, making it easier for an obligee to bring a revocatory action. See Fraud, supra Chapter 4, Article 2.

the obligor, by his act or failure to act, causes or increases his insolvency. The potential right of an obligee should be considered as being in existence for the purpose of a revocatory action, whenever that right is subject to a **suspensive term** or, even, when the obligee's right is subject to a **suspensive condition**.³ A right subject to a **term** is a right vested in the obligee although the performance owed by the obligor to the obligee is delayed. An obligor should not be allowed to take advantage, at the expense of his obligee, of the right he had not to perform immediately.⁴

Furthermore, as **Art. 1782** states very clearly, justifying thereby the right of the obligee to bring a revocatory action, **"When the obligation is such that its performance requires the solvency of the obligor, the term is regarded as nonexistent if the obligor is found to be insolvent."**⁵

Although a right granted under a **suspensive condition** is not actually vested in the obligee, nevertheless if the condition should happen it will have a retroactive "vesting" effect back to the time the right was granted. It follows that a creditor under a **suspensive condition** should be given the right to bring a revocatory action as a lawful measure to preserve his right.⁶

Thus, whether there exists a **suspensive term** under **Art. 1783** or a **suspensive condition** under **Art. 1771** one can look at the revocatory action as a "lawful measure" taken by the obligee "to preserve his right."⁷

As regards the obligor's act or result of a failure to act it must have caused or increased the insolvency of the obligor. **Art. 2037** provides an explanation of the meaning of insolvency for the purpose of the revocatory action: **"An obligor is insolvent when the total of his liabilities exceeds the total of his fairly appraised assets."**⁸

Furthermore, the act or result of a failure to act on the part of the obligor must not be or have been *strictly personal* to that obligor. The legal distinction made between heritable rights or obligations on the one hand and strictly personal rights or obligations on the other hand, leads to deny to an obligee the right to bring a revocatory action in the event his obligor failed to exercise a strictly personal right so recognized under the law. For example, should a husband-obligor be entitled to "support" from his wife under the law,⁹ an obligee of the husband should not have the right to a revocatory action because of the husband-obligor's result of a failure to act to seek 'his' support from his wife. Likewise, a creditor should not have the right to bring an action for the divorce

---

³ On Term and Condition, see Précis, Louisiana Law of Obligations in General, § 2.2-A.1 and § 2.2-B.1.

⁴ "Performance of an obligation not subject to a term is due immediately." Art. 1777(2).

⁵ See Précis, Louisiana Law of Obligations in General.

⁶ See LSA-C.C. Art. 1771; see Précis, Louisiana Law of Obligations in General, § 2.2.- B.2.B.

⁷ See Précis, Louisiana Law of Obligations in General.

⁸ See LSA-C.C. Art. 2037 in Appendix I; see also LSA-C.C.P. Art. 2723 on appraisal of property in Appendix II.

⁹ See LSA-C.C. Art. 98.

of his obligor from the latter's spouse.[10] Neither should an obligee be allowed to bring a revocatory action against his obligor when the latter is "a successor" since **"A successor is not obligated to accept his rights to succeed. He may accept some of those rights and renounce others."** Art. 947.

§ 11.1.2. PRINCIPAL EFFECT OF A REVOCATORY ACTION: NULLITY OF THE ACT.

A reading of Articles 2036, 2038, 2040 leads one to state that the effect of a revocatory action is to have a juridical act or contract *annulled*. Therefore the rules governing nullity or dissolution[11] of contracts should apply.

Actually, the outcome of a revocatory action is not to "annul" an act or contract between the obligor and a third person but, rather, to declare that the act or contract cannot be "opposed" to the obligee who brings the revocatory action. Indeed, that act or contract will remain binding between the parties but the obligee who brings the revocatory action will be allowed to ignore the existence of the act or contract to the extent that his own right as an obligee was endangered by his obligor's act or failure to act. In a sense, the purpose of the revocatory action is to make the juridical act or contract between the obligor and the other party *res inter alios acta*[12] vis-à-vis the obligee with the consequence that the obligee can consider the act or contract as "non-existent" as far as he is concerned. It is interesting to read in **Art. 2039** that **"An obligee may attack a gratuitous contract. . . ."** The use of the verb "attack" accurately describes the legal purpose or effect of the revocatory action.[13]

The ultimate effects of the right of the obligee to consider the act or contract as 'non existent' and un-opposable against him depend on whether the act or contract between the obligor and his co-contractor was onerous or gratuitous.

§ 11.1.3. REVOCATORY ACTION AND ONEROUS CONTRACTS.

Art. 2038 provides as follows: "An obligee may annul an onerous contract made by the obligor with a person who knew or should have known that the contract would cause or increase the obligor's insolvency. In that case, the person is entitled to recover what he gave in return only to the extent that it has inured to the benefit of the obligor's creditors.

An obligee may annul an onerous contract made by the obligor with a person who did not know that the contract would cause or increase the obligor's insolvency, but in that case that person is entitled to recover as much as he gave to the obligor. That lack of knowledge is presumed when

---

[10] On Heritable and Strictly Personal Rights and Obligations, see Précis, Louisiana Law of Obligations in General, § 2.1.2.

[11] See supra Nullity, Chapter 9, Article 2.

[12] See supra Effects of Contracts, Chapter 8.

[13] LSA-C.C. Art. 2039: "An obligee may attack a gratuitous contract. . . ."

that person has given at least four-fifths of the value of the thing obtained in return from the obligor."

As regards a revocatory action meant to "attack" an onerous contract entered into between the obligor and his co-contractor, **Art. 2038** contemplates two different situations depending on the presumed good or bad faith of the "co-contractor" of the onerous contract.[14] To better help understand the somewhat intricate situations that are contemplated by this **Art. 2038**, we have chosen to give a name to each of the three parties involved: the obligee who brings the revocatory-pauliana action will be "Paulus"; Paulus' obligor will be "Ulpian", who will be in a contractual relationship with a co-contractor (the "person" in **Art. 2038**) by the name of "Gaius".

In Situation 1, Paulus is "attacking'" **"an onerous contract made by the obligor (Ulpian) with a person (Gaius) who knew or should have known that the (onerous) contract would cause or increase the obligor's (Ulpian's) insolvency." Art. 2038(1)**. It is important to add here this excerpt from the second paragraph of **Art. 2038**, to the effect that "[the] **lack of knowledge (by Gaius) is presumed when that person (Gaius) has given at least four-fifths of the value of the thing obtained in return from the obligor (Ulpian)."** This second sentence of **Art. 2038(2)** creates a presumption of bad faith on the part of any person (such as Gaius) who "gives" the obligor (Ulpian) less than four-fifths of the "fairly appraised" value of the "asset(s)" he acquired from the obligor (Ulpian). Because of the precise mathematical formula given, four-fifths, it appears that the presumption cannot be rebutted. In addition, the clear availability given in the immediately preceding sentence of Art. 2038(2) to the person (Gaius) to show that she did not know that she had caused or increased the insolvency of the obligor (Ulpian) is "cut-off" by the second sentence which presumes lack of knowledge only if the person (Gaius) gave at least four-fifths. The only hope that the person (Gaius) has to "show" her good faith so as to recover the total amount of her payment, is for a court to "fairly appraise" the asset transferred by the obligor (Ulpian) in an amount such that the person (Gaius) would have made a payment above the limit of four-fifths.[15]

In Situation 1 we assume that Paulus holds a credit of 200 against Ulpian. Let us assume also that Ulpian has a patrimony worth 150 and that one item, a painting, in his total patrimony of 150 is worth 100. At that moment in time Ulpian is already partially insolvent vis-à-vis Paulus in an amount of 50. Now Ulpian enters a sale of his painting with Gaius, the buyer, for an amount of 50. Thereby Ulpian has increased his insolvency vis-à-vis Paulus by another 50 (painting worth 100 sold for 50 equals a deficiency in amount of 50).

---

[14] On Gratuitous and Onerous Contracts, see supra Chapter 1, Article 2.

[15] "Fraud" (or bad faith) having been deleted as a second requirement imposed on the obligee Paulus to prove in addition to the insolvency of his obligor, the application of the mathematical formula is now all that is required to restrict or not the right of the person (Gaius) to recover her payment. Under the law of the 1870 civil Code, before the 1984 revision of the law of Obligations, then Article 1978 stated that "No contract shall be avoided by this action but such as are made in fraud of creditors. . . ."

Under the second paragraph of 2038, because Gaius has paid far less than four-fifths (actually one half) of the value of the painting worth 100, Gaius will be presumed to have had the knowledge that he had contributed to an increase of Ulpian's insolvency at the expense of Ulpian's creditor, Paulus. Now enters Paulus and his revocatory action. Because Ulpian has increased his insolvency, Paulus may bring a revocatory (Pauliana) action to attack (annul) the sale of the painting made by Ulpian to Gaius so as to annul that sale and bring Ulpian's patrimony back to the value it had before the sale of the painting to Gaius. Thus Ulpian will, first of all, keep the 50 received from Gaius as the price the latter paid for the painting actually worth 100. An additional 50 will be taken out of the value of the painting which could be sold by Paulus for a price in money. Ultimately, Gaius would get back 50, the price he paid for the painting and no more. An alternative solution to this problem would be for Gaius to return the indivisible thing, the painting, to Ulpian who would then return the price of 50 he received from Gaius. Gaius contributed to an increase of Ulpian's patrimony up to (100-50) or (50) and not 150.

In Situation 2, Paulus is owed 200 by Ulpian who has 200 in his patrimony. Paulus, if he acts on time and if he is the only creditor, could be paid his 200 out of Ulpian's patrimony. But Ulpian, later on, disposes by onerous contract with Gaius of the 200 in his patrimony for a payment from Gaius in the amount of 50. Again, Gaius, when paying 50, paid far less than four-fifths of the 200 in value he received from Ulpian. Now Paulus, who had a right worth 200 over Ulpian's patrimony, will find only 50 in that patrimony. He is "short" of 150. When bringing a revocatory action against Ulpian and Gaius jointly sued, Paulus will find 50 in Ulpian's patrimony and Gaius will have to return directly to Paulus the 150 that he had received from Ulpian. Paulus who brought the revocatory action to attack that onerous contract between Ulpian and Gaius will receive 200, his due, whereas Gaius will be out of pocket in the amount of 50. One could say that the mathematical formula has cost Gaius 50 for his "mathematical bad faith".

The lesson that may be drawn from the strict mathematical application of this Article is that one should not feel safe when making a "good deal" too "good a deal", i.e. when paying less than four-fifths the value of an acquisition by onerous title. To be safe, it is wiser to pay at least four-fifths because in that situation (Situation 3) **"the person (Gaius) is entitled to recover as much as he gave to the obligor (Ulpian)." Art. 2038 (2).**[16]

§ 11.1.4. REVOCATORY ACTION AND GRATUITOUS CONTRACTS.

As regards "gratuitous contracts", **Art. 2039** states very clearly, in a few words, that **"An obligee may attack a gratuitous contract made by the obligor whether or not the other party knew that the contract would cause or increase the obligor's insolvency."** The reason for this rule of law is that a gratuitous juridical act cannot legally justify the enrichment of a person (Gaius) at the expense of an obligee (Paulus) whose "onerous" right against the obligor

---

[16] The same advice could be given to those buyers who buy at a lesionary price. See Précis, Louisiana Law of Sale and Lease, § 2.5.1.

(Ulpian) existed before the latter entered a gratuitous juridical act benefiting the person (Gaius). When required to "return" the totality or part of the "gift" he received, the person (Gaius) is not suffering any monetary or economic prejudice. Gaius' patrimony could not be "unjustly" enriched at the expense of Paulus.[17]

§ 11.1.5. EXCEPTIONS.

As stated above, an obligee could not bring a revocatory action whenever he would interfere with his obligor's strictly personal rights vis-à-vis a third person.[18]

Art. 2040 adds explicitly the following exception: **"An obligee may not annul a contract made by the obligor in the regular course of his business."**

§ 11.1.6. ADDITIONAL REQUIREMENTS AND EFFECTS OF A REVOCATORY ACTION.

Besides the fundamental requirements of insolvency of the obligor and of the existence of the right of an obligee to demand performance of his obligation by the obligor, there are two additional requirements that determine the exercise of the pauliana action. One additional requirement is the proper timing of the exercise of his right by the obligee. Under **Art. 2041 "The action of the obligee must be brought within one year from the time he learned of the act, or the result of the failure to act, of the obligor that the obligee seeks to annul, but never after three years from the date of that act or result."** Thus, an obligee is faced with a peremptory period of three years from the time his obligor entered the juridical act with a person, or from the result of the obligor's failure to act, which means that beyond the three years the obligee will no longer have the right to bring a revocatory action. Within these three years, the obligee must bring the revocatory action within one year "from the time he learned or should have learned of the act, or the result of the failure to act." It is obviously difficult to give practical illustrations of such instances when an obligee "learned" and even more when he "should have learned" of the obligor's act or result of his failure to act. Should such a case have to be litigated it is to be expected that the court will have much discretion in its analysis of the facts, the circumstances and the "timing" of the learning. Obligees should be vigilant in the exercise of their rights on their obligors.

This Article raises an additional question. Since the action by the obligee may not be initiated immediately after the act between the obligor and the third person has been entered into, as much as two years may have gone by between that latter time and the time the action is initiated by the obligee. At which point in time must the "insolvency" of the obligor be determined or "his assets be fairly appraised"? At the time the act was entered into or the time the obligee learns of the act and brings his action against both the obligor and the third person? In the case of a sale with "lesion", the appraisal of the value of the property is made

---

[17] See LSA-C.C. Art. 2298 on Enrichment without cause.

[18] See supra Revocatory Action, Conditions for the Existence of a Revocatory Action, § 11.1.1.

as of the time the sale *was* entered and not the time when the seller brings his action in lesion.[19] However, in this instance the contract of sale is between the seller and "his" buyer, so that the seller should be fully informed of the value of the property at the time of "his sale". In a revocatory action, the obligee is not a party to the juridical act between his obligor and the third person and the obligee may not learn of this act until months if not years later. In this instance of the revocatory action, the fair appraisal of the obligor's assets should be made at the time the obligee learns or should have learned of the act.

In addition, and this is a second requirement, the obligee will have to "join" the third person in his attack against the act because the obligor and the third person are, somewhat, like "joint" obligors,[20] each one being held for a different amount. In addition, **"In an action to annul either his obligor's act, or the result of his obligor's failure to act, the obligee must join the obligor and the third persons involved in that act of failure to act."** Art. 2042(1). As such, the third person will be allowed to raise the defense of the benefit of discussion[21] as stated in Art. 2042(2) **"A third person joined in the action may plead discussion of the obligor's assets."**

As regards an important additional effect of a revocatory action, it is stated in **Art. 2043: "If an obligee establishes his right to annul his obligor's act, or the result of his obligor's failure to act, that act or result shall be annulled only to the extent that it affects the obligee's right."** In other words, the benefit of the revocatory action is personal to the obligee who brings that action. Whatever assets that obligee can retrieve from the obligor and the third person, these assets will be "his", they will not fall in the patrimony of the obligor where some other obligees of his could lay claim to them. The benefit of the revocatory action against an obligor is not to be shared by the obligee-plaintiff with any other spectator-obligee. Therein lies the fundamental difference between the revocatory action and the oblique action.

ARTICLE 2
THE OBLIQUE ACTION

A single Article, **Art. 2044**, provides an obligee with an additional remedy against his obligor in the event the **"obligor causes or increases his insolvency by failing to exercise a right. . . ."** In that case **"the obligee may exercise it himself, unless the right is strictly personal to the obligor. For that purpose, the obligee must join in the suit his obligor and the third person against whom that right is asserted."** This right of action of the obligee is known as the "oblique action".

The legal meaning of the adjective "oblique" in the name of this action is easy to explain. We have seen that the revocatory or pauliana action is an action that belongs to the obligee as an "obligee" and, therefore, it is an action that the

---

[19] On Lesion in a contract of sale, see Précis, Louisiana Law of Sale and Lease § 2.5.1. p. 32 et seq.

[20] On Joint Obligations see Précis, Louisiana Law of Obligations in General § 3.2.1. p. 56 et seq.

[21] "Discussion is the right of a secondary obligor to compel the creditor to enforce the obligation against the property of the primary obligor or . . . against other property affected . . . before enforcing it against the property of the secondary obligor. . . ." LSA-C.C.P. Art. 5151.

obligee brings for his own personal benefit. Whatever the obligee recovers from the obligor and the latter's co-contractor, he does recover for "himself". The opposite occurs in an oblique action because the obligee takes in his hands a right of action which belongs to his "obligor" and, therefore, the obligee is actually bringing that action as if the obligor himself were the plaintiff. In other words, the obligee cannot reach "directly", as is the case in a revocatory action, a third person co-contractor of "the" obligor who is herself indebted to "that" obligor unless the obligee goes "through" (obliquely) his obligor's patrimony to find in it a right of action that the obligor holds against the third person but that, for some reason, the obligor "fails to exercise". By failing to exercise his right against the third person as his own debtor co-contractor, the obligor may cause or increase his insolvency to the detriment of his obligees. Since this right of the obligor against his own debtor may have a monetary or patrimonial value, the obligor should not be allowed to deprive his obligees of their own right to be paid out of that obligor's patrimony. If the obligor remains indifferent to the rights of his obligees, the benefit of an oblique action in the hands of the obligees will give its full meaning and purpose to **Art. 3182** according to which "**Whoever has bound himself personally, is obliged to fulfill his engagements out of all his property, movable and immovable, present and future.**" Since the "property" of the obligor "**is the common pledge of his creditors**" (Art. 3182), the latter can include in that "property" the obligor's rights which have a monetary value.

The wording of the first part of the first sentence of **Art. 2044, "If an obligor causes or increases his insolvency by failing to exercise a right . . .",** seems to intend to restrict the oblique action to the "failing to exercise a right". Yet, one may ask: what difference is there between **"the result of a failure to act"** in **Art. 2036** on the revocatory action, and the **"failing to exercise a right"** for an oblique action? Is there not a "result" following necessarily a "failure to exercise a right"? The distinction, if ever one was intended, is only in the words chosen and not in the result of "a failure to act" or the "failing to exercise a right". The only consideration that matters or should matter to obligees in both actions is whether or not the obligor causes or increases his insolvency to their detriment.

Once an obligee can ascertain that his obligor has caused or increased his insolvency, that obligee will have to select that right or those rights of his obligor that the latter "fails to exercise". Not every right of an obligor can be exercised by his obligee because the obligor is still in charge of his patrimony and no "stranger" should be allowed, without limitations, to interfere with the obligor's management of his patrimony. These limitations find their justification in the fact that the obligee intends to "substitute" himself to his "negligent or indifferent" obligor in the exercise of a right that belongs to the obligor. Thus, rights which are "personal" to the obligor cannot fall in the hands of the obligee.[22] In addition, those rights of the obligor that he himself could not exercise, cannot either fall into the hands of an obligee who is only a "substituted" party plaintiff against the third person co-contractor of the obligor. For example, if the obligor's right of action against his own debtor-third person is subject to a suspensive term or a suspensive condition, the obligor himself cannot bring an action until the

---

[22] Art. 2044: ". . . the obligee may exercise it himself, unless the right is strictly personal to the obligor." See supra Revocatory Action and Personal Rights of an Obligor, Article 1.

expiration of the suspensive term or the occurrence of the suspensive condition. In these instances, the obligor does not "fail to exercise a right"; his own contractual relationship with another suspends his own right of action against another. Furthermore, the third person sued by an obligee of his own obligee through an oblique action can oppose to the suing obligee all the exceptions and defenses he could raise against his own obligee, although obligor of the suing obligee.[23]

As to the outcome of the oblique action, it is the opposite of the outcome of the revocatory action. Should an obligee be successful in bringing an oblique action, the benefit of the action will be shared by *all* the obligees. The reason is that the suing obligee was exercising a right vested in the obligor himself, as if that obligor was exercising his own right. It is perfectly logical, therefore, for the benefit of the oblique action to be shared by all. Since all the obligees-creditors may not be "equal" in ranking, it could happen that the suing creditor may have acted, entirely or in part, for the benefit of privileged creditors or secured creditors so that, in the long run, the obligee-plaintiff, despite stepping forward and taking the initiative, may be left with nothing or very little to receive out of the obligor's patrimony.

There can be no prescription proper to an oblique action since the prescriptive period to be taken into account is that of the "right" that the obligor "failed to exercise". If the prescriptive period of the action, the principal action, that the obligor had on account of a right he held against a co-contractor has expired, no oblique action can be available as it itself expired with the principal action.

---

[23] Such defenses could be the nullity of the contract with his own obligee, or compensation between himself and his own obligee, or prescription of the action.

APPENDIX I

Louisiana Civil Code 2010
Title 4 Conventional Obligations or Contracts
(Acts 1984, No. 331, § 1, eff. Jan. 1, 1985)

Art. 1906
A contract is an agreement by two or more parties whereby obligations are created, modified, or extinguished.

Art. 1907
A contract is unilateral when the party who accepts the obligation of the other does not assume a reciprocal obligation.

Art. 1908
A contract is bilateral, or synallagmatic, when the parties obligate themselves reciprocally, so that the obligation of each party is correlative to the obligation of the other.

Art. 1909
A contract is onerous when each of the parties obtains an advantage in exchange for his obligation.

Art. 1910
A contract is gratuitous when one party obligates himself towards another for the benefit of the latter, without obtaining any advantage in return.

Art. 1911
A contract is commutative when the performance of the obligation of each party is correlative to the performance of the other.

Art. 1912
A contract is aleatory when, because of its nature or according to the parties' intent, the performance of either party's obligation, or the extent of the performance, depends on an uncertain event.

Art. 1913
A contract is accessory when it is made to provide security for the performance of an obligation. Suretyship, mortgage, pledge, and other types of security agreements are examples of such a contract.

When the secured obligation arises from a contract, either between the same or other parties, that contract is the principal contract.

Art. 1914
Nominate contracts are those given a special designation such as sale, lease, loan, or insurance.

Innominate contracts are those with no special designation.

Art. 1915
All contracts, nominate and innominate, are subject to the rules of this title.

Art. 1916

Nominate contracts are subject to the special rules of the respective titles when those rules modify, complement, or depart from the rules of this title.

Art. 1917

The rules of this title are applicable also to obligations that arise from sources other than contract to the extent that those rules are compatible with the nature of those obligations.

Art. 1918

All persons have capacity to contract, except unemancipated minors, interdicts, and persons deprived of reason at the time of contracting.

Art. 1919

A contract made by a person without legal capacity is relatively null and may be rescinded only at the request of that person or his legal representative.

Art. 1920

Immediately after discovering the incapacity, a party, who at the time of contracting was ignorant of the incapacity of the other party, may require from that party, if the incapacity has ceased, or from the legal representative if it has not, that the contract be confirmed or rescinded.

Art. 1921

Upon rescission of a contract on the ground of incapacity, each party or his legal representative shall restore to the other what he has received thereunder. When restoration is impossible or impracticable, the court may award compensation to the party to whom restoration cannot be made.

Art. 1922

A fully emancipated minor has full contractual capacity.

Art. 1923

A contract by an unemancipated minor may be rescinded on grounds of incapacity except when made for the purpose of providing the minor with something necessary for his support or education, or for a purpose related to his business.

Art. 1924

The mere representation of majority by an unemancipated minor does not preclude an action for rescission of the contract. When the other party reasonably relies on the minor's representation of majority, the contract may not be rescinded.

Art. 1925

A noninterdicted person, who was deprived of reason at the time of contracting, may obtain rescission of an onerous contract upon the ground of incapacity only upon showing that the other party knew or should have known that person's incapacity.

Art. 1926

A contract made by a noninterdicted person deprived of reason at the time of contracting may be attacked after his death, on the ground of incapacity, only when the contract is gratuitous, or it evidences lack of understanding, or was made within thirty days of his death, or when application for interdiction was filed before his death.

Art. 1927

A contract is formed by the consent of the parties established through offer and acceptance.

Unless the law prescribes a certain formality for the intended contract, offer and acceptance may be made orally, in writing, or by action or inaction that under the circumstances is clearly indicative of consent.

Unless otherwise specified in the offer, there need not be conformity between the manner in which the offer is made and the manner in which the acceptance is made.

Art. 1928

An offer that specifies a period of time for acceptance is irrevocable during that time.

When the offeror manifests an intent to give the offeree a delay within which to accept, without specifying a time, the offer is irrevocable for a reasonable time.

Art. 1929

An irrevocable offer expires if not accepted within the time prescribed in the preceding Article.

Art. 1930

An offer not irrevocable under Civil Code Article 1928 may be revoked before it is accepted.

Art. 1931

A revocable offer expires if not accepted within a reasonable time.

Art. 1932

An offer expires by the death or incapacity of the offeror or the offeree before it has been accepted.

Art. 1933

An option is a contract whereby the parties agree that the offeror is bound by his offer for a specified period of time and that the offeree may accept within that time.

Art. 1934

An acceptance of an irrevocable offer is effective when received by the offeror.

Art. 1935

Unless otherwise specified by the offer or the law, an acceptance of a revocable offer, made in a manner and by a medium suggested by the offer or in a reasonable manner and by a reasonable medium, is effective when transmitted by the offeree.

Art. 1936

A medium or a manner of acceptance is reasonable if it is the one used in making the offer or one customary in similar transactions at the time and place the offer is received, unless circumstances known to the offeree indicate otherwise.

Art. 1937

A revocation of a revocable offer is effective when received by the offeree prior to acceptance.

Art. 1938

A written revocation, rejection, or acceptance is received when it comes into the possession of the addressee or of a person authorized by him to receive it, or when it is deposited in a place the addressee has indicated as the place for this or similar communications to be deposited for him.

Art. 1939

When an offeror invites an offeree to accept by performance and, according to usage or the nature or the terms of the contract, it is contemplated that the performance will be completed if commenced, a contract is formed when the offeree begins the requested performance.

Art. 1940

When, according to usage or the nature of the contract, or its own terms, an offer made to a particular offeree can be accepted only by rendering a completed performance, the offeror cannot revoke the offer, once the offeree has begun to perform, for the reasonable time necessary to complete the performance. The offeree, however, is not bound to complete the performance he has begun.

The offeror's duty of performance is conditional on completion or tender of the requested performance.

Art. 1941

When commencement of the performance either constitutes acceptance or makes the offer irrevocable, the offeree must give prompt notice of that commencement unless the offeror knows or should know that the offeree has begun to perform. An offeree who fails to give the notice is liable for damages.

Art. 1942

When, because of special circumstances, the offeree's silence leads the offeror reasonably to believe that a contract has been formed, the offer is deemed accepted.

Art. 1943

An acceptance not in accordance with the terms of the offer is deemed to be a counteroffer.

Art. 1944

An offer of a reward made to the public is binding upon the offeror even if the one who performs the requested act does not know of the offer.

Art. 1945

An offer of reward made to the public may be revoked before completion of the requested act, provided the revocation is made by the same or an equally effective means as the offer.

Art. 1946

Unless otherwise stipulated in the offer made to the public, or otherwise implied from the nature of the act, when several persons have performed the requested act, the reward belongs to the first one giving notice of his completion of performance to the offeror.

Art. 1947

When, in the absence of a legal requirement, the parties have contemplated a certain form, it is presumed that they do not intend to be bound until the contract is executed in that form.

Art. 1948

Consent may be vitiated by error, fraud, or duress.

Art. 1949

Error vitiates consent only when it concerns a cause without which the obligation would not have been incurred and that cause was known or should have been known to the other party.

Art. 1950

Error may concern a cause when it bears on the nature of the contract, or the thing that is the contractual object or a substantial quality of that thing, or the person or the qualities of the other party, or the law, or any other circumstance that the parties regarded, or should in good faith have regarded, as a cause of the obligation.

Art. 1951

A party may not avail himself of his error if the other party is willing to perform the contract as intended by the party in error.

Art. 1952

A party who obtains rescission on grounds of his own error is liable for the loss thereby sustained by the other party unless the latter knew or should have known of the error.

The court may refuse rescission when the effective protection of the other party's interest requires that the contract be upheld. In that case, a reasonable compensation for the loss he has sustained may be granted to the party to whom rescission is refused.

Art. 1953

Fraud is a misrepresentation or a suppression of the truth made with the intention either to obtain an unjust advantage for one party or to cause a loss or inconvenience to the other. Fraud may also result from silence or inaction.

Art. 1954

Fraud does not vitiate consent when the party against whom the fraud was directed could have ascertained the truth without difficulty, inconvenience, or special skill.

This exception does not apply when a relation of confidence has reasonably induced a party to rely on the other's assertions or representations.

Art. 1955

Error induced by fraud need not concern the cause of the obligation to vitiate consent, but it must concern a circumstance that has substantially influenced that consent.

Art. 1956

Fraud committed by a third person vitiates the consent of a contracting party if the other party knew or should have known of the fraud.

Art. 1957

Fraud need only be proved by a preponderance of the evidence and may be established by circumstantial evidence.

Art. 1958

The party against whom rescission is granted because of fraud is liable for damages and attorney fees.

Art. 1959

Consent is vitiated when it has been obtained by duress of such a nature as to cause a reasonable fear of unjust and considerable injury to a party's person, property, or reputation.

Age, health, disposition, and other personal circumstances of a party must be taken into account in determining reasonableness of the fear.

Art. 1960

Duress vitiates consent also when the threatened injury is directed against the spouse, an ascendant, or descendant of the contracting party.

If the threatened injury is directed against other persons, the granting of relief is left to the discretion of the court.

Art. 1961

Consent is vitiated even when duress has been exerted by a third person.

Art. 1962

A threat of doing a lawful act or a threat of exercising a right does not constitute duress.

A threat of doing an act that is lawful in appearance only may constitute duress.

Art. 1963

A contract made with a third person to secure the means of preventing threatened injury may not be rescinded for duress if that person is in good faith and not in collusion with the party exerting duress.

Art. 1964

When rescission is granted because of duress exerted or known by a party to the contract, the other party may recover damages and attorney fees.

When rescission is granted because of duress exerted by a third person, the parties to the contract who are innocent of the duress may recover damages and attorney fees from the third person.

Art. 1965

A contract may be annulled on grounds of lesion only in those cases provided by law.

Art. 1966

An obligation cannot exist without a lawful cause.

Art. 1967

Cause is the reason why a party obligates himself.

A party may be obligated by a promise when he knew or should have known that the promise would induce the other party to rely on it to his detriment and the other party was reasonable in so relying. Recovery may be limited to the expenses incurred or the damages suffered as a result of the promisee's reliance on the promise. Reliance on a gratuitous promise made without required formalities is not reasonable.

Art. 1968

The cause of an obligation is unlawful when the enforcement of the obligation would produce a result prohibited by law or against public policy.

Art. 1969

An obligation may be valid even though its cause is not expressed.

Art. 1970

When the expression of a cause in a contractual obligation is untrue, the obligation is still effective if a valid cause can be shown.

Art. 1971

Parties are free to contract for any object that is lawful, possible, and determined or determinable.

Art. 1972

A contractual object is possible or impossible according to its own nature and not according to the parties' ability to perform.

Art. 1973

The object of a contract must be determined at least as to its kind.

The quantity of a contractual object may be undetermined, provided it is determinable.

Art. 1974

If the determination of the quantity of the object has been left to the discretion of a third person, the quantity of an object is determinable.

If the parties fail to name a person, or if the person named is unable or unwilling to make the determination, the quantity may be determined by the court.

Art. 1975

The quantity of a contractual object may be determined by the output of one party or the requirements of the other.

In such a case, output or requirements must be measured in good faith.

Art. 1976

Future things may be the object of a contract.

The succession of a living person may not be the object of a contract other than an antenuptial agreement. Such a succession may not be renounced.

Art. 1977

The object of a contract may be that a third person will incur an obligation or render a performance.

The party who promised that obligation or performance is liable for damages if the third person does not bind himself or does not perform.

Art. 1978

A contracting party may stipulate a benefit for a third person called a third party beneficiary.

Once the third party has manifested his intention to avail himself of the benefit, the parties may not dissolve the contract by mutual consent without the beneficiary's agreement.

Art. 1979

The stipulation may be revoked only by the stipulator and only before the third party has manifested his intention of availing himself of the benefit.

If the promisor has an interest in performing, however, the stipulation may not be revoked without his consent.

Art. 1980

In case of revocation or refusal of the stipulation, the promisor shall render performance to the stipulator.

Art. 1981

The stipulation gives the third party beneficiary the right to demand performance from the promisor.

Also the stipulator, for the benefit of the third party, may demand performance from the promisor.

Art. 1982

The promisor may raise against the beneficiary such defenses based on the contract as he may have raised against the stipulator.

Art. 1983

Contracts have the effect of law for the parties and may be dissolved only through the consent of the parties or on grounds provided by law. Contracts must be performed in good faith.

Art. 1984

Rights and obligations arising from a contract are heritable and assignable unless the law, the terms of the contract or its nature preclude such effects.

Art. 1985

Contracts may produce effects for third parties only when provided by law.

Art. 1986

Upon an obligor's failure to perform an obligation to deliver a thing, or not to do an act, or to execute an instrument, the court shall grant specific performance plus damages for delay if the obligee so demands. If specific performance is impracticable, the court may allow damages to the obligee.

Upon a failure to perform an obligation that has another object, such as an obligation to do, the granting of specific performance is at the discretion of the court.

Art. 1987

The obligor may be restrained from doing anything in violation of an obligation not to do.

Art. 1988

A failure to perform an obligation to execute an instrument gives the obligee the right to a judgment that shall stand for the act.

Art. 1989

Damages for delay in the performance of an obligation are owed from the time the obligor is put in default.

Other damages are owed from the time the obligor has failed to perform.

Art. 1990

When a term for the performance of an obligation is either fixed, or is clearly determinable by the circumstances, the obligor is put in default by the mere arrival of that term. In other cases, the obligor must be put in default by the obligee, but not before performance is due.

Art. 1991

An obligee may put the obligor in default by a written request of performance, or by an oral request of performance made before two witnesses, or by filing suit for performance, or by a specific provision of the contract.

Art. 1992

If an obligee bears the risk of the thing that is the object of the performance, the risk devolves upon the obligor who has been put in default for failure to deliver that thing.

Art. 1993

In case of reciprocal obligations, the obligor of one may not be put in default unless the obligor of the other has performed or is ready to perform his own obligation.

Art. 1994

An obligor is liable for the damages caused by his failure to perform a conventional obligation.

A failure to perform results from nonperformance, defective performance, or delay in performance.

Art. 1995

Damages are measured by the loss sustained by the obligee and the profit of which he has been deprived.

Art. 1996

An obligor in good faith is liable only for the damages that were foreseeable at the time the contract was made.

Art. 1997

An obligor in bad faith is liable for all the damages, foreseeable or not, that are a direct consequence of his failure to perform.

Art. 1998

Damages for nonpecuniary loss may be recovered when the contract, because of its nature, is intended to gratify a nonpecuniary interest and, because of the circumstances surrounding the formation or the nonperformance of the contract, the obligor knew, or should have known, that his failure to perform would cause that kind of loss.

Regardless of the nature of the contract, these damages may be recovered also when the obligor intended, through his failure, to aggrieve the feelings of the obligee.

Art. 1999

When damages are insusceptible of precise measurement, much discretion shall be left to the court for the reasonable assessment of these damages.

Art. 2000

When the object of the performance is a sum of money, damages for delay in performance are measured by the interest on that sum from the time it is due, at the rate agreed by the parties or, in the absence of agreement, at the rate of legal interest as fixed by R.S. 9:3500. The obligee may recover these damages without having to prove any loss, and whatever loss he may have suffered he can recover no more. If the parties, by written contract, have expressly agreed that the obligor shall also be liable for the obligee's attorney fees in a fixed or determinable amount, the obligee is entitled to that amount as well.

Art. 2001

Interest on accrued interest may be recovered as damages only when it is added to the principal by a new agreement of the parties made after the interest has accrued.

Art. 2002

An obligee must make reasonable efforts to mitigate the damage caused by the obligor's failure to perform. When an obligee fails to make these efforts, the obligor may demand that the damages be accordingly reduced.

Art. 2003

An obligee may not recover damages when his own bad faith has caused the obligor's failure to perform or when, at the time of the contract, he has concealed from the obligor facts that he knew or should have known would cause a failure.

If the obligee's negligence contributes to the obligor's failure to perform, the damages are reduced in proportion to that negligence.

Art. 2004

Any clause is null that, in advance, excludes or limits the liability of one party for intentional or gross fault that causes damage to the other party.

Any clause is null that, in advance, excludes or limits the liability of one party for causing physical injury to the other party.

Art. 2005

Parties may stipulate the damages to be recovered in case of nonperformance, defective performance, or delay in performance of an obligation.

That stipulation gives rise to a secondary obligation for the purpose of enforcing the principal one.

Art. 2006

Nullity of the principal obligation renders the stipulated damages clause null.

Nullity of the stipulated damages clause does not render the principal obligation null.

Art. 2007

An obligee may demand either the stipulated damages or performance of the principal obligation, but he may not demand both unless the damages have been stipulated for mere delay.

Art. 2008

An obligor whose failure to perform the principal obligation is justified by a valid excuse is also relieved of liability for stipulated damages.

Art. 2009

An obligee who avails himself of a stipulated damages clause need not prove the actual damage caused by the obligor's nonperformance, defective performance, or delay in performance.

Art. 2010

An obligee may not avail himself of a clause stipulating damages for delay unless the obligor has been put in default.

Art. 2011

Stipulated damages for nonperformance may be reduced in proportion to the benefit derived by the obligee from any partial performance rendered by the obligor.

Art. 2012

Stipulated damages may not be modified by the court unless they are so manifestly unreasonable as to be contrary to public policy.

Art. 2013

When the obligor fails to perform, the obligee has a right to the judicial dissolution of the contract or, according to the circumstances, to regard the contract as dissolved. In either case, the obligee may recover damages.

In an action involving judicial dissolution, the obligor who failed to perform may be granted, according to the circumstances, an additional time to perform.

Art. 2014

A contract may not be dissolved when the obligor has rendered a substantial part of the performance and the part not rendered does not substantially impair the interest of the obligee.

Art. 2015

Upon a party's failure to perform, the other may serve him a notice to perform within a certain time, with a warning that, unless performance is rendered within that time, the contract shall be deemed dissolved. The time allowed for that purpose must be reasonable according to the circumstances.

The notice to perform is subject to the requirements governing a putting of the obligor in default and, for the recovery of damages for delay, shall have the same effect as a putting of the obligor in default.

Art. 2016

When a delayed performance would no longer be of value to the obligee or when it is evident that the obligor will not perform, the obligee may regard the contract as dissolved without any notice to the obligor.

Art. 2017

The parties may expressly agree that the contract shall be dissolved for the failure to perform a particular obligation. In that case, the contract is deemed dissolved at the time it provides for or, in the absence of such a provision, at the time the obligee gives notice to the obligor that he avails himself of the dissolution clause.

Art. 2018

Upon dissolution of a contract, the parties shall be restored to the situation that existed before the contract was made. If restoration in kind is impossible or impracticable, the court may award damages.

If partial performance has been rendered and that performance is of value to the party seeking to dissolve the contract, the dissolution does not preclude recovery for that performance, whether in contract or quasi-contract.

Art. 2019

In contracts providing for continuous or periodic performance, the effect of the dissolution shall not be extended to any performance already rendered.

Art. 2020

When a contract has been made by more than two parties, one party's failure to perform may not cause dissolution of the contract for the other parties, unless the performance that failed was essential to the contract.

Art. 2021

Dissolution of a contract does not impair the rights acquired through an onerous contract by a third party in good faith.

If the contract involves immovable property, the principles of recordation apply to a third person acquiring an interest in the property whether by onerous or gratuitous title.

Art. 2022

Either party to a commutative contract may refuse to perform his obligation if the other has failed to perform or does not offer to perform his own at the same time, if the performances are due simultaneously.

Art. 2023

If the situation of a party, financial or otherwise, has become such as to clearly endanger his ability to perform an obligation, the other party may demand in writing that adequate security be given and, upon failure to give that security, that party may withhold or discontinue his own performance.

Art. 2024

A contract of unspecified duration may be terminated at the will of either party by giving notice, reasonable in time and form, to the other party.

Art. 2025

A contract is a simulation when, by mutual agreement, it does not express the true intent of the parties.

If the true intent of the parties is expressed in a separate writing, that writing is a counterletter.

Art. 2026

A simulation is absolute when the parties intend that their contract shall produce no effects between them. That simulation, therefore, can have no effects between the parties.

Art. 2027

A simulation is relative when the parties intend that their contract shall produce effects between them though different from those recited in their contract. A relative simulation produces between the parties the effects they intended if all requirements for those effects have been met.

Art. 2028

Any simulation, either absolute or relative, may have effects as to third persons.

Counterletters can have no effects against third persons in good faith.

Art. 2029

A contract is null when the requirements for its formation have not been met.

Art. 2030

A contract is absolutely null when it violates a rule of public order, as when the object of a contract is illicit or immoral. A contract that is absolutely null may not be confirmed. Absolute nullity may be invoked by any person or may be declared by the court on its own initiative.

Art. 2031

A contract is relatively null when it violates a rule intended for the protection of private parties, as when a party lacked capacity or did not give free consent at the time the contract was made. A contract that is only relatively null may be confirmed.

Relative nullity may be invoked only by those persons for whose interest the ground for nullity was established, and may not be declared by the court on its own initiative.

Art. 2032

Action for annulment of an absolutely null contract does not prescribe.

Action of annulment of a relatively null contract must be brought within five years from the time the ground for nullity either ceased, as in the case of incapacity or duress, or was discovered, as in the case of error or fraud.

Nullity may be raised at any time as a defense against an action on the contract, even after the action for annulment has prescribed.

Art. 2033

An absolutely null contract, or a relatively null contract that has been declared null by the court, is deemed never to have existed. The parties must be restored to the situation that existed before the contract was made. If it is impossible or impracticable to make restoration in kind, it may be made through an award of damages.

Nevertheless, a performance rendered under a contract that is absolutely null because its object or its cause is illicit or immoral may not be recovered by a party who knew or should have known of the defect that makes the contract null. The performance may be recovered, however, when that party invokes the nullity to withdraw from the contract before its purpose is achieved and also in exceptional situations when, in the discretion of the court, that recovery would further the interest of justice.

Absolute nullity may be raised as a defense even by a party who, at the time the contract was made, knew or should have known of the defect that makes the contract null.

Art. 2034

Nullity of a provision does not render the whole contract null unless, from the nature of the provision or the intention of the parties, it can be presumed that the contract would not have been made without the null provision.

Art. 2035

Nullity of a contract does not impair the rights acquired through an onerous contract by a third party in good faith.

If the contract involves immovable property, the principles of recordation apply to a third person acquiring an interest in the property whether by onerous or gratuitous title.

Art. 2036

An obligee has a right to annul an act of the obligor, or the result of a failure to act of the obligor, made or effected after the right of the obligee arose, that causes or increases the obligor's insolvency.

Art. 2037

An obligor is insolvent when the total of his liabilities exceeds the total of his fairly appraised assets.

Art. 2038

An obligee may annul an onerous contract made by the obligor with a person who knew or should have known that the contract would cause or increase the obligor's insolvency. In that case, the person is entitled to recover what he gave in return only to the extent that it has inured to the benefit of the obligor's creditors.

An obligee may annul an onerous contract made by the obligor with a person who did not know that the contract would cause or increase the obligor's insolvency, but in that case that person is entitled to recover as much as he gave to the obligor. That lack of knowledge is presumed when that person has given at least four-fifths of the value of the thing obtained in return from the obligor.

Art. 2039

An obligee may attack a gratuitous contract made by the obligor whether or not the other party knew that the contract would cause or increase the obligor's insolvency.

Art. 2040

An obligee may not annul a contract made by the obligor in the regular course of his business.

Art. 2041

The action of the obligee must be brought within one year from the time he learned or should have learned of the act, or the result of the failure to act, of the obligor that the obligee seeks to annul, but never after three years from the date of that act or result.

Art. 2042

In an action to annul either his obligor's act, or the result of his obligor's failure to act, the obligee must join the obligor and the third persons involved in that act or failure to act.

A third person joined in the action may plead discussion of the obligor's assets.

Art. 2043

If an obligee establishes his right to annul his obligor's act, or the result of his obligor's failure to act, that act or result shall be annulled only to the extent that it affects the obligee's right.

Art. 2044

If an obligor causes or increases his insolvency by failing to exercise a right, the obligee may exercise it himself, unless the right is strictly personal to the obligor.

For that purpose, the obligee must join in the suit his obligor and the third person against whom that right is asserted.

Art. 2045

Interpretation of a contract is the determination of the common intent of the parties.

Art. 2046

When the words of a contract are clear and explicit and lead to no absurd consequences, no further interpretation may be made in search of the parties' intent.

Art. 2047

The words of a contract must be given their generally prevailing meaning. Words of art and technical terms must be given their technical meaning when the contract involves a technical matter.

Art. 2048

Words susceptible of different meanings must be interpreted as having the meaning that best conforms to the object of the contract.

Art. 2049

A provision susceptible of different meanings must be interpreted with a meaning that renders it effective and not with one that renders it ineffective.

Art. 2050

Each provision in a contract must be interpreted in light of the other provisions so that each is given the meaning suggested by the contract as a whole.

Art. 2051

Although a contract is worded in general terms, it must be interpreted to cover only those things it appears the parties intended to include.

Art. 2052

When the parties intend a contract of general scope but, to eliminate doubt, include a provision that describes a specific situation, interpretation must not restrict the scope of the contract to that situation alone.

Art. 2053

A doubtful provision must be interpreted in light of the nature of the contract, equity, usages, the conduct of the parties before and after the formation of the contract, and of other contracts of a like nature between the same parties.

Art. 2054

When the parties made no provision for a particular situation, it must be assumed that they intended to bind themselves not only to the express provisions of the contract, but also to whatever the law, equity, or usage regards as implied in a contract of that kind or necessary for the contract to achieve its purpose.

Art. 2055

Equity, as intended in the preceding articles, is based on the principles that no one is allowed to take unfair advantage of another and that no one is allowed to enrich himself unjustly at the expense of another.

Usage, as intended in the preceding articles, is a practice regularly observed in affairs of a nature identical or similar to the object of a contract subject to interpretation.

Art. 2056

In case of doubt that cannot be otherwise resolved, a provision in a contract must be interpreted against the party who furnished its text.

A contract executed in a standard form of one party must be interpreted, in case of doubt, in favor of the other party.

Art. 2057

In case of doubt that cannot be otherwise resolved, a contract must be interpreted against the obligee and in favor of the obligor of a particular obligation.

Yet, if the doubt arises from lack of a necessary explanation that one party should have given, or from negligence or fault of one party, the contract must be interpreted in a manner favorable to the other party whether obligee or obligor.

APPENDIX II

Louisiana Code of Civil Procedure 2010

C.C.P. Art. 1005

The answer shall set forth affirmatively negligence, or fault of the plaintiff and others, duress, error or mistake, estoppel, extinguishment of the obligation in any manner, failure of consideration, fraud, illegality, injury by fellow servant, and any other matter constituting an affirmative defense. If a party has mistakenly designated an affirmative defense as a peremptory exception or as an incidental demand, or a peremptory exception as an affirmative defense, and if justice so requires, the court, on such terms as it may prescribe, shall treat the pleading as if there had been a proper designation.

C.C.P. Art. 2291

A judgment for the payment of money may be executed by a writ of fieri facias directing the seizure and sale of property of the judgment debtor.

C.C.P. Art. 2501

A party in whose favor a judgment of possession has been rendered may obtain from the clerk a writ of possession directing the sheriff to seize and deliver the property to him if it is movable property, or to compel the party in possession to vacate the property by use of force, if necessary, if it is immovable.

C.C.P. Art. 2631

Executory proceedings are those which are used to effect the seizure and sale of property, without previous citation and judgment, to enforce a mortgage or privilege thereon evidenced by an authentic act importing a confession of judgment, and in other cases allowed by law.

C.C.P. Art. 2638

If the plaintiff is entitled thereto, the court shall order the issuance of a writ of seizure and sale commanding the sheriff to seize and sell the property affected by the mortgage or privilege, as prayed for and according to law.

C.C.P. Art. 2723

Prior to the sale, the property seized must be appraised in accordance with law, unless appraisal has been waived in the act evidencing the mortgage, the security agreement, or the document creating the privilege and plaintiff has prayed that the property be sold without appraisal, and the order directing the issuance of the writ of seizure and sale has directed that the property be sold as prayed for. There is no requirement that seized property subject to a security interest under Chapter 9 of the Louisiana Commercial Laws (R.S. 10:9-101, et seq.), be appraised prior to the judicial sale thereof.

C.C.P. Art. 3501

A writ of attachment or of sequestration shall issue only when the nature of the claim and the amount thereof, if any, and the grounds relied upon for the issuance of the writ clearly appear from specific facts shown by the petition verified by, or by the separate affidavit of, the petitioner, his counsel or agent.

The applicant shall furnish security as required by law for the payment of the damages the defendant may sustain when the writ is obtained wrongfully.

C.C.P. Art. 3601

A. An injunction shall be issued in cases where irreparable injury, loss, or damage may otherwise result to the applicant, or in other cases specifically provided by law; provided, however, that no court shall have jurisdiction to issue, or cause to be issued, any temporary restraining order, preliminary injunction, or permanent injunction against any state department, board, or agency, or any officer, administrator, or head thereof, or any officer of the state of Louisiana in any suit involving the expenditure of public funds under any statute or law of this state to compel the expenditure of state funds when the director of such department, board, or agency or the governor shall certify that the expenditure of such funds would have the effect of creating a deficit in the funds of said agency or be in violation of the requirements placed upon the expenditure of such funds by the legislature.

B. No court shall issue a temporary restraining order in cases where the issuance shall stay or enjoin the enforcement of a child support order when the Department of Social Services is providing services, except for good cause shown by written reasons made a part of the record.

C. During the pendency of an action for an injunction the court may issue a temporary restraining order, a preliminary injunction, or both, except in cases where prohibited, in accordance with the provisions of this Chapter.

D. Except as otherwise provided by law, an application for injunctive relief shall be by petition.

C.C.P. Art. 3603

A. A temporary restraining order shall be granted without notice when:

(1) It clearly appears from specific facts shown by a verified petition or by supporting affidavit that immediate and irreparable injury, loss, or damage will result to the applicant before the adverse party or his attorney can be heard in opposition, and

(2) The applicant's attorney certifies to the court in writing the efforts which have been made to give the notice or the reasons supporting his claim that notice should not be required.

B. The verification or the affidavit may be made by the plaintiff, or by his counsel, or by his agent.

C. No court shall issue a temporary restraining order in cases where the issuance shall stay or enjoin the enforcement of a child support order when the Department of Social Services is providing services, except for good cause shown by written reasons made a part of the record.

C.C.P. Art. 4733

If the lessee or occupant does not comply with the judgment of eviction within twenty-four hours after its rendition, the court shall issue immediately a warrant directed to and commanding its sheriff, constable, or marshal to deliver possession of the premises to the lessor or owner.

C.C.P. Art. 5151

Discussion is the right of a secondary obligor to compel the creditor to enforce the obligation against the property of the primary obligor or, if the obligation is a legal or judicial mortgage, against other property affected thereby, before enforcing it against the property of the secondary obligor.

APPENDIX III

Cases — Illustrations

CHAPTER I — CLASSIFICATION OF CONTRACTS

Orkin Exterminating Company v. Foti	302 So.2d 593 (1974)

CHAPTER II — CAPACITY

Fernandez v. Hebert	61 So.2d 404 (2007)
Fidelity Financial Servs. Inc. v. McCoy	392 So.2d 118 (1980)

CHAPTER III — CONSENT

Ever-Tite Roofing Corp. v. Green	83 So.2d 449 (1955)
Johnson v. Capital City Ford Co., Inc.	85 So.2d 75 (1955)
The National Co., Inc. v. Navarro	149 So.2d 648 (1963)
Wagenvoord Broadcasting Co., Inc. v. Canal Automatic Transmission Service, Inc.	176 So.2d 188 (1965)

CHAPTER IV — INTEGRITY OF CONSENT

Article I — Error

Bischoff v. Brothers of the Sacred Heart	416 So.2d 348 (1982)
Deutschmann v. Standard Fur Co., Inc.	331 So.2d 219 (1976)
Griffin v. Seismic Services, Inc.	259 So.2d 923 (1972)
Wise v. Prescott	151 So.2d 356 (1963)

Article II — Fraud

Boucher, Wilkinson, Gueymard v. Division of Employment Security	169 So.2d 674 (1964)

Article III — Duress [Violence]

Board of Commissioners of the Port of New Orleans v. Turner Marine Bulk, Inc.	629 So.2d 1278 (1993)
In re Succession of Hollis	987 So.2d 387 (2008)
Wilson v. Aetna Casualty & Surety Co.	228 So.2d 229 (1969)

Article IV — Lesion

O'Brien v. LeGette	223 So.2d 165 (1969)

CHAPTER V — CAUSE

Barnett v. Board of Trustees for State Colleges and Universities	809 So.2d 184 (2001)
Davis-Delcambre Motors, Inc. v. Simon (Court of Appeal)	154 So.2d 775 (1963)
Davis-Delcambre Motors, Inc. v. Simon (Supreme Court)	246 La. 105 (1964)
W.T. West v. Loe Pipe Yard, et al.	125 So.2d 469 (1960)
Wooley v. Lucksinger	961 So.2d 1225 (2007)

CHAPTER VI — OBJECT AND MATTER OF CONTRACTS

Cryer v. M&M Manufacturing Co., Inc.	273 So.2d 818 (1972)
TAC Amusement Co. v. Henry	238 So.2d 398 (1970)
The Springs Thunder Agency, Inc. v. Odom Insurance Agency, Inc.	237 So.2d 96 (1970)

CHAPTER VII — THIRD PARTY BENEFICIARY-STIPULATION POUR AUTRUI

Andrepont v. Acadia Drilling Co.	208 So.2d 737 (1968)
Joseph v. Hospital Service District No. 2 for the Parish of St. Mary	39 So.2d 1206 (2006)
McKee v. Southfield School	613 So.2d 659 (1993)

CHAPTER VIII — EFFECTS OF CONVENTIONAL OBLIGATIONS OR CONTRACTS

American Creosote Works v. Boland Machine & Mfg. Co.	35 So.2d 749 (1948)

Article I — General Effects of All Contracts: Effect of Law and Good Faith

Leon v. Dupre	144 So.2d 667 (1962)

Article II — Specific Performance and Putting in Default

Associated Acquisitions, L.L.C. v. Carbone Properties of Audubon, L.L.C.	962 So.2d 1102 (2007)
Fletcher v. Rachou	323 So.2d 163 (1975)
J. Weingarten, Inc. v. Northgate Mall, Inc.	404 So.2d 896 (1981)

Article III — Damages

Bourne v. Rein Chrysler-Plymouth, Inc.	463 So.2d 1356 (1985)
Chaudoir v. Porsche Cars of N. Am.	667 So.2d 569 (1995)
Lombardo v. Deshotel	647 So.2d 1086 (1994)

Meador v. Toyota of Jefferson, Inc.   332 So.2d 433 (1976)

CHAPTER IX — DISSOLUTION AND NULLITY

Mennella v. Kurt E. Schon E.A.I., Ltd.	979 F.2d 357 (1992)
Owen v. Owen (Court of Appeal)	25 So.2d 283 (1976)
Owen v. Owen (Supreme Court)	336 So.2d 792 (1976)
Peacock v. Peacock	674 So.2d 1030 (1996)
Voitier, Sr. v. Antique Art Gallery	524 So.2d 80 (1988)
Wilkerson v. Wilkerson	62 So.2d 1137 (2007)

CHAPTER X — INTERPRETATION OF CONTRACTS

Aguillard v. Auction Management Corp.	908 So.2d 1 (2005)
Giamanco v. Fairbanks (Court of Appeal)	218 So.2d 346 (1969)
Giamanco v. Fairbanks (Supreme Court)	230 So.2d 65 (1969)

CHAPTER XI — SIMULATION, REVOCATORY AND OBLIQUE ACTIONS

London Towne Condominiums Homeowner's Assoc. v. London Towne Co.	939 So.2d 1127 (2006)
National Bank of Bossier City v. Hardcastle	204 So.2d 142 (1967)
Succession of Boning	248 So.2d 385 (1971)
Succession of Elizabeth E. Terral [Simulation]	312 So.2d 296 (1975)

INDEX

A

ACCEPTANCE

    Consent [See infra]

    Medium, 3.1.2.2

    Notice of . . ., 3.1.2

    Performance as . . ., 3.1.2

    Reception, 3.1.2

    Revocation, Chapter 3, Article 2

    Silence, 3.1.2

    Time, 3.1.2

ACT

    [See Précis, Louisiana Law of Obligations in General]

ACTION

    Breach [See Effects of Contracts, infra]

    Nullity [See infra]

    Oblique [See infra]

    Prescription, 9.2.2

    Revocatory (Pauliana) [See infra]

AGREEMENT

    [See Contract, infra]

ALEATORY CONTRACT

    [See Contract, infra]

ALTERNATIVE OBLIGATION

    [See Précis, Louisiana Law of Obligations in General]

B

BILATERAL CONTRACT

    [See Contract, infra]

C

CAPACITY

    Confirmation, 2.2.1

    Emancipated minor, Chapter 2, Article 2

    Interdict, Chapter 2, Article 2

    Minor, 2.2.1

    Noninterdicted person, Chapter 2, Article 2

    Ratification, 2.2.1

    Unemancipated minor Chapter 2, Article 2

CAUSE

    [See Contract, infra]

    Consideration, Chapter 5

    Definition, Chapter 5, Article 1

    Detrimental reliance, 5.1.2

    Error, 5.1.2

    Expressed, 5.1.1, 5.1.2

    Lawful, 5.1.1, 5.1.2C

COMMUTATIVE

    [See Contract, infra]

COMPENSATION

    [See Précis, Louisiana Law of Obligations in General]

CONDITION

    [See Précis, Louisiana Law of Obligations in General]

CONFIRMATION

    [See Capacity, supra]

CONFUSION

    [See Précis, Louisiana Law of Obligations in General]

CONSENT

    [See Contract, infra]

    Acceptance [See supra]

    Conduct, 3.1.2

    Express, 3.1.2

    Form, 3.1.2

Offer [See infra]

Vices of [See Vices, infra]

CONSIDERATION

[See Cause, supra]

COUNTEROFFER

[See Offer, infra]

CONTRACT

Effects of [See EFFECTS]

Accessory, Chapter 1, Article 4

Aleatory, Chapter 1, Article 3

Bilateral, Chapter 1, Article 1

Capacity [See supra]

Cause [See supra]

Commutative, Chapter 1, Article 3

Consent [See supra]

Definition, Chapter 1

Gratuitous, Chapter 1, Article 2

Innominate, Chapter 1, Article 5

Interpretation [See infra]

Matter of Contracts [See infra]

Nominate, Chapter 1, Article 5

Nullity [See infra]

Object [See infra]

Onerous, Chapter 1, Article 2

Option [See Vices of Consent]

Principal, Chapter 1, Article 4

Standard form contracts [See Interpretation, supra]

Synallagmatic, Chapter 1, Article 1

Unilateral, Chapter 1, Article 1

CONVENTIONAL OBLIGATION

[See Contract, supra]

COUNTER-LETTER

[See Simulation, infra]

D

DAMAGES
- [See Duress, infra]
- [See Effects . . . , infra]
- [See Fraud, infra]
- Attorney fees, 8.3.2.B
- Interest, 8.3.2
- Limitation of liability, 8.3.2
- Measure of, 8.3.2.A
- Mitigation, 8.3.2.A
- Moratory, 8.2.2.A
- Non-Pecuniary loss, 8.3.2.B
- Obligor: bad faith, 8.3.2.A
- Obligor: good faith, 8.3.2.A
- Role of court, 8.3.1
- Stipulated damages [see infra]

DEFAULT, PUTTING IN, 9.1.2
- [See Effects of Contracts, infra]
- Manners of . . .
- Risk, 8.2.2.C
- Term, 8.2.2

DELIVERY
- [See Précis, Louisiana Law of Sale and Lease]

DETERMINABLE
- [See Object, infra]

DETRIMENTAL RELIANCE
- [See Cause, supra]

DISSOLUTION
- Continuous/Periodic performance, 9.1.3
- Dissolution clause, 9.1.2
- Effects of, 9.1.3
- Notice to perform, 9.1.2
- Right to, 9.1.2

Security, 9.1.1

Substantial performance, 9.1.1

Third party, 9.1.1

DONATION

[See Contract, gratuitous, supra]

DURESS

[See Vices of Consent, infra]

Against Third person, 4.3.1

By Third person, 4.3.2

Damages, 4.3.3

Nature, Chapter 4, Article 3

E

EFFECTS OF CONTRACTS

Damages [See Damages, supra]

General effects, Chapter 8, Article 1

Good faith performance, 8.1.1

Obligations of successors, 8.1.1

Putting in default, 8.2.2

Rights of successors, 8.1.1

Specific performance, 8.2.1

Stipulated damages [See Stipulated damages, infra]

Term, 8.1.1

Third parties, 8.1.1

ERROR

[See Fraud, infra]

Cause, 4.1.1, 4.1.2

Law, 4.1.3.B

Nature, 4.1.1

Person, 4.1.3.C

Quality, 4.1.2

Rescission, 4.1.4

Thing/Object, 4.1.2, 4.1.3.A

EXTINCTION of Obligations, Chapter 9, Article 1

[See Précis, Louisiana Law of Obligations in General]

F

FAITH, good

[See Damages, supra]

[See Précis on Louisiana Law of Obligations in General]

FORM

Formality, Chapter 1, Article 2; 1.6.1

FRAUD

Contract [See supra]

Damages [See supra]

Error induced, 4.2.2.B

Fraud by third person, 4.2.2.B

Proof, 4.2.3

Vices of consent [See Vices of Consent, infra]

G

GIVING IN PAYMENT

H

HOPE

[See Object, infra]

I

IMPOSSIBILITY OF PERFORMANCE

[See Précis on Louisiana Law of Obligations in General]

INNOMINATE CONTRACT

[See Contract, supra]

INCAPACITY

[See Capacity, supra]

INTERPRETATION

Absence of provision, 10.2.2

Equity, 10.2.1

General terms, 10.1

In favor of obligor, 10.2.1

Intent, 10.2.1

Meanings of words, 10.1

Nature of contract, 10.2.1

Standard form contracts, 10.1

Usage, 10.2.1

L

LESION

[See Vices of Consent, infra]

[See Précis on Louisiana Law of Sale and Lease]

M

MINOR

[See Capacity, supra]

MITIGATION

[See Damages, supra]

MORAL DAMAGES

[See Non-Pecuniary loss, Damages, supra]

MORATORY DAMAGES

[See Damages, supra]

MATTER [OF CONTRACT]

[See Object, infra]

N

NOVATION

[See Précis on Louisiana Law of Obligations in General]

NULLITY

Absolute, Chapter 9, Article 2

Action, 9.2.2

Defense, 9.2.2

Effects, 9.2.2

Relative, Chapter 9, Article 2

Third party, 9.2.2

O

OBJECT

Determinable, Chapter 6, Article 1

    Determined, 6.1.2.A

    Future thing, 6.1.3

    Hope, 6.1.3

    Impossible, 6.1.3

    Option, 6.2.1

    Possible, 6.2.1

    Stipulation pour autrui, Chapter 7

    Third person, 6.1.2.B

OBLIGATION[S]

    [See Précis on Louisiana Law of Obligations in General]

OBLIQUE ACTION

    Action, Chapter 11

    Failure to exercise a right, Chapter 11, Article 1

    Insolvency, Chapter 11, Article 1

OFFER

    [See Consent, supra]

    [See Contract, supra]

    Counteroffer, 3.2.1.1

    Death, 3.1.1.4

    Expiration, 3.1.2.2

    Incapacity, 3.1.1.4

    Irrevocable, 3.1.1.4; Chapter 3, Article 2

    Medium, 3.1.1.3

    Revocable, 3.1.1.4; Chapter 3, Article 2

    Revocation3.1.1.4; Chapter 3, Article 2

    Reward, Chapter 3, Article 3

    Time, 3.1.1.1

    To public, Chapter 3, Article 3

ONEROUS CONTRACT

    [See Contract, supra]

OPTION

    [See Object, supra]

    [See Précis on Louisiana Law of Sale and Lease]

P

PAULIANA ACTION

[See Revocatory Action, infra]

PERFORMANCE

[See Dissolution, supra]

[See Précis on Louisiana Law of Obligations in General]

PRESCRIPTION

[See Action, supra]

PROOF

Contract, 1.6.1

Putting in default [See Default, supra]

R

RATIFICATION

[See Capacity, supra]

RELIANCE

[See Detrimental Reliance, supra]

REMISSION

[See Précis on Louisiana Law of Obligations in General]

RESCISSION

[See Capacity, supra; Error, supra]

RESOLUTORY

[See Précis on Louisiana Law of Obligations in General, Conditional Obligations]

RETROACTIVITY

REVOCATORY ACTION

[See Pauliana Action, supra]

Act, Chapter 11

Assets returned, 11.1.3

Course of business, 11.1.5

Four-fifths, 11.1.3

Gratuitous contract, 11.1.4

Insolvency, 11.1.6

Joint action, 11.1.6

Onerous contract, 11.1.3

Prescription, 11.1.6

Result of failure to act, Chapter 11, Article 1

REWARD

[See Offer, supra]

S

SIMULATION

Absolute, 8.1.1.B.1

Counterletter, 8.1.1.B

Definition, 8.1.1.B.1

Relative, 8.1.1.B.1

Third persons

SOLIDARY

[See Précis on Louisiana Law of Obligations in General]

SPECIFIC PERFORMANCE

[See Effects of Contracts, supra]

[See Précis on Louisiana Law of Obligations in General]

STIPULATED DAMAGES

[See Damages, supra]

STIPULATION POUR AUTRUI

[See Object, supra]

[See Third Party Beneficiary, infra]

SUSPENSIVE CONDITION

[See Précis on Louisiana Law of Obligations in General, Conditional Obligations]

SYNALLAGMATIC CONTRACT

[See Contract, supra]

T

TERM

[See Précis on Louisiana Law of Obligations in General]

THING

[See Object, supra]

THIRD PARTY BENEFICIARY

Concept, Chapter 7

Defenses, 7.3.3

Object [See supra]

Revocation, 7.3.2

Rights of beneficiary, 7.3.2

Rights of promisor, 7.3.2

Rights of stipulator, 7.3.2

Stipulation pour autrui [See supra]

THREAT

[See Vices of Consent, infra]

U

UNILATERAL CONTRACT

[See Contract, supra]

V

VICE(S) OF CONSENT

Duress (Violence) [See supra]

Error [See supra]

Fraud [See supra]

Lesion [See supra]

Threats, Chapter 4, Article 3; 4.3.1

VIOLENCE

[See Vices of Consent, Duress, supra]